Starting Your Career in Broadcasting

Working On and Off the Air in Radio and Television

Chris Schneider

**ALLWORTH
PRESS**
NEW YORK

11   10   09   08   07   5   4   3   2   1

Published by Allworth Press
An imprint of Allworth Communications, Inc.
10 East 23rd Street, New York, NY 10010

Cover design by Derek Bacchus
Interior design by Mary Belibasakis
Page composition/typography by Integra Software Services, Pvt. Ltd., Pondicherry, India
Cover photo by Michael Alonzo

Library of Congress Cataloging-in-Publication Data

Schneider, Chris.
  Starting your career in broadcasting: working on and off the air in radio and television / Chris Schneider.
      p. cm.
  Includes bibliographical references and index.
  ISBN-13: 978-1-58115-489-4 (pbk.)
  ISBN-10: 1-58115-489-5 (pbk.)
  1. Broadcasting—Vocational guidance.   I. Title.

PN1990.55.S36 2007
384.54023—dc22

                                                                                    2007005027

Acknowledgements

Thank you to my wife Michelle for her support and wonderful editing. To my mentor Mary Beth Sweeney and her understanding husband Joe, who were key in helping me to the career I have been so blessed with. Thank you to my friend and computer guru Doug Helton, who keeps my machines, running. Thank you to all the wonderful celebrities who gave selflessly of themselves to share wonderful stories and who contributed great advice to this book. Thank you to all the teachers and leaders at universities and career schools for offering me their stories and wisdom to pass along; I will be calling a few more of you soon for the next edition. Thank you to all the great friends, colleagues, leaders, and even rivals that I have worked with over the years for enriching my life and helping shape my career. And thank you to my Lord and Savior Jesus Christ for blessing me with an amazing journey of destiny.

CONTENTS

103

CHAPTER 11

BEING GOOD ON THE AIR

❧ *Get as Much Work on the Air as Possible* ❧ *Practice off the Air* ❧ *Listen and Learn from Major Market Talent* ❧

111

CHAPTER 12

HOW TOP RADIO AND TELEVISION PERSONALITIES IMPROVED THEMSELVES ON THE AIR

❧ *Hone Your Voice* ❧ *Lampley Thrown into the Fire on National Television* ❧ *Painful Early Air-Checks* ❧ *Lamp's Keys* ❧ *Syler's Rise* ❧ *How Costas Got Better* ❧ ❧ *Kingsley's Improvement Path* ❧ *Detours Can Be Learning Tools* ❧ *Berman on the Ground Floor* ❧ *Berman: Mr. Nice Guy* ❧ *ESPN Boss's Improvement Advice* ❧ ❧ *Communicating One to One* ❧ *Improvement Keys to Remember* ❧

119

CHAPTER 13

THE BIG BREAK

❧ *Big Breaks and Huge Breaks* ❧ *Bonaduce's Huge Break* ❧ *Tuna's Huge Break* ❧ ❧ *King's Rise To Greatness* ❧ *Costas—The Wonder Kid* ❧ *Help Make Your Breaks* ❧ *Syler, Intern to National Star* ❧ *You Never Know Who's Watching* ❧ ❧ *Sometimes You Have to Take a Chance* ❧ *Tragedy into Triumph* ❧ *Big Breaks Come in All Sizes* ❧

127

CHAPTER 14

DID THEY REALLY SAY THAT?

❧ *School Slips* ❧ *Costas Blows It* ❧ *My Little Slip* ❧ *Berman Caught with His Pants Down* ❧ *Berman Met His Wife on the Job* ❧ *The Flying Skirt* ❧ *Kingsley's Ace in the Hole* ❧ *Pulling the Chair Out* ❧ *An Inconspicuous Star* ❧ *Shake and Bake* ❧ *Snow Days and Hot Copy* ❧ *What Are Friends For?* ❧ *Humor Is Good* ❧ ❧ *Equipment Malfunction* ❧ *Just Plain Weird* ❧ *Creative, and Proud of It* ❧

137

CHAPTER 15

THE UPS AND THE DOWNS

❧ *Near-Death Eye-Opener* ❧ *Money Problems for the King* ❧ *Kingsley Back with the Parents* ❧ *Packing up and Moving On* ❧ *Passed Over for the Perfect Job* ❧

Introduction:
Why and How I Wrote This Book

My name is Chris Schneider. I have been talking on radio and television for nearly thirty years, mostly as a sportscaster. I am the Sports Director and Morning Drive Sports Anchor on KRLD and the Texas State Networks in Dallas. My journey over the years has taken me from a little town in Wyoming where I grew up to working in some of the world's greatest cities. I have worked as a sportscaster and talk show host in Los Angeles, London, Chicago, Cincinnati, and Dallas. I have had the privilege of working on the air for some incredible organizations, including ESPN International, the BBC, Prime Sports, and CBS, alongside a host of incredibly talented people.

Working on the air is a fascinating thing to do for a living, but it is not without its challenges. Many of the wonderful people I have worked with over the years, whether they be disc jockeys, news or sports anchors, or talk show hosts, swore that they would write a book someday about their strange, amazing, and occasionally unbelievable experiences in this business. To my knowledge none of them have, so I decided that I would.

I decided to write this book because there is no real how-to guide for starting or improving a career in radio and/or television. In this age of how-to books, it is pretty rare to find an area that has not already been covered. You can get career advice on just about everything, including how to sell, dress, talk, and think, but there are no books that offer solid advice on getting started in broadcasting.

I first started writing this book after a meeting with a literary agent a few years ago. He was not so sure that the novel I had written would be a success, but he was fascinated by my long career on the air in radio and television. He was enthralled by stories I told him about working with stars that he listened to and watched every day. He told me that if I could write a book outlining my vast knowledge of the broadcasting industry, the book would sell itself. He asked me how my career on the air got started, and I told him the following true story:

HOW I GOT STARTED IN THE BIZ

I was working as a bus boy at a restaurant in Torrington, Wyoming, the little town where I grew up. Torrington consisted of only five thousand people, but it was still a big city to me. After all, I had lived in a town even smaller than that a few years earlier; it had a population of ten people, and six of those ten were in my family. I knew that I had to be on the radio the first time I saw the TV sitcom *WKRP in Cincinnati*. I was eleven years old and absolutely sure that everyone else felt the same way. I was worried that they would take all of the on-air jobs before I was old enough to get one.

One day after my shift busing tables at the restaurant I walked several miles out of town to the local radio station to apply for a job. I dodged the water puddles on the side of the paved two-lane highway heading west until I reached the gravel driveway that led up to the station's studios. After a deep breath and big swallow, I pushed open the unlocked front door and walked into a dark, empty room. There was a small light that beckoned from somewhere down a hallway in the back. I knew this could be the biggest moment of my life, my only shot at what I knew I was born to do. I walked toward the light until a shadow appeared.

"Hello?" I asked.

A scruffy looking man with blue jeans and a dirty red-and-white checkered shirt was startled from his intense examination of the sports page.

"What the...?" A look of horror and surprise flashed across his face. "What do you want?" he asked looking me over, his fear quickly transformed to amusement as a smile creased the corners of his mouth.

I said, "Who do I talk to about getting a job?" I forced the words out, hoping they did not sound as ridiculous as I felt when I uttered them.

"What?"

I could tell his surprise was real, but it was too late to turn back now.

"I would like to fill out an application to be a disc jockey." I was pleased that the words sounded so confident.

"How old are you?" he asked, taking a sip of coffee. He was certainly still amused, but now I detected a small amount of respect in his voice.

"Eleven." I knew it was over as soon as I said it.

"Sorry, kid. You're way too young to get a job here."

"How old do I have to be?" I asked the question before the full force of his statement denying me a job hit home.

"I think you've got to be eighteen or something."

He watched me with pitying amusement while I stole one last look around the high-tech studio and the green, yellow, and red blinking lights coming from an unbelievably impressive machine. There were felt-lined turntables (record players) where the radio gods played music, all part of a cockpit-like desk that was the heart of a real radio studio. I left without saying another word, nor did I get one from Mr. Radio. I consoled myself on the long walk back to town that I would try again when I was older, but that did not make me feel much better.

Five years later, when my parents decided to move to a bigger town (there are no cities in Wyoming, only towns), I was all for it. I knew my chances to get a job in radio would be better. Even at that age, I knew location mattered.

The new town, Casper, had a population of fifty thousand people, ten times the size of little Torrington. From day one in my new metropolis, I listened closely to the radio stations, and one station in particular caught my ear. KATI-AM played my favorite music, had great DJs, and great sportscasters. That was my station!

I had my next run-in with broadcasting when I was a sixteen-year-old sophomore in high school. Making new friends was slow, but I had a few, mostly from playing sports. My new school had some very good teams that year, winning the state championships in basketball and track and field. The radio station that covered us was KATI. To me, it was a sign from God.

The main sportscaster at the station called the play-by-play of our high school games; his name was Bob Coleman. After we won the state championship in basketball, the school called an assembly. Mr. Coleman was there to give a speech and help us celebrate. But the actual speech was less significant than his huge presence. He didn't have to say much because he was a star, and he knew it. His voice was as smooth and strong in person as it sounded on the radio. He said he was happy to be there and that he felt honored to cover the team. I sat there in the stands, and I knew what I had to do with my life: I had to get a job in radio no matter what it took.

When the assembly ended, I quickly walked back home, fired up the old brown Chevy station wagon I had named "Grace," and drove to the radio station. It took me a while to find it. The station was located in a double-wide trailer behind a Holiday Inn, beside the North Platte River running through the middle of town.

A lovely dark-haired lady greeted me when I opened the front door and entered the lobby. "Can I help you?"

"Uh, yeah, uh..." waves of embarrassment put a lock-down on my voice. I though, "What in the hell am I doing?"

"Are you here to pick up a prize?"

I was sure she thought that I had a serious learning disability. What the heck, I figured, I'm here. "Yeah, I'm sorry. I would like to fill out an application to be a DJ."

I said it! Five years after my first attempt, I still felt stupid, I was still too young for the high-profile, incredibly professional job of being on the air. I knew it, but I still had to try.

The secretary smiled and made a call. I figured that she was alerting the entire staff to come and have a good laugh.

Soon afterwards, a tall, bearded man walked up to me and said, "Hi, my name is Fred Leemhius. I'm the program director here. Can I help you?"

I had heard that deep booming voice before, on the air. I realized I was talking to a real DJ. "Yes sir, I would like to fill out an application to be a disc jockey."

"All right, follow me."

They were taking me seriously! I followed the tall, bearded man down a narrow hallway with big glass windows on both sides. A glance to my right revealed the cockpit-like command center studio that I had been dreaming of for five years now. A bit further down the hall I saw what looked like a small newsroom, and to the left an incredibly high-tech-looking place I figured was the production studio. I was in heaven!

Fred led me to an empty desk at the end of the hallway and put a one-page application and a pen in front of me. He said he would return shortly.

It was a standard job application with all the usual questions. I was a little disappointed; I figured there would be some sort of FBI or CIA background search involved:

Name: Chris Schneider

Experience: high school speech class

Age: 16

Sex: no, still working on it

Explain why you want this job: I want to be a *dis* jockey (I didn't even know how to spell disc jockey), I want to be on the air. I will work anytime, any place and for anybody.

I buzzed through the questions without any trouble. I was filled with a new confidence. They were actually taking me seriously. Then I heard a familiar voice coming from down the hallway. It was Bob Coleman, my hero. The only superstar I cared about was just feet away.

"Are you finished?" The program director's booming voice snapped me back to reality.

"Yes, sir."

"All right. Well, we appreciate your interest, we'll let you know."

Before I knew what hit me, I was ushered out the front door and was back in my brown station wagon, pulling away from the little trailer beside the river. I knew I had just come in close contact with something bigger than this world.

After not hearing from Fred for three weeks, I mustered the courage to call the station and ask for him.

"Hello, KATI radio."

"Yes," I said, "Fred Leemhius please." Click. I was briefly put on hold.

"Fred Leemhius."

"Yeah." My heart froze. Here I was again, about ready to blow what I knew was my life's calling. "Mr. Leemhius, this is Chris Schneider. I filled out an application to be a DJ several weeks ago. I wanted to see if you liked it." *If he liked it?* Oh no, I could not believe I had just said that.

"Yeah, Chris, I liked it just fine, but we don't have any openings right now. If we do, we'll look at your application again, okay?"

"Okay, thanks!" I hung up quickly and whooped out a celebratory howl. I still had a chance.

Every Thursday thereafter, I called Fred as soon as I got home from school. Sometimes I got through to him, sometimes I just left a message, but the answer was always the same: still no openings.

Three months after filling out the application I came home from school on a Thursday, and there was a message waiting for me on the counter by the phone. "Call Fred at KATI." My heart stopped, my knees buckled, and I lost my breath all at once.

"*Mom!*" I screamed down the stairs where she was working, "Did you take this message?"

"Yes."

"What does it mean?"

"I don't know," she replied. "Maybe you have the job."

I did have the job. At sixteen, my broadcasting career was underway.

I HAVE BEEN BLESSED

For the last three decades or so I have jocked music, called play-by-play, hosted local and national talk shows, anchored news and sports, programmed entire stations, voiced commercials, and have done just about everything else there is to do on the air. I have worked in London, Dallas, Los Angeles, Chicago, and Cincinnati, and I have had the amazing privilege of interviewing hundreds of star athletes, actors, musicians, authors, and other public figures. The media business can be fickle sometimes, so I have been on top of the world as well as down-and-out at different stages of my career.

JOINED BY THE BEST

Despite all of my experience on the air, I soon found out after I began writing this book that my stories and experiences were not nearly enough. I needed anecdotes and advice from other notable on-air veterans to make a really great book. I wanted to write a book that would give the reader a well-rounded tutorial with experiences, stories, and advice from a lot of different sources. So I started making some calls.

First, I called a couple of guys I had worked with in Los Angeles a few years earlier: legendary disc jockey Charlie Tuna and well-known Olympic and boxing host Jim Lampley. I had the privilege of working with both of them at KMPC, an all-sports station in Los Angeles. Jim and Charlie were kind enough to offer me their time as well as regale me with wonderful stories and hard-earned wisdom. I continued making calls, and before long I had talked with the great Bob Costas of NBC and HBO fame, Chris Berman from ESPN and ABC, and Larry King of CNN. A couple of the top women in the business were happy to give me their time and wisdom, as well as Rene Syler, former host of the *Early Show* on CBS, and E.D. Hill from the Fox News Channel. To round things out, former Dallas Cowboy quarterback Troy Aikman, Fox NFL analyst and Pro Football Hall of Famer, and former child acting star Danny Bonaduce, among others, joined me as well.

When I needed expert opinions and advice on the best broadcast/ journalism/mass communications programs at universities around the country, I talked with some of the best teachers and administrators who were more than kind enough to offer their expertise. When I needed information on career broadcast schools, once again the top people in the industry kindly and selflessly offered their time and wisdom. Without all of these wonderful people it would have been impossible to write this book.

Talking with each of these stars, teachers, and experts was not only a privilege for me but great fun as well. Chris Berman, for instance, made me laugh with his off-the-cuff stories for several hours one afternoon between sportscasts I was doing live in Dallas. When I would go back on the air, we would hang up in the middle of a story, then Berman would call me back a few minutes later when I was done to finish the story. Berman would get so caught up in spinning his yarns that he would throw in an expletive here and there, and then apologize, saying he hoped I could still use the story in the book.

I talked with Larry King for a few minutes before he went on the air live to host his talk show on CNN. He was not the least bit nervous about either our interview or his upcoming show. Funny, for a guy who was too scared to talk the first time he opened the microphone (I will tell you about that later in the book).

I interviewed all of these wonderful radio and television stars, teachers, and experts on the phone over the course of several years. I have tried to weave their stories, experiences, and advice into a coherent work that is both entertaining and informative in the hopes of helping the reader get a career on the air started. If you are already in the radio or television business with ambitions of moving up, the anecdotes and advice in the book are designed to help you as well.

YOU ARE NOT ALONE

Many times, we feel like we are alone in the universe when it comes to following our calling in this business. I am here to say that you are not alone. There is a fraternity of us who felt the same need to be on the air, communicating with somebody on the other side of the microphone.

I just told you how my career got started; in this book you will hear how some real broadcasting greats got their start. These true stories will also give you ideas on how you might get started. Depending on your circumstances, there are several different paths to choose, and there are ways to make the most out of the position you currently find yourself in. If you are able to get a job on the air, this book will show how you can make yourself better in order to move up the ladder faster. On the other hand, if you have to start your career with a job off the air, then this book will give you ideas on how you can try to parlay that into on-air work.

We will also take a look at the differences between university broadcasting programs and career school courses. There are advantages and disadvantages to each. The university route is the best, offering a well-rounded education that will serve you well for the rest of your life. That being said, I realize that some are not in the position to go to college, and career broadcast schools, which offer quicker, more concentrated programs, are the best route. We will take a look at both choices.

When I was first getting started in this business, I tried to talk to anyone and everyone whom I considered better or more experienced than me, so that I could learn their tricks and learn from their mistakes. It is my hope that I can pass these experiences along to you. In my interviews with star personalities featured in the book, I ask about their growing pains, their biggest mistakes, and things they would have done differently. I hope this will be a great learning tool in your climb up the ladder.

If you are going to have a successful career on the air, you will likely need to experience a few big breaks. Both I and my friends in the book have experienced these amazing opportunities. I will tell you about these big breaks and help you understand how to make some for yourself too.

Along with giving you advice on how to get a broadcasting career started, and ways to improve your talents and skills to advance, I hope this book makes you laugh as well. As I mentioned earlier, just about everybody in the business says at some point that they are going to write a book about it. They say that because of some of the fun, strange, and wacky things that happen. I will relay my experiences, as well as those of my friends and colleagues, for your enjoyment. As your career progresses, you will experience similarly unbelievable moments as well, and when you do, you can sit back and laugh, knowing your experiences are in the same league as some of the biggest names in the business.

Thank you for taking the time to read *Starting Your Career in Broadcasting*! It is my hope you find it entertaining, educational, and inspiring.

The Big Bang! How Top Radio and Television Stars Got Their Start

"The dream" was Larry King's first conscious thought. Charlie Tuna was inspired by a disc jockey in Nebraska. Bob Costas was energized by New York legends. Jim Lampley stumbled into broadcasting. It got Bob Kingsley through painful nights after falling ill with polio as a child. E.D. Hill first knew it would be her life's purpose while doing a writing assignment in the sixth grade. It hit me while I was watching *WKRP in Cincinnati.* "It" is the dream, the desire, and the need to be on the air, whether it be radio or television. Every successful air personality had to start somewhere. Without fail, those beginnings were rife with embarrassment, mistakes, luck, and learning. Some were easier than others, many improbable, but all captivating.

LARRY KING: BORN TO BE IN BROADCASTING

I found out after my first few years in the business that I was not the only person who thought that being on the air was what he was born to do; other notable figures have had that same sensation, like CNN icon Larry King. "It was my earliest memory, to be a broadcaster. I used to point to the radio, they tell me, when I was four or five years old and try to imitate announcers, and that's all I ever wanted to do." Being on the air was never a question for Larry—it was a necessity. "I never wanted to do anything else. When other kids would say 'I want to be a fireman or a cop,' I never wanted to be anything but a broadcaster. After high school, I knocked around a bunch of odd jobs and, finally, at age twenty-two I went down to Miami, knocked on doors, and got a job."

Larry's first air-shift was on May 1, 1957. He invented the national radio talk show, as we know it today, hosting an overnight call-in show on the Mutual Radio Network for almost two decades. He has interviewed nearly every major personality on both radio and CNN's *Larry King Live.*

So are there any surprises in the way his career has gone? "I always thought I'd be a sportscaster. Sports was my avocation, still is. It's still the first thing I read in the newspaper everyday."

What was the spark? What made Larry King need to be on the air? King admits, "I don't know what it was, but I had a genuine attraction to radio and then to television when it came in. And now I've spent forty-nine years on radio and forty-six on television—I've always done both."

CHRIS BERMAN

ESPN & ABC superstar personality Chris Berman had the itch to be on the air at an early age, too. When I asked him if he had always wanted to be in this business, he said, "Yes, I mean always. My mother and father tell me of times that I turned down the sound of hockey games on TV on Saturday night and did my own announcing. They would have to ask me to please close the door.

"When I was in high school, now this is the early seventies, believe it or not, we had this little screw-in-the-light-bulb campus radio station. So I announced the football games on Saturday. Now, who really listened? Well, on a nice day, uh, no one. If it was raining, some of the parents would sit in the cars and listen to a few minutes of the game. So I had a chance to do a little of it in high school. I knew this was what I wanted to do. I thought I was pretty good at it, considering I was seventeen."

BOB KINGSLEY

Bob Kingsley has been the host of a couple of the world's most listened-to programs, the *American Country Countdown* and now *Bob Kingsley's Country Top 40*. His love for radio goes back to when he was a polio-stricken child: "That's all I had was that radio there. I could move my arm, my hand, just enough to turn the dial, particularly during the evening. The soap opera stuff during the day I wasn't a big fan of, but in the evening when the *Green Hornet* and the *Fat Man* and all those great old radio shows were on. I was—what, six or seven—and it stayed with me. To be able to be involved in it today, I still think it's a marvelous medium."

E.D. HILL

E.D. Hill co-hosts Fox News Channel's *Fox News Live* every weekday morning and is the author of the inspirational book *Going Places*.[1] Her life has taken her from a junior high student in Hong Kong to a VJ (video jockey) for VH1 to the

E.D. Hill, full of energy in junior high.

hallowed halls of Harvard University, among other places, but she has known since the sixth grade that she was destined to be on the air.

"I was given a writing assignment about a news event I had experienced, which was a police chase of drug smugglers on the China Sea. I was a little girl watching that, so I wrote about it. I got a good grade on my paper and it made me realize I wanted to be a journalist. I wasn't quite sure what type of journalism I wanted to go into, but I knew I wanted to be a journalist."

Once E.D. had caught the broadcasting bug, she started having strange thoughts. "When I was out fishing, I always dreamed of being a Babe Winkleman, you know, having my own fishing show. I thought, 'Man that would be the life!'"

Fishing shows aside, it took E.D. quite a while to find out what kind of on air job she really wanted to pursue. "Through high school and college I kind of pared it down; I was a punk rock DJ, I wrote, I worked in radio, TV, film, and then I realized I wanted to be a TV reporter."

CHARLIE TUNA

I was on staff with Los Angeles Morning Drive radio legend Charlie Tuna and longtime

Photos courtesy of E.D. Hill & Fox News Channel

E.D. is an industry leader now.

ABC, NBC, and HBO commentator Jim Lampley at 710-AM KMPC in Los Angeles when it was an all-sports station. Charlie now has his own star on the Hollywood Walk of Fame, but his beginnings were a bit more humble. He got started by practicing at home, alone in his room, in Kearney, Nebraska, at the age of five. "I'd talk like I was introducing records and talking to people on the radio." Charlie chuckles, remembering, "You sit in a little room all by yourself and make believe you have an audience, kind of like you do today."

Tuna was inspired by listening to local disc jockey Jack Lewis. "This was 1949 and he started talking about things like UFOs and flying saucers which were just starting to get talked about. It was just fascinating to me. Then, when I was eleven years old, I had him on my paper route and I would tremble every time I had to go up to him to collect money. I could never speak. I couldn't even look at the guy—he was it."

Charlie Tuna got his first break as a DJ at a junior high sock hop. "The kids thought, 'Wow, he's really good.' I thought, 'Well, I've been practicing in my room at home for years.' I wound up being the first guy they paid for doing that. They gave me twenty-five bucks a week, I guess, and all the concessions I wanted, candy or soda pop. From there, the kids were always encouraging me to go down and audition at the local radio station. I was very shy but my dad knew one of the chief engineers. He asked if I could get an audition, so I went down and cut a tape in their production studio. They gave me the standard, 'don't call us we'll call you,' and about six months later, they did."

JIM LAMPLEY

Jim Lampley started "fiddling around with broadcasting" in college. "I definitely was not a kid who grew up knowing what he wanted to do, especially being a sportscaster. I actually got started in politics. I worked for a U.S. Senate campaign in North Carolina when I finished undergraduate school, but when we lost the campaign I had to think of something else to do. I signed up for graduate school in mass communications."

Jim was soon hired by ABC to do sideline reports during college football games, but only after he was first rejected for being too arrogant during a talent search that included a nationwide field of 432 candidates. The network was looking for a new, young face to put on their college football broadcasts and figured that looking at college students might be a good idea.

"My whole sportscasting career is an accident as the result of that talent hunt, which took place in 1974. I told a guy named Dick Ebersol, who happened to be Roone Arlidge's personal assistant at the time, that they were absolutely crazy. That this was all a big ego trip for them and I hoped they had fun. On my screening form, someone wrote, 'Arrogant, Abrasive, Alienated, Antagonistic.' It infamously became known as the 'Four A's.' Later in the hiring process ABC was having trouble finding someone they could be really confident about putting on the air. So, Roone Arlidge, remembering the abrasive but confident young man who had told them off, said, 'Let me see him.'" The rest is history.

BOB COSTAS

Bob Costas has become an icon in the broadcasting business, working for HBO and NBC as a sportscaster and talk show host. Bob now anchors NBC's *Football Night In America*, covers the Olympics, hosts shows on HBO, and fills in as a back up for Larry King on CNN.

Did he know he wanted to be on the air from an early age? "Yes. I think I first entertained thoughts of being a sports broadcaster when I was ten or eleven years old." Growing up in New York, Bob was inspired by legends in the business, "Mel Allen, Red Barber, Jack Buck, Vin Scully, Jim McKay, Lindsey Nelson. I went to Syracuse because I had heard they had an excellent program, not just in journalism but in broadcasting. At that time, there weren't that many high-profile universities that actually had a concentration in broadcasting, so I went there because of that reputation. You could work on the campus radio and television stations as an undergraduate so you got some hands-on experience. That was an important and useful first step to just start there."

WILLIAMS, COURIC, GIBSON, CRONKITE, & KEILLOR

NBC Evening News anchor Brian Williams started his broadcasting career in little Pittsburg, Kansas, "doing everything but operating the transmitter," at KOAM-TV. CBS's Katie Couric started her career off the air, as a desk assistant for the ABC Bureau in Washington. She moved on to CNN to be an assignment editor and later a show producer before her meteoric rise to stardom. ABC's Charles Gibson got his start in college radio at the University of Princeton.

CBS News legend Walter Cronkite worked in public relations, newspapers, and small Midwestern radio stations before joining United Press in 1939 to cover World War II. After joining CBS in 1950, one of Cronkite's earliest jobs included working with a puppet named Charlemagne on the *CBS Morning Show*. Another legend, Garrison Keillor, started broadcasting at the University of Minnesota. After graduating, Keillor wrote for the *New Yorker* magazine before being inspired to create a widely reknowned live radio variety show.

That is how some of the greats in our business got their careers off the ground, so the next question is, how do *you* get your career in broadcasting started? We will start looking at that in chapter 2.

End Note

[1] Hill, E.D. *Going Places*. New York: HarperCollins Publishers, 2005.

2

Is Broadcasting Right for You?

In the radio and television business, there are about as many ways to get hired as there are to get fired—not quite, but close. When all is said and done, the ways to get started boil down to a basic six:

⚜ Get an on-air position in a small market.

⚜ Get a job off the air in a small, medium, or large market.

⚜ Be a celebrity. This is usually reserved for athletes and lawyers, but there are some exceptions.

⚜ Go to either a university or career broadcast school and work at school radio and television stations.

⚜ Work in public access television and/or podcasting.

⚜ Buy time on the air.

These are all valid ways to get a broadcasting career started. Each have their advantages and disadvantages, and we will take an in-depth look at them all in the next few chapters.

Before we get to that, let's start with a fundamentally important question: Is this a good time to be thinking about a career in the broadcasting business in the first place? "I think it still is," says Bob Costas. "I think there are more outlets than there have ever been. That's obvious with the proliferation of cable TV. Not all of it is at a high level of skill or thought. Anytime you increase anything, you're going to dilute the quality to some extent, but even with that there are more opportunities for people who do have ability to get a chance and maybe make an impression. When I was starting out in the early 1970s, there were fewer places to broadcast than there are now. It's still an exciting and worthwhile area."

Del Cockrell founded the American Broadcasting School (ABS) thirty-four years ago and now has five schools located in Oklahoma and Texas. He agrees with Costas: "I think there's always a demand for good personalities." Numbers would tend to agree, with 80 to 90 percent of his students finding a job in the broadcast industry after graduation. The number of students at career broadcast trade schools and university programs has grown over the last decade, indicating that interest is increasing.

"It's much bigger," says Kent Collins, chairman of the Broadcast News Department at the University of Missouri School of Journalism. Interest is increasing for jobs, "on the air or behind the scenes. We produce producers who are going into the large markets, people who are starting their careers in places like Kansas City, Cincinnati, and New Orleans, right out of school because the demand for newscast producers is so great." The National Broadcasters Training Network agrees: "In the dawn of the increasingly digitized millennium, interest in broadcasting careers is at its peak. People from communications, media, and technical backgrounds are all flocking to this diverse field, which seems to offer a vocation for everyone."[1]

As Mr. Collins indicates, not all jobs in broadcasting are in front of the microphone. There are a lot of good positions behind the scenes. Bruce Gilbert is the general manager of ESPN Radio. "My dad was in the radio business all his life, so that's all I've ever known. I started hanging out in radio stations when I was a few years old. I fell in love with the vibe, thought it was the coolest thing. I was on the air from the time I was fourteen. When I realized I sucked real bad on the air, I decided to get into management." That choice has worked out well for Bruce, as he has programmed successful talk stations in major markets including Pittsburgh and Dallas before moving to ESPN Radio.

How does Bruce Gilbert advise those who have their mind set on a career in broadcasting? "Do anything you can to get a show in any town, no matter how small, that has a radio station. Get off this belief that you can start in a top-ten market as a talk talent or as a disc jockey, because you need to go learn stuff at a smaller station and get paid nothing for it. In fact, I've even told people who want to do talk shows: if you have to, find a way to buy the time so that you can pay for your way on the air. It'll be worth the investment if that's what you really want to do, so that you can get some real tape and you can really get a feel for what it's like to do live radio."

BEING ON THE AIR MEANS MORE THAN BEING A STAR

Many people think they want a job on the air to become a celebrity, a star. That is definitely an aspect of the job, and if you want to be on the air you should have a certain amount of that desire. But being on the air is much more than just being a star; it is also a responsibility to the viewer or listener, many times without appreciation, and it is also more hard work than glamour. Long-time British journalist Tony Harcup describes the lifestyle this way in his book, *Journalism*: "Being a journalist is not like working in a baked bean factory—journalists have a more *social* role that goes beyond the production of commodities to sell in the marketplace. Journalists *inform* society about itself and make *public* that which would otherwise be private. Rather an important job you might think. But public opinion polls frequently remind us that, in the league table of trustworthiness, journalists vie for bottom place with politicians and real estate agents . . ."[2]

If you are serious about a career on the air, you should be prepared to start out on the bottom, in a small market, making small money. Almost every major star started out this way and then moved up the ladder. That being said, there are always miraculous stories too. Like Jim Lampley's, whose first job was with a major TV network. How does he advise those just starting out? "I've told thousands that I don't know as much about this as most of the people they're going to approach. Unlike most of my peers, I didn't follow a logical path and go up a ladder from local stations to some kind of regional exposure to networks. So, I don't really know what to tell people."

We will hear more about Jim's improbable career beginnings a bit later, but the best way to prepare for a career on the air is to expect to start small and slowly move up. If you should be fortunate to get your start in a medium or major market, then all the better.

RADIO/TV DEREGULATION HAS POSITIVES AND NEGATIVES

Industry deregulation during the last few years has allowed a few larger companies to buy up a large percentage of radio and television stations across the country. This has enabled them to shrink their workforce. The good news for beginners is that since these companies own more stations, there is less competition for ratings. This allows younger and more inexperienced personalities a better shot at getting jobs, both on and off the air, in bigger markets right away.

THE BROADCASTING ROLLER COASTER

Working in the broadcast business, whether it be radio or television, is a business of wonderful, glorious highs and challenging, scary lows, more so than in other professions. Here is how author Andrew Boyd describes our business in his book *Broadcast Journalism:* "Ask most journalists what they think about their chosen profession and the chances are they will bemoan the anti-social hours, unreasonable stress, flogging to meet constant deadlines, time wasted draped over the telephone, destruction of family life and home existence, but when the griping is over and you ask them what else they would rather do the chances are they would shrug, smile and tell you, '*nothing*.'"

Boyd goes on to say, "Few professions can match broadcast journalism for its rewards in terms of job satisfaction, interest, variety, sheer challenge—and for the select few—fame and wealth."[3]

How do you know if you should make the leap into broadcasting or not? Larry King has an answer. "If someone can talk you out of it, you are not meant to be in it. If I can say to someone, 'Hey, it's a tough business, there are a lot of people that want to be in this business' and you say, 'Well maybe I won't go in,' then don't go in, because competition is fierce. See, you gotta love it. Not like it. Love it! I don't know anyone in the business who doesn't love it. They may not love their current radio station, or television station. They may wish they had a better gig, but I never met anyone who said, 'Boy I wish I were a detective!' You gotta want it! That is half the battle if you want it, and the other half is talent. If you have talent and you want it, there always seems to be an opening."

Former child star Danny Bonaduce, a veteran Los Angeles morning-drive radio star and co-host of syndicated TV shows agrees: "Radio is one of the few arms of the entertainment industry where you can still make millions of dollars just because you are clever enough. Where you can kind of work your way into it. Everybody I know who is in radio, I don't know one person with a degree in broadcasting. What I know are people who were interns, and swept up around the radio station starting at thirteen years old. Then they got the night job and then they got the weekend job, then they got the afternoon job, then they got the morning show!"

If you have the burning desire to be on the air or in the broadcast business in some capacity, the next step is to find out which of the six options mentioned earlier is the best for you and to get started. Even though there are just a few basic paths, the number of ways to travel these paths varies largely depending on the person involved, along with his or her personality, and his current situation in life. We will find out that for some it will be best to go to broadcasting school, for others university, and still others to start out at a little town radio station. It will be up to you to figure out the path that best suits your talents and allows you to attain the position and success that you strive for. I will attempt to help you make the choice in the following chapters.

End Notes

[1] *www.learn-by-doing.com*

[2] Harcup, Tony. *Journalism*. London: Sage Publications Inc., 2003.

[3] Boyd, Andrew. *Broadcast Journalism*. Oxford: Focal Press, 2000.

Broadcasting Success

"Success is not a specific destination; it is a *direction you choose*. It is a process, a never-ending journey. It is your constant progress toward your highest purpose, your vision, and the life of your dreams—in all areas. I know a lot of people who are highly successful in the financial arena who are not happy or fulfilled. They are not truly successful. Other people have great relationships, but are not succeeding financially. None of these people are truly successful."

—Personal Growth Expert James Arthur Ray,
The Science of Success[1]

You are the only person who can define what success is to you. To many people in the broadcast business success means moving up to bigger and bigger markets, which offer more listeners and more money. There are others, however, who rightfully consider success finding a nice little town where they love to live and work on the air. This is just as much of a success as the person who wants to find fame and fortune in a large market. Finding happiness is success. Victory in any endeavor is being able to achieve what you desire; it does not necessarily depend on fame and money.

If it is your desire to move up the ladder in the broadcast industry, this chapter will give you some ideas on how best to do that. There are several key elements you will need to bring together in order to give yourself the best chance of advancement. The combination of these elements all working together will be driven by the strength of your desire to move up.

KEY ELEMENTS IN MOVING UP THE LADDER

⬥ Network. Get to know as many people in the business as possible. Make friends and acquaintances. Know what the broadcasters and stations in your area are doing.

⬥ Study the industry trade magazines to learn the business, the slang, and to keep up with job openings.

⬥ Start putting together a list of stations in markets you would like to work and their vital information.

Each of these steps will bring you closer to your dream of a career in the broadcast business.

NETWORK: GET TO KNOW AS MANY PEOPLE AS POSSIBLE

Networking is important in every business. It is even more essential in the entertainment industry. Start by getting to know the people at your own station. Find out whom you can learn from as well as those who hold influence. These people are not necessarily the same.

You can learn on-air skills from some, like on-air personalities and production directors, who many times have little or no influence at the station. At the same time, many people who have great influence are not on the air. Each proves very valuable in his or her own way; however, be smart and learn from all of them as best you can.

At every chance, meet and be friendly with people from other stations as well. Become their friends. You will learn a lot about how other stations operate. You will find out who holds the power as well as when they have an opening you might be interested in. I personally have received job offers from people at rival stations or networks that I had met at a party or out at dinner or after having an acquaintance drop my name to their boss. These connections are priceless when you are looking to advance your career.

Right Place at the Right Time

One of the most important elements to success in this business is being in the right place at the right time. Part of that is luck; the other part is just plain and simple hard work—the work it takes to be in the right place at the right time.

Business advisor and professional networker Heather White offers advice on how to meet and greet for success in *Networking for Business Success*:

> So my purpose in networking is to meet a person/company who may not otherwise take my telephone calls or reply to my letters, and develop a long-term relationship.

> 1. My initial questions are "who do I want to meet and why?" and/or "what do I want to learn and why?"

> 2. I consider my overall objective, i.e., short-term, is to establish rapport and get an appointment; long-term, to win a contract, enhance my profile, receive referrals or whatever else I might be aiming at.

> 3. To meet my "who" I consider where they gather and attend their events.

> 4. To know what is going on I subscribe to a number of relevant mailing lists.

> 5. I am clear about the image I wish to create . . .[2]

Networking Never Stops

Networking happens at all times of the day, when you are working and when you're not, when you are out with friends or at a business gathering. Always have your eye open to meeting and establishing a relationship with those who might be able to help you in some way down the line. Remember that many times these other people are networking too and are hoping that you might be able to help them in some way in the future. Top-selling author and master motivator Zig Zigler has some good advice on how to best handle this situation in his book *Over The Top*: "To get what you want in life you just need to help enough other people get what they want."[3]

STUDY INDUSTRY TRADE MAGAZINES

Other than just being around the day-to-day operation of a station and hanging out with radio/TV types, industry trade magazines and industry Web sites are the best sources to get inside information on the broadcasting business and find out about job openings. The top sources for information are magazines like *Radio & Records* (R&R) and *Billboard* and Web sites such as InsideRadio.com, tvspy.com, tvjobs.com, and newsblues.com.

Almost all radio and television stations subscribe to one or more of these magazines or get information off their Web sites. *R&R* has a subscription rate of about eight thousand magazines per week, with a "pass around" readership of nearly ninety thousand a week. That means a lot of people are reading the magazines lying around the station.

You can also buy your own, of course, which may be a good idea when you are seriously looking for a new job. That way you will have the list of job openings in each edition that you can keep for yourself. This is, by far, the best way to keep up with job openings at stations and companies around the country.

Buying your own magazine will also allow you to avoid those awkward moments when you get the station's copy from your boss, and he or she asks if you are looking for a job. You do not want to burn any bridges in this business, so try to avoid lying.

If you don't want to pay for a subscription, most of these magazines are available at your local public library or at a local journalism school library.

Plenty of Places to Get Info

There has been an avalanche of new industry Web sites that have popped up in recent years, and most are gone just as quickly. There are a few, however, that are a great source for job openings and industry news and gossip, most notably TVSpy.com,[4] TVJobs.com,[5] and Newsblues.com.[6] *Radio & Records Magazine*[7] is usually a great source of everything important that is going on in the broadcasting business. It also has the best job listings. Insideradio.com[8] provides more nuts-and-bolts information on in the business. It will give you more information about what the FCC is up to and what labor issues station chains are facing, as well as other inside industry news. *Billboard Magazine*[9] is more geared toward the musical aspects of the business. If you are a disc jockey or work at a music station, then *Billboard* may be a useful tool for you to keep up with the music business.

COMPILE A LIST OF ESSENTIAL INFORMATION

Start a list of radio and television stations that you would be interested in. A database of this information will allow you to establish contacts and relationships with people at different stations and help you learn about and get a foot in the door when an opportunity arises.

Put together station call letters and addresses, as well as the names of ownership, the program director, news director, sports director, operation manager, board op, and every other significant person you can find who works at the station. This will be your database of information for sending out audition packages. You will be able to reference this database when you decide to start looking for a new job and sending out CDs and resumes. Keep the information that you think you will need and organize it in a way that you can understand. It does not have to be pretty, and it does not have to be perfect, but you must keep the information up to date. Keep track of whom you talked to at which stations and make notes of the date you talked (most conversations will happen via email or phone, not in person) and the content of your conversation. When you keep detailed records, the next time you contact anyone to whom you have spoken before, you will be able to remind him of your previous conversation. You also need to keep track of what was on the audition tape you mailed to these contacts so that you will be sure to send them fresh material every time.

Keeping Stress Down

When you decide to start the process of moving up the ladder and looking for a new job, it is important to get into the right frame of mind to keep stress at a minimum. I always found it psychologically and emotionally difficult when that time came because of the ups and downs of the process. Having the right mental attitude makes it easier to do all the different tasks and makes stress more manageable. First, you have to make a good audition tape. You must be vigilant to record as much quality on-air work as possible and then edit it so that you look and sound your best. Then you will need to put together a list of stations you are targeting, get call letters, as well as their mailing addresses, program director/news director information, etc. Before you mail out any audition CDs or DVDs, it would be wise to double-check to make sure you have the correct mailing address and contact information, due to the high rate of turnover in the business. You must also make sure you have a top-notch résumé to go with your audition tape and a good cover letter introducing yourself (more on this later in the book). Envelopes and postage will be the final step.

Keeping up with all of these things can be stressful, but less so if you have prepared your mind for the ups and downs inherent in searching for a new job. Do not let yourself get too high or too low. Realize that there will be good days and bad days. There will be days when everything goes well and sounds good and other days when nothing goes right. Keep an even keel and continue to work with a professional attitude. Also know going in that you will get rejections from program directors and other station management; that is just part of the way it works. Every great talent has been rejected at one time or another, one way or another, multiple times before ultimately finding success.

Hearing from a program director or news director is, of course, what you are working and hoping for, but it too will bring a certain amount of pressure that you must be ready for. More than likely you will be asked to make a second audition tape, and hopefully the program director will want to set a time for a face-to-face meeting. Part of what the hiring manager is looking at in the evaluation process is the way you handle this stress.

Along with keeping an even temperament, the best way to handle the pressure of all these different elements of moving up the ladder is to make the whole process a part of your daily life. Keep your database and your air-check tapes up to date on a regular basis. You will find that the stress hits you the hardest when you try to flip a switch telling yourself that you have to get everything done at once. If you keep up with it all, always having a résumé, always having a decent audition tape, etc., and always having these things ready to drop in the mail, you will not have to deal with the terrible stress of doing it all at once.

Staying up to date on all these materials in your quest to rise to the top will also allow you to send out audition packages to different stations on a regular basis, one a week, two a month, whatever you feel comfortable with. When you do hear back from an interested program director, you will be prepared to impress.

SETTING YOURSELF APART

As you begin your quest to catch the attention of news directors and program directors, you will need to find ways to set yourself apart. You will want to have the best recordings of your work, the most impressive résumé that you can put together and a cover letter that expresses who you are in a way that will entice the program director. In his book, *Broadcast Journalism*, author Andrew Boyd gives an idea of what kind of person these people are looking to hire: "Intelligence, curiosity, creativity, and writing ability are basic qualities. Added to this our paragon will need that essential spark. Vitality, vivacity, energy, drive, enthusiasm—call it what you will—news editors are looking for that extra something that will set one applicant above all others."[10]

After hiring people over the years at major market stations in Pittsburgh and Dallas, and now at ESPN Radio, Bruce Gilbert has seen a lot of ways people have tried to get his attention. "I had somebody send me a great big huge sneaker once and their resume was inside the sneaker. On the toe of the sneaker they had written, 'I just want to get my foot in the door.' I had a guy once, that I did end up hiring actually for a morning show, his big thing on the outside of his envelope was, 'magic moon rocks inside.' Now, nobody really knows what that means but it was clever enough to catch my eye, it was like a cereal box with magic moon rocks inside and there was his résumé and tape. He happened to be very good on the air so I did end up hiring him. Little tricks like that I think are fun, and I think it shows creativity and this is a creative business. I have to admit, I am a sucker for some of that creative stuff."

On the other side of the coin, Gilbert has received some pretty bad packages as well. "I've gotten hand-written résumés or letters just hen-scratched. Believe it or not, you'll think I'm making this up, but I really did get one in crayon once. From a guy that was just a regular Joe who thought he should be on the radio because, 'all his friends told him he was good.' It's just really surprising that people believe that's going to, I guess it did catch my eye, but if they believe that's going to get them the job that's a little bit scary. Of course I probably, at the same time that I got that letter in crayon, I probably had actual disc jockeys filling out the log in crayon, so maybe it wasn't that far fetched anyway."

WORK, ABILITY, LUCK, TIME, AND WEIGHT

While there may be some creative ways that you can get the attention of program directors or station managers, the basics of climbing the ladder are really just common sense. Rene Syler, former co-host of the *Early Show* on CBS alongside Harry Smith, Hanna Storm, and Julie Chen, explains, "You know people say, 'Oh, nice guys finish last, that this business isn't for nice people,' and I totally disagree. I didn't get to where I am by stabbing anybody in the back or whatever. I was just myself and kept my eye on, day in and day out, doing a good job. I think that's how you get ahead, day in and day out doing a good job."

Here are some of Bob Costas' thoughts on climbing the broadcasting ladder: "You have to have luck and circumstances, but if you don't have a willingness to work hard and if you don't have some ability, then luck doesn't really matter much. Nobody is successful just based on luck, but you can't be successful without some luck."

We usually play a part in making luck happen for ourselves by working hard to be in the right place at the right time and being prepared. Being prepared means that you have kept up with the business and know what is going on in the industry. It means you have worked hard to grow in your ability to be good on the air. It means your confidence level is such that you know you can perform when called upon. Costas describes his formula for success: "The willingness to work hard to be prepared, but at the same time not to be wedded to that preparation. To be able to react to something as it happens and be spontaneous."

Chris Berman credits one main element for his success in the business: "Time. We realize very quickly there is no substitution for time. I think I moved up the ladder because people enjoyed what I did. I was told early in

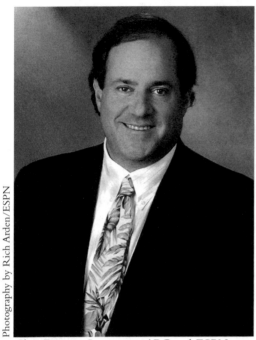

Photography by Rich Arden/ESPN

Chris Berman: Superstar at ABC and ESPN.

my career, by someone who had been in the business a long time, 'The very weight of what you do will eventually take you to where you want to go.' I was very touched by that. You know, we're all impatient when we're young, but in the end I think he was right."

The key phrase Chris Berman built his career on consists of six words: "the weight of what you do." That weight consists of some pretty powerful things according to Chris: "Knowing your subject matter, I think being passionate about it, being informative and entertaining about it, and the fact that you're consistent every night.

That's what it is, it's the general bulk of your work not, 'Eh boy, that was a good highlight that night wasn't it?' Well, you have to be able to say, 'That was a good highlight every night!' I would never want to be judged any other way than that."

OFFICE POLITICS

Another big part of playing the game and moving up the ladder is the office politics. Berman went about that part of the business thinking, "You try not to play them but you can't be oblivious to it either. Part of it is having the people in the decision-making process just know who you are a little bit. I don't know if that's playing politics, maybe they just don't know who you are and their only image of you is just like

Photography by ESPN

Berman in the early days.

a fan off the screen. Let them know what you're about. I think to play politics too much is, uh, if that's what you're doing primarily they'll see through that and you'll be put in places where you're not going to succeed and the public will see that."

In other words, there are always going to be job politics going on around you. The best way to handle these politics is to make sure you maintain good communication with your coworkers, especially your bosses. At times there will be coworkers who lie about you, and who will stab you in the back to make you look bad. If you maintain a good relationship and communication with the other workers and bosses, these attempts to hurt you will fail. Your bosses will know the difference because they know you, and the friends that work alongside you will defend you.

TUNA MAGIC

Charlie Tuna has been a radio star in Los Angeles for decades. His journey started out very humbly in a small Midwestern town, "A friend of mine, who I hired at the station in Kearney, Nebraska, we both decided that if were going to go anywhere we'd get our first tickets [broadcasters used to be required to get a license from the FCC to be on the air, the licenses were known as tickets. We are no longer required to have a license to be on the air]. So we went down to Dallas, to Elkins Broadcast School, and we got our first class radio license. It was like a six-week course but it wound up being four weeks for us. You have to go and take theory and pass the two FCC tests."

Charlie went back to Nebraska with his first-class radio license still wondering if he would ever be able to move out of the little town and fulfill his dreams. His buddy, in the meantime, applied for an on-air position in Wichita, Kansas, on the way home from Dallas and got the job.

"I was thinking I was going to be in Kearney the rest of my life, I just didn't see myself going anywhere bigger than Kearney. I wanted to work at KOMA in Oklahoma City because it was the station that all the kids would cruise Main Street listening to at night but I thought, ah that's just a dream. He went down to Wichita and started working, and about three months later he called me and told me they had another opening."

Charlie Tuna's career was on the move. He went from Wichita to Oklahoma City to Boston and then to Los Angeles, but none of it would have happened if he had not taken the chance of going to Dallas for broadcasting school. The key to it all, according to Charlie, is this: "I've always told people who want to get into the business to be prepared to do about twenty hours a day between on and off the air as far as just work. But also remember, I'm going to work twenty-one hours just to beat you."

E.D.'S FIRST JOB

After figuring out that she wanted to be a television news reporter in college, E.D. Hill wasted no time looking for her first job after graduation. "I spent the summer going out and driving from station to station. I went along parts of the East Coast. I went along parts of the North, in Minnesota. I sent my tapes out all over, really, just all over, everywhere."

While she is a big star now, seen by millions daily around the world on the Fox News Channel, E.D. found breaking into the business and getting that first job on the air was anything but easy. "I was turned down for hundreds of jobs, hundreds. I used to take every rejection letter and tape it, one to the next, on my walls. Everyday when I walked out of my apartment I would look at every rejection letter I had ever gotten and it inspired me to do better that day. It sounds kind of sick, but it's how I inspired myself."

The hard work paid off. E.D. got her first job as a reporter at KDLH in Duluth, Minnesota. "I worked three weekdays and on the weekend. It was long hours and a hard job. They were perfectionists, which was wonderful. It was an exacting, demanding station, so there was a level of professionalism that I have rarely seen since then which is amazing, a small station like that. It was great, great training. I was there thirteen months."

YOUR CHANCES OF MOVING UP

Larry King is optimistic about the chances of moving up the ladder in the broadcast business these days. "If you have talent, and you want it, there always seems to be an opening. In other words, there is no great broadcaster in Missoula, Montana, *unless* he doesn't want to leave Missoula. If you're terrific, and you're a jock or a sports guy and you're on in Missoula, Montana, and you are age thirty, if you want to leave Missoula, you will definitely get a job in a bigger market. So you could be great, if you want to stay in Missoula that's fine, but the openings always occur. I'd say that the field is unlimited, but the competition is vicious."

King's keys to beating the competition on the way up the ladder: "Perseverance up off the floor. Opportunistic. Ambition, I guess, is the word."

Bob Kingsley thinks the formula is pretty simple. "There's only one way to go about it and that's just go do it. By virtue of being out there and, you know, just getting after it all the time. Hanging out at the right places and being there all the time and pretty much convincing people you know what you were doing, whether you do or not. That's how I got this gig, the countdown. Somebody just mentioned my name one night to Tom Rounds who owned Watermark with Casey Casum and they were thinking about doing the same thing that Casey does [Top 40 Countdown], only with country. I produced it for the first four years and the guy that was there left, and I started voicing it in '78, and it just worked out. Gosh, talk about a lucky disc jockey."

Luck always seems to have a hand in moving up the ladder of success, but if you will notice, all the luck is preceded by plenty of hard work. There are a lot of keys to success: honing your voice, networking, keeping up with the trade magazines and Web sites, keeping a list of vital industry information, and going the extra mile. The road to success has to start somewhere, in broadcasting that can mean going to college or a career school. We will take a look at these paths in chapter 4.

End Notes

[1] Arthur, Ray James. *The Science of Success*. La Jolla, CA: James Ray International, 1999.

[2] White, Heather. *Networking for Business Success*. London: WritersPrintShop, 2004.

[3] Ziglar, Zig. *Over the Top: Moving from Survival to Stability, from Stability to Success, from Success to Significance*. Nashville, TN: Thomas Nelson, 1998.

[4] *www.tvspy.com*

[5] *www.tvjobs.com*

[6] *www.newsblues.com*

[7] *www.radioandrecords.com*

[8] *www.insideradio.com*

[9] *www.billboard.com*

[10] Boyd, Andrew. *Broadcast Journalism*. Oxford: Focal Press, 2000.

Getting Started on the Air

Although it is not impossible, the chances of getting an on-air job in a larger market, having little or no previous experience, are not very good. It is very possible, however, to get an on-air job in a small town. If you are willing to relocate or already live in a smaller market, this is a fantastic way to get a broadcasting career started.

Major markets, or larger cities, such as New York, Los Angeles, Chicago, and Dallas, are in a constant state of having their ratings monitored. With only a few weeks off in between the spring, summer, fall, and winter ratings books, monitoring happens year round. In most cases, at major market stations these ratings are the bottom line. If an air personality's numbers go down, he could find himself out of a job. If the ratings go up, more than likely, his salary will too. I have seen it happen where a personality gets a raise one ratings period and gets fired the next. Ratings make the world go around in big-city broadcasting. You can learn more about how the ratings work in appendix C, but right now lets focus on how to get a career on the air off the ground.

STARTING SMALL

Ratings being what they are in big cities, the best chance of getting into broadcasting, with a job on the air, is by starting in a small town. Not only is it more practical to get a job in a small market, it also allows you to make mistakes and learn the arts and skills of being an on-air personality without too much pressure. Ratings are still important at small stations, but there is less competition and most of the on-air talent will be closer to your level. For someone just starting a career on the air, the main focus should be learning how to improve your craft, not worrying about whether or not you will have a job in a few weeks. This is why it is so important, not to mention advantageous, to get your first on air job in a smaller town.

Although Fox News Channel anchor E.D. Hill's first job in Duluth, Minnesota, paid her almost nothing, she considers being able to start out in a small town a great advantage. "It's interesting, nowadays, I have young women who come up to me here at Fox and they'll say, 'Oh, I want to do exactly what you do.' I say, 'that's terrific, how do you intend to start?' They say, 'Well, I don't want to start in a small town, you know, I live near New York so I want to start right around here,' or, 'I live in Miami, I really want to start in Miami.' They don't want to mess with the small town. I'm like, 'Listen, if everybody felt that way, no one would have a job.'"

Obviously E.D. feels strongly that the best way to get an on-air career off the ground is by getting started in a small market. "The fact of the matter is, you have to start in the small town. There is really a good reason for that. Regardless of who you are, you're going to make mistakes and it's a lot better to make 'em when there's 13,000 people watching you then 1.3 million people watching you. When you make a mistake at the big level, everybody notices and everybody remembers. Fortunately you get the chance to make the mistakes at the small level where people are a whole lot more forgiving and the papers generally don't have a media correspondent so they aren't going to write it up. I don't think people really appreciate that enough."

Del Cockrell of the American Broadcasting Schools agrees: "Remember, you've got to start at the bottom. You start at maybe a Chickasha, Oklahoma, radio station and work your way up. Then the sky's the limit. We have a lot of graduates who make very good money in this business after getting out and going one, two, or three radio stations down the road."

SHOW ME THE MAGIC

Once you are able to secure your first job on the air, strange, if not amazing, things can happen. Take Charlie Tuna, for instance. He got his first job at a little station in Kearney, Nebraska, when he was sixteen and quickly got a boost to his career. "The morning man got sick one time and, uh, it's a funny story because he was a little drunk and lost his teeth in the toilet when he threw up. So they asked me to do the morning show in an emergency and I did. They decided to keep me on, so I wound up when I was sixteen years old doing mornings. Then I'd run out of the station about 8:05 for a nine o'clock class at school. That was it. That was the beginning of everything."

COSTAS' FIRST JOB

Bob Costas had a little seasoning, having gone to college, but still got his first paying job on the air in a smaller market. "It's something I hadn't calculated, but it soon struck me, you were, in a way, better off being in Syracuse because it's much more likely you could get a paying job at a real station in that local market than if you were going to college and the local market is Chicago or New York. I had a job when I was a senior at Syracuse broadcasting sports on radio and doing some fill-in stuff on television, and that was really helpful in helping me build a résumé early on."

As happens so often in the broadcast business, the element as important as anything else is being in the right place at the right time. Costas worked hard to make sure that he was in a position to get his initial air job. "A friend left WSYR in Syracuse for a job in Cincinnati, leaving open a play-by-play position calling minor league hockey games. He recommended me for the job and I just kinda fell into it because I don't think they had the time to do an extensive talent search. I remember it paid thirty dollars a game and five dollars a day—meal money on the road." That is not a lot of money, but money is not the most important factor when you are laying the corner stones of your career. "I would have paid them! If I had any money I would have paid them to do it!"

BERMAN'S FIRST JOB

Chris Berman's first paying position out of college was in an even smaller town. "I got a job at WERI at Westerly, Rhode Island. I got a job doing everything. I was a disc jockey, I read the news."

Those were the days when records were still made of vinyl, not compact discs, and were played on turntables, otherwise known as record players.

"Oh yeah. I played, uh, last week when I heard 'How Deep Is Your Love' by the Bee Gees, 'cause this was '77–'78, I played that f-ing record maybe 800 times! Yes, I queued up the records. In that year, I learned everything. I was disc jockey. I read the news. I did swap shows that small town stations do. I did 'open mic' once a week, you know, they call in [talk show], and I ran the board late at night, you know we carried the Red Sox games. So you really do everything, you work six days a week and they say we'll give you one day off. Well thanks a lot."

Berman's advice for those interested in a broadcasting career: "The most important thing we do is to communicate. I didn't say communications. I'm not saying it's bad, I'm not saying taking journalism or communications courses is bad, but don't think you must go to a college. Will it help you get your first job out of school? Maybe a little. I majored in American History, it's turned out okay. Now, what did I have to do in American History? I had to write. I had to read. I had to speak. Isn't that what we do? The most important thing is to communicate, not necessarily communications."

SIZE MATTERS

I did not know it at the time, but living in a small town when I started my career was a great blessing. My first air shift was from midnight to 6 AM on the weekends. I was just sixteen years old and had absolutely no previous experience. When you start off in a small town, do not be surprised if that first on-air job offers a little less money than what you dreamed it would. Don't expect big money right away and be ready to put in the hours and time you must in order to hone the craft of being good on the air. You will have to be willing to go the extra mile and work the extra hours in order to learn how to use your voice and to find tones and inflections that are enjoyable to listen to. It is no different than Michael Jordan spending extra time in the gym or a musician or actor in training.

In the Introduction, I described how I got my first radio job at the age of sixteen. It was at a small market radio station in Wyoming. For all the big breaks and acts of God that have helped me along the path of my career, this was the most important break because it got me into "the biz."

At that little station in Wyoming, I worked every shift that I could possibly get to learn the art of being on the air and to cultivate the skills it takes to be successful. When I was eighteen years old and a senior in high school, I was offered a full-time job as a disc jockey doing the overnight shift, midnight to 6 AM Monday through Friday. I had been working on the air for over two years and had dreamed of an opportunity like this one, so I readily accepted the position, not knowing what a terrible schedule I was getting myself into.

I got off the air at six in the morning. After recording commercials in the production room for another thirty minutes to an hour, I would drive home to try and get some sleep before school. My first class was at eight o'clock. As a senior, I had a light schedule with only a half day of classes, so I would be back home at one in the afternoon, again trying to catch some sleep before heading off to baseball practice at five in the afternoon. When practice was over at eight o'clock, I was back in bed, trying to catch another catnap until eleven o'clock, when I had to get ready to go back to work.

The schedule was such that I began to understand how someone could lose touch with reality. I woke up three different times a day, not knowing if it was morning, noon, or night, if I was going to work, school, or practice. Even harder was just trying to get to sleep in the first place because I was always keyed up from my latest activity.

As difficult as the schedule was, my first full-time job on the air was a priceless jump-start to my career. I had a job and was labeled a rising star. Even in a small market it helps to have a positive label. When I graduated from high school, instead of going to college with all my friends, I chose to continue climbing the ladder of my radio career. I wondered several times, especially during situations when my job was in jeopardy or I had no idea where my career was going, if I had made the right decision. Right now, it is easy to say that I did.

GETTING IN THE DOOR

The best way to get a job at a small market station is to get to know the program director (PD). There are a couple of key things you can do to help your chances of being hired.

Make an appointment to meet the program directors in person at the different stations that interest you. You must convince them that you are serious and that you are reliable. When you are getting to know a program director, play to his or her ego. Make each PD feel like he is the most talented person that you have ever met and that you would like to learn at the feet of the master.

More than likely, you will not be hired on the spot at your initial meeting. Do not let this bother you. It is normal. Stay in contact with the program directors and call them on a regular basis. Make sure you are available when they are ready to hire you.

Being in the right place at the right time is the biggest key to being successful in the broadcast business. Many times less talented people get a job because they made it easier for a manager to hire them. You must put yourself in a position where it is easy for the program director to hire you. You will need to do this if you are going to be a success not only in getting your first job but other jobs in the future.

KING'S FIRST JOB

CNN's Larry King put himself in the right place at the right time when the broadcasting industry was in its early stages. Larry got his first on-air job in Miami. "After high school I knocked around a bunch of odd jobs and then finally at age twenty-two went down to Miami, knocked on doors, got a job. A small station gave me a voice test and said, 'If you want to hang around here they usually have openings.' It was a very non-union town, with a lot of stations. An opening developed and I got a job as an all-around disc jockey, sports and news. That was May 1, 1957, a couple days before Herb Score was hit in the head by that line drive [at a Cleveland Indians game], because I remember talking about it on the air."

Larry remembers his first air shift as if it were yesterday: "Oh absolutely! I was scared to death! It was 9 AM on that morning and I, I, words weren't coming out of my mouth. The general manager kicked open the door to the studio and said, 'This is a communications business!' I did something that day that I do to this day. I brought the audience into my dilemma. I said it's my first day on the air and I'm nervous. Once I did that I completely relaxed, and I was never nervous again."

FACE-TO-FACE INTERVIEWS

There are few things that are certain in any business, but there is one situation that you can pretty much count on in any field. Sooner or later you will have to have a face-to-face interview in order to get a job. You can have the best audition tape and a great résumé and still lose a job because you come off the wrong way when you meet a prospective boss.

Tyler Cox, one of the nation's top program directors, is based in Dallas and is the former national program director, news/talk, for Salem Broadcasting.

He and Bruce Gilbert, general manager at ESPN Radio, have had about as many face-to-face interviews over the years as anyone in the business. What is it that catches their attention? Mr. Cox says it is "People who have done their homework, who come in and have an understanding about what your station's about. Who can even speak off the cuff and fluently, someone who expresses a working knowledge of what the radio station is about. It doesn't have to be exactly accurate but someone who does their homework and knows what they're talking about, and who they're talking to goes a long way."

Some of this "homework" Mr. Cox refers to also includes getting information on the people you are trying to get to hire you. Find out where they are from, where they grew up, and where they went to school. You may have something in common. At a top-five market radio station I worked for, we were looking to fill a sports talk show position. The program director and I were going through tapes and résumés and he came across a package from

Photography by Lori Conrad

Tyler Cox, program director in Dallas, author John Grisham, and Chris Schneider.

a guy who grew up in the same town that he did. The first comment out of my PD's mouth when he saw it was, "If this guy would have done his homework, he would have know we were from the same hometown!" That kind of homework would have given the applicant an inside advantage. Sometimes the little things make the difference in getting the job or not.

ESPN's Bruce Gilbert says, "The thing that impresses me is just genuine, honest people. I think that unfortunately our business is full of too many phonies, people who are trying to falsely impress you. I like just genuine people who are honest about who they are, who have a lot of self-confidence in what they're all about and no pretense as far as what makes them tick. People who can, you know in our business, people who can entertain you. If they can entertain you in an interview, then I feel like they can probably entertain an audience. I like people who can be emotional and positive and also sometimes humorous, and be just a well-rounded, genuine person. Someone who is very one-dimensional and all they think about or talk about or live eat and breathe is radio, that's probably not a real good person. I'm not going to be that excited about them."

Bruce Gilbert, general manager, ESPN Radio.

WHAT TURNS THEM OFF

On the other hand, there are plenty of things that can turn a program director off. Stay away from doing what these job-seekers did that made a negative impression. Tyler Cox says, "It's an applicant who hasn't done his or her homework, who doesn't know what the radio station's format is about, who doesn't know what's going on in the marketplace, who doesn't have a clue of what the competitive landscape is about."

Bruce Gilbert explains, "The stuff that turns me off is just those people that do have a false sort of belief in themselves that they're the greatest and they're the best. I guess you look out for that large ego and that 'I-can-do-anything' attitude and 'I don't need to learn anything because I've got it all figured out.'

"I want people who are still looking to learn and who have had a lot of life experience. You know it's funny, the people who have been through the most in life are usually the best on the radio because they've experienced some really down times in life and had some very difficult moments. I think those have made them stronger and made them wiser and more relate-able to the audience 'cause most of the people listening have had to go through hard times too."

Before setting up a face-to-face interview with you, a program director will usually ask you to send him a cover letter and a résumé. You must take these things very seriously; they represent you in your absence. The program director will equate you to what you've written, and that can have a big impact. Tyler Cox explains, "We are in the spoken word communication business, so you better know how to write. Poor writing skills are just a real put-off. That's increasingly true for no matter what industry you're looking at, but man, when you're dealing with spoken word radio, you better know how to write." We will go into more detail on good cover letters and résumés later in the book.

MAKING THE AUDITION TAPE

Small market program directors are always looking to hire people for positions that are difficult to fill. These are usually overnight or weekend shifts. You may be able to secure a part-time position without an air-check tape—I did. However, in order to get a full-time position, a voice- or videotape will probably be required.

So, how do you get a tape of yourself without being in the business? This is where having gone to broadcast school, in one form or another, comes in handy. Not only do you learn how to use the equipment when you are at these schools, but you can make yourself an audition tape, and many times the schools will help their students find a job after graduation.

As convenient as that is, it is not a necessity. There are several ways around this little problem, but again, it requires some dedication on your part.

Advances in technology today, including karaoke machines, computers, and CD/DVD recorders, allow you to have a better sound system in your home than what we had in our early radio and television stations. The idea may sound hokey, but taping yourself at home is not only an option, it is a must, if it is your only way to make a voice-check tape. Work on recording yourself on tape until you feel comfortable with what you have recorded and how you look and sound. Then make copies of it to hand out to the different PDs or hiring managers you are in touch with.

This is not the only option. If you are able to establish a good relationship with a certain program director or station manager, ask him if you can sit in on one of his sessions in the production room. Usually small stations record many of their own commercials. More than likely, if you have established a good relationship with this person, he will say yes. If he says no, you can offer to buy time in his production room to make your tape. The cost should be minimal.

I did this for one of my first television jobs in Dallas. I was working full-time as the sports director at the USA Radio Network, but I also wanted to break into the local television market. I watched the local stations and noticed that one of them did short news and sports features during movies in the evening. I called the station and asked the production manager what it would cost to make a tape in their studio. She told me it would cost about $400 (it cost more because it was a big city, and it was in television). I bit the bullet, paid the money, and made the tape. It was nothing special, just a couple minutes of me talking about the big news and sports stories of the day, but it was enough to show that I could look decent and sound good on television. It worked. The station manager liked what he saw, and a couple of weeks later they asked the newscaster whose job I wanted to leave. The production manager asked me if I would like to take over, and I happily accepted.

The option of using a station's own production room to make your tape has several great advantages. It is yet another way for you to get to know the person doing the hiring, another way for you to prove to them you are serious, and of course, gives you an opening to make a tape for them. I would advise that you first practice on your equipment at home. When you do get the chance to make a tape of yourself in the production room, it may be a one-time shot, and you will need to be ready for the moment.

WHAT THEY'RE LOOKING FOR IN THE TAPE

What the program director or news director is looking for most in an aircheck tape is that you do not have a major speech impediment and that you can communicate on the air in a pleasing fashion. If you have real talent, all the better! If you do have a speech impediment but are still determined to be in the business, do not give up. In chapter 9 we will see a list of many great people who overcame a speech impediment to go onto greatness. We will also hear from a former NFL quarterback who overcame a lisp and who now has big jobs on the air in both radio and television. Many speech impediments and heavy accents can be overcome with training and practice.

TERMS OF EMPLOYMENT AND CONTRACTS

For those just starting out in the business, there are usually no contracts to be signed or major terms of employment involved. It is usually a simple verbal agreement to pay you a certain amount for working certain shifts. The contracts will come when you move up to medium and major markets, but not always. Many major market stations choose not to put many of their employees under contract.

Some markets are unionized, and others are not. The main union for radio and television personalities in the United States is the American Federation of Television and Radio Artists, or AFTRA.[1] When you work at a union station, naturally you will be asked to join if you are not already a member. This is something I would highly recommend because the union will make sure that you get a fair and legitimate deal. AFTRA has worked very hard over the years to make sure radio and television talents are not taken advantage of by employers.

If you live in a non-union market, then you are on your own. When it comes to contracts, it is *always* a good idea to read them through thoroughly, write down questions that come up, and highlight paragraphs that you do not understand (do not feel stupid—every contract is full of dense wording that can be difficult to understand). Seek the council of a lawyer or person you trust who can give you good advice. Do not be afraid to bring these questions up with your future employers—they expect you to. Negotiating for yourself with a future boss can always be tricky. Obviously you do not want to make an enemy of the person you are going to work for. Remember that negotiation does not necessitate a confrontation. When you negotiate, you can be smart, tough, and kind all at the same time.

Until you gain a little star power, you need the work more than the station needs you, so these contracts will almost always be weighted in the favor of the company. For instance, you will likely have a "no compete" clause, which usually says that if you quit, you cannot work for a competing station in the market for a certain amount of time, usually six months to a year. Under contract many times you are also deemed an "exempt employee," meaning they do not have to pay you overtime. This usually applies to management as well.

During your contract negotiations, you will determine your salary and what you will be doing. The contract should also stipulate things like vacation time, sick days, how much you will get paid for station appearances, your compensation as on-air spokesman for a sponsor, and how many sponsorships you can have going at one time. You may also be able to add some incentives, like a bonus if ratings go up during your air shift.

It has been my experience that companies put clauses in the contract that they may be happy to take out if you ask. Many times they are open to the idea of adding bonuses for ratings increases too, since that is a win–win situation for everyone. When you get to be one of the top personalities in a large market, you can hire an agent to take care of all these details for you.

In this chapter we focused on how to get a job on the air. Keep in mind that there is much, much more to broadcasting than just being on the air. There are great positions off the air that are essential to a station's success that you may be better suited for. We will discuss these in chapter 5.

End Note

1 *www.aftra.org/aftra/aftra.htm*

5

Getting Started off the Air

If you cannot get a job on the air at a small market station, or you cannot relocate, the next best option is to get an off-air job somewhere nearby where you can get your career started. Many major stars, including Katie Couric and Rene Syler, got started in the business this way.

Syler, former co-host of *The Early Show* on CBS, started her broadcasting career by getting an off-air job as an intern. She then became a news anchor in Reno before moving up the ladder to Birmingham, Dallas, and then New York.

Rene tells us how she got her start: "I called around to some TV stations in Sacramento, California, where I'm from, and got on as an intern at the Fox station and basically learned everything in about, it makes it sound so shallow, but I learned a lot in about six months and then got a TV job in Reno. Now when I say I learned everything in six months, I mean I learned enough to get a job. Learning is a constant thing."

Rene used those six months well, learning some very important things in order to get her first job on the air. "Just the basics of learning good story-telling in terms of story-telling in television is different from print, or even radio because you have to incorporate the pictures. So I learned about 'see-dog, say-dog,' making the pictures reinforce the words, that kind of thing. (See-dog, say-dog is a common phrase in television. It basically means to enhance the pictures on the screen with your words of description). Also, my first TV job I had to edit videotape, so I had to learn how to edit. I got a real sort of 'crash course' in television there, but I was never on the air in Sacramento. My first experience on the air was in Reno.

As for how she got that first on-air job in Reno after being an off-air intern for six months, Rene says "I dropped a tape off [at the TV station] and then I drove back home, and then they called me. Then I went back up there for an interview, you know it was one of those things, it paid fifteen thousand dollars a year as a cub reporter. Fifteen grand! There was no wiggle room, it was like, take it or leave it, and because I wanted to get in the business I took it. You know, I made more money waiting tables than I did my first year in television. Because it was what I wanted to do, I just kind of looked at it as a learning experience. I looked at it as grad school."

PAYING THE DUES

Rene found out that her school of hard knocks also meant paying her dues going through some tight times monetarily. "I could basically pay my rent and a couple of other little things and that was it. It was really difficult because to be on the air you still have to look good, that means you still have to have clothes and you have to have makeup and you have to have hair treatments and all that stuff. That's hard to do when you're taking home $494 dollars every two weeks! My rent was $450!"

Fox News star E.D. Hill had similar money problems while working at her first on-air job in Minnesota. "When you go to stations that are that small, you make so little money that you have to keep moving. You are just desperate to move, whether you like the place or not, you're desperate to move because you've just got to start earning more money. I recall that I was eligible for those bread and cheese giveaways because I was making such a small salary. It was the overtime that saved me. I started anchoring on the weekends, and I was the assignment editor, producer, and anchor and frequently reported, so I would get a lot of overtime hours on the weekend. Six months into it I started sending my tapes out and I got a job as an anchor in Waco, Texas. A huge increase in salary."

DIFFERENT KINDS OF OFF-AIR JOBS

There are a lot of off-the-air jobs that are in constant need of being filled at radio and television stations. Training at university and career broadcasting schools will definitely give you a better chance to land any of these jobs, but many times stations will be willing to train you if you are willing to work the less desired shifts. Here are some of the positions:

BOARD OPERATORS

Informally known as board ops, these are people who run radio control boards at large market and some medium market stations, and at all television stations. Everything that goes on the air goes through the master control room. The control board consists of a varying number channels that run audio and/or video that goes on the air. Each one of these channels has a volume control called a "slider" or "pot," which allows the board op to adjust what goes on the air. Hands-on training for this position is desired, but many times stations will be willing to train new board ops.

In Los Angeles, we liked to call our board op the traffic cop, because he was in charge of making sure all the different things going on the air got on in the right order and sounded good. When I do a sportscast, my board operator is making sure that my fellow anchors and I get on the air, along with our audio cuts, traffic reports, and live reports. On top of all that, he runs the commercials that are logged (so that we can all get paid) and keeps different people informed as to what is going on. He is the one who has to inform the traffic reporter to keep her reports short or she will not get on the air due to breaking news, which the board op has to make sure gets on as well.

This is an important job with a lot of different challenges. Most of us who started working at small radio stations had to run our own control board, so we got the best of both worlds, being on the air and learning how to work the equipment as well.

COPY WRITERS

Copy writers produce scripts for commercials, public service announcements (PSAs), promotional events, and other written information the station runs on the air.

Commercials that run on the air come from several different sources. There are national and regional commercials that are produced by a professional recording studio and sent to the station to play, as is. There are a lot of commercials, however, that each station has to produce by itself. At almost all stations, production directors are in charge of putting these together. In major markets, broadcasters who are asked to voice these commercials usually get a talent fee or are paid for it. At small market stations, it is considered just part of the job for an air talent to voice commercials. This is in your best interest, as a matter of fact, because it gives you more of a chance to hone your voice and get better on the air.

Copy writers are the creative and talented people who write these scripts. Their job is to sell whatever the commercial is pitching in the time allowed. Commercials usually run ten, thirty, or sixty seconds.

Duties for the copy writer do not end there. There are station promos that need to be written. You have heard them many times on the air: "Come join us at the Happy Mart this afternoon and get a free hot dog while you meet morning man Jack," or something similar to that. Those have to be written by somebody, and usually it is the copy writer.

A part of each station's licensing agreement includes doing a certain amount of good for the local public. In order to accomplish this, most stations run PSAs. An example of this would be something like, "Help out the local Red Cross today by giving blood here at the station." These are usually written by the copy writer. Some stations do not hire copy writers anymore, requiring the production directors and air talent to write their own copy. If you desire to be a copy writer, you will probably be required to prove that you can actually write creatively when you are interviewed for the job. Bring some examples of your writing that showcase your writing skills.

TRAFFIC DEPARTMENT

The traffic department consists of the people and computers that put together the logs (pages) that tell board operators what commercials to run and at what time. This position requires working with just about everyone in the station. Since their job is to log commercials, the traffic department (traffic) has to deal with salespeople. When a sale is made and a commercial is produced, traffic has to make sure it gets played on the air, and at the right time. They make sure the commercial, also known as a "spot," is run on the air as many times as it is supposed to. If a special time slot was purchased for the spot to run, traffic makes sure it is on the log to run at that time.

Traffic also works closely with the board op, who will eventually play the commercial, and the program director, who oversees the format to make sure that commercial breaks are taken at the right time. The general manager, operations manager, and sales manager are always watching the bottom line, and they stay in contact with the traffic department to make sure that sales are being made and that those clients are paying their bills. Many entry-level positions in the traffic department require no previous experience, but a working knowledge of computers and the business helps.

ACCOUNT EXECUTIVES

Account executives, also known as salespeople or marketing representatives, sell commercials that will air on the station. It is common for salespeople to make more money than everyone else in the building, with the exception of the general manager, operations manager, and sales manager. Without sales, very little would happen in radio and television because without commercials running on the air, no one gets paid.

There is just as much, if not more, competition between stations for good salespeople as there is for good air talent. The salesperson's job is more than selling commercials; she is also a key ambassador of the station in the community. It is the job of some account executives to deal with regional and national agencies. This is not only an important source of money for the station, but is the only way important people around the area come into direct contact with the station. Depending on the size of the station looking to hire a salesperson, experience may or not be necessary. Many times a station will hire a new salesperson and pay her a minimum salary for six months. If the person has not reached a certain level of sales at the end of that six-month period, she will be asked to leave. It is not for the faint hearted, but the rewards can be very nice.

PRODUCERS

Producers work with on-air hosts to put talk shows together. Duties are varied but usually include setting up interviews, screening phone calls, setting up on-air bits to entertain the listener, and making sure everything goes smoothly on the show. There can be a lot of power that goes with this position. The producer is a gatekeeper of sorts, with a great deal of sway over who makes it on the air and who does not. Usually a certain amount of experience or training as a producer is required for this position. Having good contacts and knowing how to track down celebrities and book interviews is important, as is being creative in coming up with show topics and bit ideas.

PROMOTIONS DEPARTMENT

This department is in charge of finding ways to get the public more interested and interactive with the station. When you hear contests running on the air, there is a good chance the promotions department came up with the idea. When a personality is out at the mall giving away free tickets to a game, or running a constest to win free tickets to a special movie screening, the promotions department is beind it. Many promotion departments also have assistants that take the station van or truck out in the public as well, sometimes even doing spots on the air. Generally no experience is necessary for entry-level positions in promotions. This is usually a good way to get your foot in the door to be on the air.

TAPE EDITORS

Tape editors are important in both radio and television. At smaller stations the air talent is usually expected to edit most of their own audio or video. At larger stations, especially news and sports intensive stations, there are positions available that are editing intensive. The main tasks for tape editors include recording audio/video feeds or reports from outside sources such as a network or a reporter filing from the field.

Much like being on the air, there is a lot of art and skill involved in being a good editor. The person in this position can make an air personality, and the station, look good or bad, depending on how well he does his job. Experience or training at a college or career school program using the audio/video equipment and editing computers is usually required for this position.

CAMERAMEN/WOMEN

Cameramen are essential in television. Photojournalists can add just as much to a story as the on-air personality. The old saying "a picture is worth a thousand words" holds true for this job. The cameraman is out on the streets with a reporter, showing the viewer what the reporter is talking about. In some cases the photojournalist will go out to cover an event without a reporter. The anchors in studio can talk over the pictures when run on the air. (Remember "see-dog, say-dog?")

Just like being on the air, this job takes talent and skill to do well. A good cameraman will make a reporter better, and vice versa. Usually experience or training in a university or career school broadcast program is required, but some small market stations are willing to train.

These are just a few of the numerous off-air positions you may want to consider in order to get your foot in the door. Some of these positions are closer to on-air work than others if that is your ultimate goal. You have a shorter road to being on the air from the producer's chair than you do from the traffic department. Nothing is impossible, however, if you are willing to put yourself in the right place at the right time.

RADIO VERSUS TV JOBS

It is a little easier to get an off-air position in radio than in television because the equipment used in television is a little more complicated. Most can learn how to run a radio control board in a matter of days, but it takes a little more time in television.

If you want to get started in television in an off-air position, the best idea is to take a class in TV equipment and production at a university, small local college, or career school. This will give you a good idea of what you will need to know and how to run the equipment. Before deciding on a particular course, call and ask a few local television news directors what they recommend that you learn. This is a wonderful way to make some valuable contacts and, at the same time, find out what you have to do to work at their station.

Follow their advice, and stay in contact with them while you are taking your class. Keep notes of when you called whom, and what was discussed— that way you will not get the station managers confused with each other and make a big mistake. Staying in touch will make it very easy for several stations to eventually hire you once you finish your courses.

IN THE "BIZ"—OFF THE AIR

Now, you have a job in the business. If you find that working off the air is what you love to do, you can focus on moving up the ladder to become the best in your field. Believe it or not, this happens quite frequently. Remember, making things happen behind the scenes in broadcasting is just as much an art as is being a star in front of the mic or camera.

Many people who have the desire to get into the business have no idea about all the magic that happens off the air, because all they have ever seen or heard has been from those on-air. Most people never know, listening to or watching a great talk show, that the producer behind the scenes made most of it happen. They don't know that a great sportscast they enjoyed was the work of an amazingly talented editor or producer who put all the tape or interviews together. Good off-air people are just as talented, respected, and, many times, powerful, as those who are on the air.

GETTING ON FROM OFF

If after getting an off-air job, your goal is still to be on air, take heart: you have made an important step on your path, but there is a lot of work still ahead to get where you want to go.

The first thing you must do is get to know the people who can help you get on the air. These people are program directors, news directors, sports directors, assignment editors, air personalities, anchors, and producers. Make yourself available to learn everything you can from them. Let them know you are willing to do whatever you have to do, professionally speaking, to make it on the air. They will let you know what those things are, but do not expect it to be easy or quick. Remember, there are people on the air who have spent years working to get to where they are. You must be willing to work twice as hard, doing both your off-air job and the extra work it takes to learn the trade and to impress the boss. Do not let the extra work you are doing to learn how to be on the air take away from the effectiveness of your off-air job. If this happens, you will lose everything. If the boss sees you doing poorly in your off-air position, his confidence in putting you on the air will diminish dramatically.

The best off-air jobs that may put you in a position to get on the air vary from station to station. Some all-talk stations allow their producers and board operators to open the microphone and join in with the hosts at any time. Other stations would never let a board op on the air but may have a promotions assistant doing broadcasts from the station's "fan van" all summer long. This is where you need to put in a little research. Study the stations, and listen closely to find out how they work. If one station lets its board operators on the air, apply for that position. At another place, if the promotions department gives you the best opportunities, go for that. Volunteer to be the one that goes out and does on-air reports. Do it for free to prove to the boss you have some talent. Be the one to go out on a remote appearance with the station's top personality. Watch and learn. You will not get your on-air position by just doing your off-air job. You must do more.

For example, when I got my first job in radio I was a part-time disc jockey. I made the announcement to everyone that I would work for anyone at anytime on the air. The offer opened some eyes. I also started hanging out with the morning man. His air name was Scott Byrd. For some reason he found me amusing, telling me that I was the only person he had ever seen that had "an attitude after being on the air for just a week." I guess I was a little cocky, and I am just lucky that he found it amusing.

Scott had the number-one rated show in town so I figured he was doing something right. I became his friend. I would come in early in the morning to watch him do his show. When he was broadcasting from a remote location, I was there to help and learn from him. I watched him closely, and when he had some free time, I would ask questions. He gave me pointers that I still use today, like taking a good healthy breath before talking so as to not run out of air in the middle of a sentence. Another good pointer, and one of the most important to remember, is to talk to one listener at a time. You may have a million people listening at once, but they only hear for themselves. The miracle of radio and television is that you can be talking to a million people and still talk to each person individually.

NEVER MISS AN OPPORTUNITY TO LEARN

Use your position at the station, whether it be in radio or television, to get to know as much as you can. For example, when you have some free time, during lunch or after five, ask the production director or a tape editor if you can sit in and watch him work his magic. Usually people in these positions will be thrilled to show you what they do. Never get in their way; if they are busy, just watch. I repeat, never, never get in their way or make a nuisance of yourself; you want to make a friend, not an enemy. When they have more time, they will be eager to show and tell. Learn from the personalities; again, stay out of their way, or you will not be invited back. Sit in with the producer running a talk show and offer to help if at all possible.

As you do this, these people will become more comfortable with you. They will show you valuable secrets and allow you to practice on the equipment. This is much easier in radio. Often, at night you can find an empty production room where you can spend all night practicing.

It is a little tougher if you are working in TV to get onto a set to practice doing a newscast. It is possible, however, to get into a production/edit booth and learn how to edit and practice on the microphone. You can learn an immense amount if you are willing to go the extra mile, spend the extra time, and make the personal contacts.

The explosion of video equipment should also help in your bid to grow in the television industry. You can easily set up your own tripod and camera and practice as if you were on the air. It is not quite as professional as doing the real thing, but it is not completely different and offers a great way to practice. Do this frequently, and get good enough so that when you feel comfortable you can show the boss what you look like on camera or what you sound like on tape. Prove to him that you do have talent.

PATIENCE IS A VIRTUE

Success will likely come in small measures. Do not get too down when it does not come fast enough. Maybe your first step into on-air work will be doing a voiceover on a commercial, maybe it is even covering a news or sports event to get interviews from newsmakers. Whatever it is you do, always take an extra step and do more than is expected. This is the best way to be noticed. If you are assigned to get tape, bring it back and offer to edit it. Now all that extra time you spent learning how to use the equipment will come in handy. Offer to voice the report, and even if the answer is no, do one later that night so the boss can hear it. When he hears you, your boss will know you are serious about being on the air. The next time you cover an event and offer to do the report, there is a decent chance he will say yes.

If you go the extra mile, you will be noticed. You may have to record reports on your own time and play them back for your bosses twenty different times, but sooner or later they will put you on the air because they know you are serious. They will also know that you can do the job.

MAKE FRIENDS

Never underestimate the importance of making friends in the right places, especially places in management. The program director, news director, sports director, general manager, and sales manager are the main people you want to get to know and befriend. It will also be very important to get to know the station's top air personalities if possible. All of these people are very influential; they can help you get to where you want to go. It is harder for people to say no if they like you.

Bob Kingsley got started in the business while in the Air Force, stationed in Iceland. "A fellow in the mess hall said they were looking for an announcer. It was like a fluke thing, man. I went over and they gave me some copy and

Bob Kingsley, one of the world's most listened to voices.

I absolutely butchered it! I thought, 'Well, that's the end of that.' I forgot about it and two days later they called and said I was in special services. [He got the job.] When I got sent back to the States I knew exactly what I wanted to do: Somehow get on the radio and play records."

Even though Bob had a little experience on the air from his military service, it was not considered to be very impressive in the real radio industry back in the States. "I had an old tape recorder and I made a little demo tape. I got in the car and started driving around. And then I went down and stayed with this friend of mine in San Diego who was a disc jockey, Don Howard, a big-time jock back in the fifties and sixties at KCBQ. He said, 'One of the reasons why no one is taking you serious is because this demo tape you've got here just really sucks!' I don't think he was near as kind as that, but I got the point. So we went in, actually got in a real studio, and we worked up a script and I went back on the road again."

Even with the new tape, Bob could not find himself a job on the air, so he had to start with a position that helps you learn about humility: sales.

Photos courtesy of Bob Kingsley

Kingsley in the early years with Willie Nelson.

"My first radio job was in Palmdale, California. It was a day-timer [only on the air during the day]. The deal was, I could come in and practice after they went off the air, but I had to sell commercials. I was there about six months and I think I sold one account and I don't think that account paid. My shot at sales was just horribly unsuccessful. While I was doing that, obviously all I could think about was getting in there and playing records."

Of course, that eventually happened. It started with a little practice while he was in the military; just enough of a taste to let him know that being on the air was what he wanted to do in life. Even though his first real job was off the air, as a salesman, it offered him the great advantage of being able to practice on the equipment at night. Bob Kingsley eventually became the host of one of the most listened-to radio shows in the world, the *American Country Countdown*, and now *Bob Kingsley's Country Top 40.*

MIRACLES DO HAPPEN

When I was working in Los Angeles at an all-sports station, a young tape editor fresh out of college spent extra time in between shifts making air-check tapes in the production room. He studied the sports pages closely and made quick friends with some of the station's top talk show hosts. He passed his air-check tapes to the program director, and it eventually paid off. Our overnight host, a bit of a hypochondriac, called in sick for his shift and Tony, the young tape editor, happened to be there that night. The program director asked him to fill in. Tony had worked hard to put himself in the right place at the right time, and he was given the opportunity. He took advantage of it, doing a good enough job that he was asked to become a part-time talk show host on the weekends.

Within a year Tony was offered the overnight show full-time. This was in Los Angeles, the second largest market in the country!

Something similar happened while I was in Dallas. A bright, hard-working intern named John was offered a board op position at our station after he graduated. One of his board shifts was on Sunday morning, and he noticed that the part-time news anchor was struggling with her sports updates. Being the sports director, I noticed it too. So John offered to do the casts for free, as part of his board shift, just to get the experience and be on the air. I worked with him off the air for a couple of months on his voice and delivery and when he was good enough, our program director agreed that he could go on the air. John has grown from doing those casts to being a part of our sports department, and he is getting invaluable experience in one of the top markets in the country. That kind of experience is priceless. He was soon also hired to do play-by-play for one of the small local universities.

Former child television star and veteran Los Angeles morning show personality Danny Bonaduce claims, "Everybody I know who is in radio, I don't know one person with a degree in broadcasting. What I know are people who were interns, and swept up around the radio station starting at thirteen [years old]. Then they got the night job and then they got the weekend job, then they got the afternoon job, then they got the morning show!"

Persistence and dedication will be the key to moving from an off-air to on-air position. Make it an easy choice for the program director or news director by being in the right place at the right time when the opportunity comes.

University and Career Broadcast Schools

The best way to build a career in the broadcasting business depends on your personal situation. If you are already out of college and in a different line of work, broadcast trade schools, known now as career schools, are probably the best option, either that or just getting a job in the business. If you are still school age, or are in the position to be able to take university classes, my recommendation is to go to college. This way you can get your start in the industry and get a good education to fall back on, in case you find that being in the biz is not for you. If you choose to go to a university, you will find yourself in some pretty good company.

In this chapter, we will hear from some major personalities who went to university to help start their career on the air. We will also find out what some of the most respected teachers of university broadcast programs have to say, as well as some highly respected leaders of career broadcast schools. Let's start out by looking at what you need to learn in order to impress those looking to hire you when you graduate. "The Jane Pauley Task Force (Society of Professional Journalists, 1996) surveyed executives at commercial TV stations and college faculty about their opinions of what broadcast journalism students should know. The task force determined that the four main needs were writing ability, a good attitude, knowledge and good work habits."[1]

UNIVERSITY PROGRAMS

Most major universities and even small colleges today have some sort of radio/TV, broadcast journalism, or mass communications program, and most of these programs are pretty good. As in everything, however, there is a hierarchy of school programs, just like you would find in college football or basketball. A survey sponsored by the Radio-Television News Directors Foundation (RTNDF) conducted by Vernon Stone of the Missouri School of Journalism asked news directors from radio and television stations around the country to rank the schools that best prepare students for a career in broadcasting. News directors turn to these university programs for entry-level hiring, as nine out of every ten TV news employees hired out of college are journalism and mass communication majors. The numbers are a little clearer for television than radio.

Responses to the question "From your experience, which school does the best job of preparing students for careers in television news?" ranked schools in this order:

1. Missouri

2. Northwestern

3. Florida

4. Washington State

5. Syracuse

6. Brigham Young

7. Ohio University

8. Columbia

9. Bowling Green

10. Texas

When news directors were asked which schools do the best job training students for a career in radio, a large majority failed to name a college or university. Of 303 news directors, only 73 named a college or university. Of the others, eleven named respected trade schools such as Brown College in Minnesota or American Broadcasting Schools, which are scattered around the Southwest. Twelve radio news directors said no school was much good and sixteen named the "school of hard knocks" or experience. Only five universities drew as many as three votes. Here are the results, ranked by number of mentions:

1. Syracuse

2. Missouri

3. Ohio University

4. Georgia

5. Texas[2]

At this point, you may be wondering about expenses. How much does it cost to attend one of the finer universities to get a broadcasting degree? As with most things, the price varies from school to school. Ivy League schools with strong broadcasting programs like Brown and Columbia are famously expensive. On the other hand, schools like Florida, BYU, Maryland, and Nebraska are a lot more affordable. For further information regarding universities and career schools, where they are, how big they are, and other notes, see appendix A at the end of the book.

The rankings above tell us several things. They show us the programs that are most respected by people doing the hiring in radio and television and show that some sort of training and education is much more necessary in television than in radio. The main reason for this is the equipment; in television, the hardware is more complicated and there is a lot more of it. Another factor, of course, is that while you can make mistakes and sound a little off on radio, no one can actually see you. On television, you can sound off and look off at the same time; it takes a little more training to have both the look and sound skills for television. This is why you find a lot of people that start off in radio and eventually move into doing television, frequently with great success. Getting the look down on camera is fairly easy for those who have figured out the art of being able to relate to the listener through radio. It can be pretty easy sometimes to spot young television personalities who skipped doing radio, because they have a harder time sounding natural on the air. Radio is a great way to learn how to relate to all viewers and listeners because the voice is the only form of connection.

WHAT YOU NEED TO LEARN

If you are going to school to start a career in broadcasting, then it would be a good idea to know what the people who do the hiring are looking for in a graduate. Tom Dickson researched this subject in his book *Mass Media Education in Transition*. "Executives in larger markets put more emphasis on liberal arts and cable courses than did those in smaller markets. Executives in smaller markets put more emphasis on marketing and sales, reading of industry publications, computer skills, and business management courses. Respondents generally expected new hires to know the basics needed to work in the industry. They were most often to name writing skills, the basics of broadcasting, knowledge of how to operate equipment, and communication skills as the most important skills or areas of knowledge."[3]

University programs have a fantastic amount to offer hungry broadcasting stars of the future. Kent Collins is the chairman of the radio/TV news department at the Missouri School of Journalism. "The School of Journalism stands alone, stands by itself. We teach advertising-public relations, newspaper-magazine and photo J. (journalism), and radio and television broadcast. Communications and all those other related skills are in different places on the campus."

Missouri has decided to separate its radio/TV program from its communications program. Collins says of this separation, "It helps them focus, and it asks them, frankly, to make some decisions before they get here as opposed to wallowing around in courses trying to make decisions. There's some intensity here to go ahead and get on with doing a lot of learning as opposed to trying to figure out where you're going when you get here."

Dona Hayes, head of the Syracuse University Broadcast journalism department, says, "The way I would define us is that we are a broadcast news department which puts the emphasis on news. Our vehicle for delivering the news is broadcast. Separately, there is a television, radio, and film department that teaches the non-journalism aspects of broadcasting: entertainment, promotion, sales, and other types of broadcast venues."

BROADCASTING SKILLS ARE TRANSFERABLE

Some students take broadcast courses to help them in other careers as well. At Missouri, according to Collins, "Some of them want to go into public relations, some of them have decided to go to law school."

Hayes sees the same thing at Syracuse. "We do have some students who go to law school after they've been in broadcast journalism. They do very well because of the type of training they get in broadcast journalism in terms of being able to write concisely, to develop an angle, and to support that angle. The performance skills that they learned are very good background for a legal career, so they tend to do quite well. We have some students who decide, for example, they want to be in public relations for various reasons, and certainly understanding the news business is a good jumping off point for that."

There is even some competition between these schools known for broadcasting prowess. "Yeah, we say unkind things about each other all the time," Collins jokes. "Syracuse is great competition, Northwestern, Maryland, and several other schools. Nebraska, I hate to mention it."

Broadcast journalism students find that they have to develop multiple skills. Hayes says, "I often say we're two-and-a-half majors. Our students have to be every bit the journalist as their print colleagues. On top of that they have to know production. On top of that they have to develop some degree of performance capability. Broadcast journalism is greater than one major."

WORKING BEHIND THE SCENES

There are some students who have neither the desire nor the capability to be on the air, but the broadcast industry has plenty of room for them too. "I think that stuff sorts itself out," continues Hayes. "We have a very good balance of emphasis here [at Syracuse] on the various on-air positions and behind-the-scenes positions. Those behind-the-scene positions are primarily in producing. Producing is where more of the jobs are. Over the course of time, it pretty much sorts itself out. The students come to find their own niche and by the time they leave, they are pretty much set on what path they want to take."

Hayes is impressed with the abilities of today's broadcast students. "When I was the age of the students I have, I don't know that I could have performed the way they do. They are remarkable in terms of coming up with ideas and executing ideas. They juggle so many balls at one time. They have other classes and other things in their lives too. I am just continually amazed."

As mentioned earlier, the broadcast business offers much more than just on-air jobs, something that the University of Missouri takes full advantage of. "Because we have an NBC affiliate, a regular commercial television station," Kent Collins explains, "you can imagine that we can teach broadcast news producing. We produce producers who are going into the large markets, not the majors, but who are starting their careers in places like Kansas City and Cincinnati and New Orleans, right out of school, because the demand for newscast producers is so great."

There are many who go into university programs looking to be on the air and find out they would rather be behind the scenes, according to Collins. "We have a lot of students that make the transition in thought once they get here. They come in thinking they want to be on camera, and after they've been around the place for awhile, they like the power and control aspects of being a newscast producer."

BERMAN'S COLLEGE EXPERIENCE

ESPN superstar Chris Berman attended Brown University to try and get his career on the air a push start. "I knew that, applying to colleges, I should go to a place that had a great radio station, but I wasn't worried about communications. I got involved with the radio the first week I was up there because," he chuckles, "my varsity sports career, once you get to college it pretty much ends."

Berman remembers a good laugh or two from his college years. "What stories weren't funny? I even did Brown baseball [play-by-play], really just to practice. I would do the middle innings, the fifth and sixth inning I would do by myself, and there was a good reason. He [his partner] always went to get the six-pack. We felt in the seventh inning we could have a beer, these were the seventies, okay, I mean Harry [Caray] did it so what the hell." (For those who don't know, Harry Caray was a renowned broadcaster for several Major League baseball teams, most notably the Chicago Cubs. He was the one who sang *Take Me Out to the Ballgame* during the seventh inning stretch at Wrigley Field.)

COSTAS' COLLEGE EXPERIENCE

Bob Costas claims that the reason he went to Syracuse in the early seventies was because of their broadcast department. "We used to drive from Syracuse down to New York or to Philadelphia or even—the longest trip I remember was to West Virginia for an NCAA Tournament game. We would put three or four of us in the car, chip in for gas money, and we'd each get to broadcast like half of the game. We were so keen to do this that we didn't even care how little sleep, how much time was involved. Just the chance to be on the air. We would trade off acting as each other's color man or play-by-play man or engineer or statistician for the chance to do it."

Photo courtesy of Bob Costas

Bob Costas, a rising star in the '70s.

A couple of internships while in college helped E.D. Hill figure out what she was going to do with her career. "I did two great internships while I was at UT [University of Texas], one at the local NBC station in Austin and one at the NBC station in San Antonio. I got there, and I knew that this was what I wanted. I think you do that. You try out different things and you determine where you fit, what gets you going. Live news was it for me. Breaking news just got my blood pumping." E.D. graduated from Texas and later went to graduate school at Harvard while working on the air in Boston.

Going to school always means a wealth of great memories for the rest of your life, even if you are concentrating on a broadcasting career.

Photography by Michael O'Neil/HBO

He is comfortable in his own success now.

Costas and his buddies would make many of their fondest memories while traveling to cover road games. "I remember one trip was a game against Fordham [University]—you know everyone had a crummy, beat-up, hand-me-down car, if they had a car at all. We made the whole trip back; a fellow named Andy McWilliams had a car, not only did the heat not work, but there was a hole in the bottom of the baseboard on the passenger's side. It must have been about five degrees below zero and we're driving through a wicked snowstorm after the Syracuse/Fordham game back from New York up to Syracuse. It must have been ten degrees in the car! I thought for sure I'd die of frostbite or hypothermia or something!

Driving back, through the snowstorm, you didn't know if you were more likely to freeze to death or drive off the road into a ditch and never be found! All just for the sake of doing half a game between Syracuse and Fordham on the campus radio station! We just did it for the love of being on the air and trying to pretend that we were Marv Albert or Marty Glickman or somebody."

E.D'S COLLEGE EXPERIENCE

E.D. Hill had to laugh and blush at the same time as she recalled the most memorable story of her college years: "When you're interning in college, wear pants if you're a girl. I recall vividly wearing one of those flouncy skirts down in Austin, Texas. As an intern you're always out carrying all the gear. So, I had a tripod in one hand and a camera or tapes or something in the other hand, and

I'm walking back to the truck with the male anchor and the photographer. We were out at the Austin airport and all the sudden one of the prop planes turned in our direction. My skirt blew over my head and stuck there! (she starts laughing). Because it's Texas and it's so hot in the dead of summer I'm not wearing a slip, I'm not wearing stockings, just my undies and that's about it! So this skirt blew over my head and I'm thinking, 'Well, I can't drop the gear!' [She's now laughing hysterically.] So I just stood there holding the tripod and the camera until the anchor finally came over and pulled the skirt from over my head. I don't know who was embarrassed more, me or him. We didn't say a thing, we got in the car and left. You'll notice I wear pants pretty often to this day!"

DIVERSIFY LEARNING

A lot of different things go into making a great on-air personality. If you are going to school to get a career on the air started, one way to help yourself is to study various subjects not directly related to broadcasting, as a broader knowledge base will help you in the long run. Author David Seidman advises in his book *Exploring Careers in Journalism* to "Go beyond journalism courses. Take as many English classes as you can. A foreign language can't hurt, either. If you like photography, take a class on that subject. If you're interested in broadcast journalism, look for classes in public speaking, debating or even acting—anything that teaches how to use your voice. Computer classes are helpful, since journalists use computers in everything from research to distribution. Don't focus on journalism alone."[4]

As you get your well-rounded education, remember that while you are learning and improving your mind, you need to work on making your voice an instrument that will sound good too. You can have the best education in the world but if no one can stand to listen to you, you are going to have a hard time getting a job. This little tidbit has caused plenty of consternation in people looking to hire talent out of college. Broadcast voice specialist Ann S. Utterback writes in the *Broadcast Voice Handbook*, "I have learned that there is much frustration among news directors about the lack of voice training that broadcast journalism students get while in college."[5]

Kent Collins of the Missouri School of Journalism advises those who want to get into the business, especially television, just for the glory of it, "If they are just starting out their college career, they need to question themselves hard as to whether they are interested in journalism or interested in TV. There are a lot of good students, good people who come to this school, and others, because they want to be on TV as opposed to doing news and sports journalism. That's a real serious issue. As far as starting their careers, the expectations are too high. They expect the money will be bigger than it is and the hours will be shorter than they are."

CAREER BROADCASTING SCHOOLS

If you are not in the position to go to college, a broadcast trade school or career school may be the best way to go. There are many highly respected schools located around the country, as mentioned earlier in the survey of news directors; Brown College, American Broadcasting School, and Specs Howard School of Broadcast Arts are among them.

Del Cockrell is the owner and founder of the American Broadcasting Schools (ABS) based in Oklahoma City. Del has been in the broadcasting business for fifty years, thirty-six of which have been spent at ABS. "We sell dreams. I picked the right thing to teach many years ago. It's not like welding, where people don't want to go to work everyday, this is fun. Usually students are here before we are, and for school that's kind of amazing. That's what we do: we sell dreams. We've got over four thousand graduates out across America. I can fly into any large city usually and hear a product of American Broadcasting Schools. Those dreams come true if they get behind it and work at it. It's like anything else, you have to start at the bottom, but once you work into it, your talent commands what you do with it and how much you make with it."

There are some differences between a university program and career broadcast school. According to Cockrell, "First of all, it's a shorter course than a two- or four-year college plan is. Ours is forty-three weeks. It's more intense, aimed at what it is, broadcasting. We don't teach history or math. We teach only one thing and we do it 90 percent hands on, as if a person is working at a very large radio station. The assignments here are everything that they have to do when they get out of this school, and then, of course, we help them with the job placement too."

Cockrell explains what students should expect to learn at career broadcasting school. "It's doing the announcing, newscasting, sportscasting. How to write and produce commercials, put all the sound effects, bells and whistles, sales, everything that they have to do primarily in radio. Then, of course, once the voice is trained, it can be used for a lot of different things, not just radio."

ABS has recently expanded its student base by using new technology and an open mind. Cockrell explains, "We now have an 'Interactive Distance Learning' program where students can take our entire curriculum from their home, over the Internet. Every graduate will have his or her own Internet radio station and we critique them in real-time. We are also introducing our curriculum in Spanish."

Rachel Tepfer has served as department chair, Radio Broadcasting, TV Production & Communications at Brown College, based just outside Minneapolis. "We've found that when people are hired into radio, they need to be able to do everything. They need to be able to be on air, they need to be able to write copy, they need to be able to edit for time, they need to be able to run a studio. They really have to be hired as someone who can do it all. We make a point of teaching journalism, of teaching Web design, Photoshop and logo design. Writing, editing . . . all in the course of the eighteen month program."

Brown College, known primarily as a media school, is now moving more toward a collegiate environment. "Our students don't just take courses in their major anymore, they also have to take general education courses. We do that to help people learn how to think. There's one side of it that says we can teach you just the skills you need, but if we can teach you how to be smarter, and process information in a smarter fashion . . . All of those skills come together to make them marketable in the long run."

The difference between Brown College and going to a university, according to Tepfer is that, "there you're talking more about theory and less opportunity to be sitting in a studio or in front of a computer, and actually working. We put tremendous pressure on the idea that you must be in the studio. We teach five different studio courses during the eighteen months."

The age of students attending career schools differs from those attending universities as well, says Tepfer. "They [career school students] tend to be a little bit older, usually between mid-twenties to even late-thirties." The percentage of graduating students placed into jobs is very impressive. At Brown, Tepfer says, "Our success rates are fantastic. We had over 90 percent of our students placed last year." The numbers at the American Broadcasting School are much the same. According to Del Cockrell, "Percentage of placement is usually 85 to 90 percent or higher. We usually have more jobs waiting than people."

Jonathan Liebman, president and CEO of the Specs Howard School of Broadcast Arts located just outside of Detroit, reported a comparable job placement percentage for his school. "Most of our students go right into the industry after graduation. We are also seeing more and more students taking advantage of partnerships and agreements we have with other colleges and universities throughout Michigan that help provide opportunities to complete their degrees. We have placed people in radio and television in most of the major markets." Lieberman continues, "We have alumni that have run camera on shows like *The West Wing* and *Lost* and in movies like *Blade* and *Bruce Almighty*. It's exciting to be able to turn on the radio in most parts of the country and hear the work of one of our 12,000 or so graduates!"

As with universities, the cost of attending courses at career schools can vary dramatically depending on the school and the length of the class. See appendix A at the end of the book for more details on career school information and locations. Students at many career broadcast schools can receive financial assistance, much like university students. According to Jonathan Liebman of Specs Howard, "It's available to students who qualify. It's all done through a well-defined process administered by the financial aid department. We participate in several loan and grant programs that are pretty much the same loan and grant programs available at traditional colleges and universities. We have a full-time, full-service financial aid department that works in conjunction with our admissions department and business office in facilitating that service for students."

There are plenty of fine broadcasting schools scattered around the country. The most respected schools are generally considered to be the ones accredited by ACCSCT (Accrediting Commission of Career Schools and Colleges of Technology) and ACCET (Accrediting Council for Continuing Education & Training).

CAREER SCHOOL STORIES

Just as in every other facet of the broadcast business, there are some great stories that come from the career broadcasting schools. Del Cockrell at ABS remembers one student. "Mike was totally blind. He and his father visited our Tulsa campus and declared Mike wanted to be in broadcasting, could he enroll? I drove to Tulsa to basically convince him that he should choose another career. Announcers need to see to read script, take meter readings, etc. Well, Mike and his father were determined. His father owned a construction company in Tulsa and suggested that I give Mike a try at attending school. He told me if I had a fear that Mike 'would hurt our equipment' that 'he would pay for it!' I assured him that was not the reluctance for enrolling Mike, but would give it a go. I took Mike to a control room, showed him how to cue up records, work the pots [volume knobs], etc. After only a few minutes Mike could operate a [control] board as well as anyone. It was amazing!

He took his lesson notes in Braille and we took the glass front off the old meters so he could read them. He labeled all the records in Braille; hell, he even found one that was lost when the rest of us couldn't!

"This experience taught me not to judge the handicapped. We have since had several seeing-impaired graduates. They are doing well in our biz. Mike's father bought a radio station in Tulsa. Mike became the PD, then manager. He once told me he didn't mind working at night. He was a trip. I'm really proud of him."

Rachel Tepfer remembers one of her students with a tear in her eye: "I got to read the name of a student at graduation who essentially had been living at shelters for the last year of their college career, and nobody knew. They just kept showing up and doing their work and was always taking care of themselves. To find out that this student had been going through so many things in their own personal life, that could have very easily been the best excuses in the world to give up. And instead, they were so passionate about the work that they were doing and really just wanted to get somewhere and make something of themselves! That's just the most exciting thing in the world. It didn't matter. It's so easy to give up on hard things, so when some-one refuses to do that it just blows your mind."

COSTAS' COLLEGE ADVICE

Looking back on how he got started, and the way the industry has evolved, Bob Costas would steer someone interested in getting into the broadcast business this way: "I would still advise them to get as well-rounded an educa-tion as possible with perhaps an emphasis on broadcasting, but not a sole emphasis. The better your frame of reference, the better you're going to be as a broadcaster. You never know, obviously, if your career or life takes a different turn, you might benefit from knowing a little bit about a number of things. I would also say that you cannot learn to be a broadcaster in a classroom. There's no prescribed course of study that you go through, you know, you go through these steps and you're a lawyer, you go through these steps and you're a doctor. It doesn't work that way for broadcasting. It's a knack more than an objective skill. You can be very bright, and you can be very willing to work hard, and you just might not have the aptitude for that particular thing. So its wise to find out if you do have that aptitude."

Bob also cautions everyone who is just starting out to be patient. It takes time to start sounding good, "You're not going to be as good as you ultimately hope to be right out of the box, but if at least you show some knack for it then you can develop and polish that skill. If you have no knack for it, you need to be honest with yourself before you waste ten years spinning your wheels. So it is good to try and find hands-on opportunities where you are really doing something on the air, you know, whether it's the campus station or some small local situation because the best way to learn and improve is hands-on."

TAKE IT SERIOUSLY

If going to school is the way you choose to get your on-air career started, make a serious decision because it will impact your entire career. The amount of dedication you put into learning will play a strong part in how far you can go. Make a serious decision, and then take your decision seriously. If you don't, no one else will.

End Notes

[1] Dickson, Tom. *Mass Media Education in Transition.* Florence, KY: Lawrence Erlbaum Associates, 1999.

[2] Survey conducted by Vernon Stone, Missouri School of Journalism, 1994.

[3] Dickson, Tom. *Mass Media Education in Transition.* Florence, KY: Lawrence Erlbaum Associates, 1999.

[4] Seidman, David. *Exploring Careers in Journalism.* New York: The Rosen Publishing Group, 2000.

[5] Utterback, Ann S. *Broadcast Voice Handbook.* Los Angeles, CA: Bonus Books, Inc., 2000.

What and How Universities Are Teaching Broadcast Students

A large percentage of broadcasters come through university broadcast/journalism/mass media/communications/radio/TV programs. With this in mind, it is important for us to take a look at what these programs are teaching and how they are teaching it. In this chapter, some of the country's best teachers at top programs will tell us how their schools prepare students for a career in broadcasting. We will learn what students must expect, learn, and know to have the best chance at success in a very competitive field.

Along with this chapter, also see appendix B in the back of the book for examples of what top university programs use to aid their teaching. This includes the Journalists Creed from the University of Missouri, Make-up 101, a vocabulary of radio/TV terms, a reporter's checklist, an example of how and what students are graded on, and more.

BALANCE THE LOAD

Many university programs try to balance classroom work with time on the air at local college radio and television stations. This helps students learn the various arts that comprise broadcasting, both in front of and behind the camera or microphone. Dr. Jim Foust of Bowling Green State University says, "The degree that we give, and the degree that most good journalism schools give, is basically a liberal arts degree. That means we are teaching people not just the nuts and bolts of doing journalism, but a broad-based education. In effect, they have to take courses in economics and history and things like that so that when they leave here they don't just know how to write a lead, they know something about the world, too. That's one of the first thing that drives what we do. The second thing is we highly encourage people to get practical experience while they're here too. So we have student media organizations, we have a couple of radio stations, we have a nightly television newscast that's all done by students. We encourage them to get involved in that kind of stuff as well."

CRITICAL THINKING

Mary Rogus of Ohio University adds, "The main thing that distinguishes the top programs from all the rest is the dual focus on technical skills and journalism. What I hear constantly from news directors and publishers is that they want two things: they want people who can write and people who can critically think and analyze information."

You may wonder just exactly what critical thinking is when it comes to journalism. Ms. Rogus says it is, "Being able to look at an issue, a problem, an angle, a story, and analyzing what the factors in the situation are and what are the consequences of various outcomes. It's more than just taking in information and memorizing facts, it is knowing what to be able to do with those facts. The other side of it is being able to communicate those facts."

Being able to communicate those facts is key in the broadcast business; after all, that is the sole reason and responsibility of the job. Before getting into teaching, Rogus spent nine years running newsrooms at various stations around the country, including in Pittsburgh, "So often I was depressed, because even in larger markets I was dealing with people who had been in the business for years, who were still at my desk after one phone call saying, 'What do I do now, this person won't talk to me. Story idea, you want me to generate my own story idea?' That's depressing."

Many professors see critical thinking and generating story ideas as one of the key things broadcast students must learn. The University of Missouri's Greely Kyle tells us, "The biggest problem I have with my students is that they can't come up with good story ideas, they really struggle with that."

Kyle has a very simple formula to teach his students this key element: "I make them do it. Every week they have to come in with three story ideas. I grade them and we discuss them, I say, 'This won't work because . . .' or, 'This is a good idea but did you think of that?' Or, 'How are you going to make this work?' And make them see the realities of it. Every week when they come in for a shift at our TV station they have to come in with story ideas, they have to have a story idea meeting. I also give them a bunch of materials, just some random magazines and newspapers and say, 'Okay, find some story ideas.' Another day I'll take them out for a walk and tell them to get story ideas. Then we'll write them down and see who's got the most. I teach them how to brainstorm, how to observe, how to look in different places for story ideas."

Just because someone can think up story ideas doesn't mean they are all good ideas. There are differences between stories that have an effect on people and those that don't. Kyle said, "A good story is going to be something that your viewers, listeners, or readers need to know, or something they really want to know. Something that is going to affect their lives or their home."

WRITING, WRITING, WRITING

The one constant topic that always comes up in my conversations with broadcasting, journalism, and communication teachers is the importance of good writing. All of the top programs teach and emphasize good broadcast writing in all of their classes. Professor Lee Thornton of the University of Maryland said, "If you desire to be a reporter or producer, above all you must know the language. You must learn how to write as broadcasters write. You must address what have been called the elements of style and you must know the proper use of the present tense, the active voice, and so forth. Writing is paramount among the things you need to know."

Steve Smith from the University of Georgia agreed, "I don't even like to call it writing because as soon as you say 'writing' it darkens back to papers they had to write in high school or early in college, and it just isn't the same. So we teach them to tell stories or to write in a very different way than they learned originally. We teach them to be as conversational as possible, tell it to me as if you were telling a friend or a family member. Describe the situation. They get hung up on the style of writing that they're taught for English class. That's not what we do. It's as different as playing football or baseball. It all revolves around story telling because at core what we do is tell stories, whether we do news or sports or whatever."

The key elements of good broadcast writing are to be concise, simple, understandable, and personable. Dr. Jim Foust of Bowling Green University said, "What I try to teach is that just because it's simplistic doesn't mean it doesn't take skill to do it and it doesn't mean that its not, once you've finished it, beautiful."

Greely Kyle of Missouri added, "Good writing is clear, it's transparent. People cannot misunderstand what you're writing. It's not enough to be understood, you have to write so that you cannot be misunderstood. Good writing is concise. You're not going to have a lot of words, especially big words that are not conversational, words that keep people from hearing what you are saying. It's clear, it's concise, it's compelling, and it's conversational."

Lee Thornton agrees: "This is writing for the ear. This is not writing for the eye; therefore, it must do certain things: it must be conversational, the active voice has a good place most of the time but not all of the time. You have to break it down to its simplest and then build it up and at the end add style."

WRITING SAMPLES

To give you an idea of what these teachers are talking about, here are some examples. The first paragraph is an example writing for the *eye*, or *print*. Paragraphs after that are examples of writing for the ear—for people listening instead of reading.

SAMPLE PARAGRAPH OF WRITING FOR THE *EYE*

Precipitation keeps following the Texas Rangers and they hardly seem to mind. Ranger starting pitcher Kevin Millwood pitched seven crisp innings, Mark Teixeira hit a tie-breaking single in the eighth, and Texas beat the New York Yankees 4–2 Monday night on another soggy day at the ballpark for the Rangers. Brad Wilkerson homered to begin the comeback from a two-run deficit, and Texas snapped an eight-game losing streak to the Yankees that dated back to last season. Michael Young and Hank Blalock each drove in a run for the Rangers, who had played only 5 1/2 innings since Wednesday because they were rained out twice in Boston over the weekend. They beat the Red Sox 6–0 on Friday night in a game cut short by showers. Mike Mussina delivered another fine outing for the Yankees, who have lost consecutive games and managed only three runs in 23 innings. Without injured sluggers Gary Sheffield and Hideki Matsui, New York has scored only 12 runs in the last five games.

SAMPLE PARAGRAPHS OF WRITING FOR THE *EAR*

Local version #1

Mother Nature keeps following the Rangers on the road, but they're not too bothered. After two straight rainouts in Boston, Kevin Millwood pitched through off-and-on showers in a 7-inning gem, and Mark Ta-sheer-a came through with the game winning single in the 8th in a 4–2 win over the Yanks. "Tex" will take it ... (sound bite here).

National version #1

Mother Nature keeps raining on the Texas Rangers, but they don't seem to mind. Ranger ace Kevin Millwood overcame showers to throw a 7-inning gem, and first baseman Mark Ta-sheer-a came through with the game winning hit in a 4–2 win over the Yankees in New York. Ta-Sheer-a is happy with the outcome ... (sound bite here).

Local version #2

After being rained out two straight days in Boston, the Rangers made the most of their series opener on the road against the Yanks. Brad Wilkerson homered—and Mark Ta-sheer-a drove in the game-winner to hand the Yanks their second straight loss, 4–2. Kevin Millwood picked up the win on the mound ... (sound bite here).

National version #2

The New York Yankees have lost two in a row, the latest setback coming at home to Texas 4–2. After two straight rainouts in Boston the Rangers offense was led by a Brad Wilkerson home run—and Mark Ta-sheer-a's game-winning single. Winning pitcher Kevin Millwood ... (sound bite here).

You will notice a lot of differences in the two different styles of writing: the style that people are going to read (newspaper or magazine) and the style that helps your listener hear what you are saying.

Writing for the eye can be cumbersome and hard to say, while writing for the ear has to be concise, straight to the point, easy to understand, and easy to say. It has to sound conversational when you speak it; you do not want to sound like you are reading, even though you are. The easiest way to sound conversational is with good writing, excellent ad-libbing, or a combination of both. Also, as you noticed in the scripts, when you are writing for the listener, you can spell in phonetics. Just make sure you are pronouncing the name correctly, and, since you are the only one who will be reading the copy, write it in a way that makes it easier for you to pronounce all the words correctly.

Another thing to take note of from the examples is that you write differently depending on who your audience is. For example, if you are doing a local broadcast, your audience will be more familiar with the team and players you are talking about, so you do not have to explain as much. If you are writing for a national audience, more than likely you will need to give a little more explanation. For instance, instead of calling them the "Rangers" you would probably need to say "Texas Rangers," and instead of calling Mark Teixeira by his nickname "Tex," as you would in the local version, you might use his full name in the national script.

OTHER ESSENTIALS

Writing is important, but it is certainly not the only thing that broadcasting programs teach. There are plenty of other essentials that need to be learned. "We teach them the technology, we teach them how to shoot video, we teach them how to use audio, we teach them the fundamentals of editing, but those are all tools in telling stories," says Georgia's Steve Smith. "Telling a TV news story, the pictures are critical; in fact, the pictures may be more critical than the words in many cases. Putting this all together is like a big beef stew. You have all these ingredients and you put them all together."

Lee Thornton of the University of Maryland says, "We teach them every position within a control room, including how to direct. We even teach them floor directing. They will never have to fill all those positions. They very well may have to do their own shooting and editing, but they'll never have to perform at all the positions that we teach them."

There are also other important essentials that top teachers try and instill in their students, things that come in handy in this business, like curiosity and passion. Dr. Jim Foust says, "Building curiosity is one of the things I really try to do. To make students more curious about things that are going on in the world and more curious about what other people are interested in, because that's where it all starts. If somebody's not curious and doesn't care about finding information, they probably won't be successful in journalism. So curiosity is a big thing."

Steve Smith of Georgia equates a good anchor or reporter to being in the medical profession, "Doctors open up bodies, well, we open up news stories. Good reporters have to get their hands on the story, they've got to get out there and talk to people, they've got to have beats where they are required, every day, to call and develop sources, to develop people who can give them information on things."

Sue Kopen Katcef of Maryland tries to instill a zeal in her students: "Passion is something everyone must possess, because in a difficult business, if passion isn't at the heart of what you do, you might not be able to make it a career. It is that fire in the belly, the passion, which will keep you going in the face of anything. If you believe in what you are doing, that you can make a difference and that you have a purpose, that will keep you going."

LEARNING TO PERFORM

Another key skill that students must learn if they want to be on the air is how to perform. Professor Lee Thornton emphasizes the performance aspect of broadcasting: "We can't get around it, for people who want to be reporters, who want to be anchors, this is a business of performance and you have to know those things. They may be easy for you, that's a gift, but some of those things also can be learned."

There are many very good journalists who find that performing is not their cup of tea. Just because a person doesn't like to perform in front of the mic or camera does not mean there isn't a job for them in the business. Just the opposite: there are a lot of great jobs available off the air that do not require you to be a performer.

If you want to be on the air but find you have trouble performing when the mic is hot, there are ways to learn. Lee Thornton explains, "I show [my students] examples of student work and professional air work that illustrates different kinds of reporting. We watch news programs and we see reporters at work. We go out and practice with a camera, bring it in and screen it to see why it worked or why it didn't work. They get so amazingly good by the end of a semester it always astonishes me."

The main tool that many universities use to teach on-air performance is actually putting their students on the air at local college radio and television stations. Ohio University's Mary Rogus says, "Our students actually produce a public affairs program that airs live on the cable station. Even their first radio class and their first television reporting class, if their stories are good enough, they know that those stories will air on one of the newscasts we produce. The students know they are working for more than just a grade, they are working at real deadlines and they are producing real product that goes out into the community."

There are big differences, according to Rogus, between campus stations and commercial stations. "The big difference between a real newsroom and us is the students are getting tons of feedback on everything they write and produce. Every morning meeting has teaching elements as well as story development. Other than that it is very real world for them."

The University of Georgia allows its students to learn on air, as well, according to Steve Smith: "We set it up like a small market news operation, which it is because it plays on the air on cable in the Athens market, which is about seventy to eighty thousand households. The first thing we say to the students is, 'Beginning right now you are a professional journalist, you're not a student anymore.' We are fortunate that we have very serious students, they realize what they are doing actually has an audience."

The University of Maryland and Lee Thornton take their on-air work seriously too. "We don't do campus news, we go all over the region. I've had students go to Philadelphia for a story, routinely they go to Annapolis; they go wherever the story is. We are on a cable station that puts them in more than 500 thousand homes, that's the equivalent of a solid medium market."

That begs the question, how do the top programs balance classroom work with hands-on work done on mic or on camera at these college stations? A lot of times students who want to be on the air find working at the campus stations much more enjoyable than what they are doing in the classroom. Dr. Foust of Bowling Green says, "What I try to make them understand is that just because you are on the air doesn't mean you are learning something. If you are not getting feedback and constructive criticism from someone who knows what they are doing, and if you are not changing in response to that, then you are actually not learning anything, you are just doing repetitive stuff. As far as balance goes, I try to make them see that both classroom and on-air work are equally important. It is not a good idea to get involved in student media so much that it starts to have a detrimental impact on your studies."

INTERNSHIPS

Another significant part of the education process at these universities is allowing their students to do internships at a radio or television station. An internship is when a student signs on to work at a station or business either for pay, for school credit, or both. Students usually find out about these positions from their teachers or on the school's job posting board. Sue Kopen Katcef of Maryland tells us: "Internships are required here. There is no option; you cannot graduate without taking an internship. You can't even begin to think about getting a foot in the door without doing an internship."

Mary Rogus of Ohio University on internships: "They are absolutely vital. We require all of our students to do at least one internship, and we encourage them to do multiple internships."

Jim Foust of Bowling Green agrees: "They are very important. It kind of plays into the whole idea of taking what you've learned in the classroom and actually being able to apply it in the real world. When you graduate, yeah, people want to see that you've got the diploma, but they also want to see what you've actually done."

These internship opportunities can vary greatly in what they offer students. Some companies allow their interns to really get involved and actually work alongside their professionals. Other companies would just rather their interns stand aside, fetch coffee, and watch. Finding an internship that allows a student to grow is important, and it is up to the student to find the right place for himself. Greely Kyle of Missouri says, "A lot of stations take interns, but not a lot of them do much with them or give them opportunities to learn."

Mary Rogus warns her students before going on internships that a lot of stations do not have formalized programs for interns. Her advice to these students is "Quite frankly the students who are most aggressive, who are constantly at somebody's elbow saying, 'What can I do? Show me how to do that' are the ones who have great experiences. The student who sits in the corner and waits to be told what to do could end up sitting in that corner for their entire internship."

Jim Foust adds, "In a lot of cases if a student goes to an internship and they are content to just sit at a desk, answer the phone, and get coffee, then in a lot of cases that's all they will learn. They have to take it upon themselves to show initiative."

Sue Kopen Katcef of Maryland reminds students going out on internships that they are leaving the protective, nurturing environment that school provides and entering the real world. "Where the real world pressures are very different and the deadlines are never-ending, that's something we can't necessarily duplicate. Being an intern allows you to observe it without having all the pressures of losing a job."

Mary Rogus adds, "The students must remember that the people working in these newsrooms have jobs to do, and one of those jobs is not babysitting the intern. You have an opportunity to have a great experience, but you have to show that you are willing and able to do something to contribute. Usually what that means is making a pain in the butt of yourself for the first couple of weeks to get up speed on the computers and the writing style and how things work in that particular place. Then you can really help."

WHERE TO INTERN

One of the big questions students must answer when looking at different internship opportunities is where is the best place to go? Jim Foust of Bowling Green reminds students that going to bigger markets isn't always the best thing. "Ideally at an internship you will get a chance to actually do something. Sometimes students will say, 'I want to go and do an internship in New York City.' In some cases that's fine, but maybe if you go to Zanesville, Ohio, or Bluefield, West Virginia, you might learn more by actually doing stuff rather than just watching people do stuff."

Along with the learning experience these internship positions offer, they also offer students a chance to start networking and to make contacts with managers, anchors, reporters, and producers at stations where they may want to get a job at in the future. If a student does a good job and makes a strong impression as an intern, there is always a possibility the station can find a position for him when he graduates. Speaking from first-hand knowledge, the station where I work in Dallas has hired at least four former students that interned for us in just the past few years.

The reason students go to these programs, take these classes, and serve these internships is to try and get themselves ready for a job in the real world. In the next chapter, we will hear from program directors and news directors from small market stations on what they are looking for when they are ready to hire someone just getting started.

What News and Program Directors Are Looking For

The reason people spend hundreds of hours and thousands of dollars studying, testing, and practicing is mainly to get a job. With that in mind, it is important to find out what hiring managers are looking for when the time comes.

Since most broadcasting careers start in smaller towns and cities, in this chapter we hear from a random sampling of news directors and program directors from small market stations. These are people who do the hiring when a position becomes available.

Some radio and television stations have specific positions that they slate for people just graduating college. Jason Wentworth is the program director of KCOW radio in Alliance, Nebraska. "We have a position here that is basically a 'program director slash production person.' It is an entry-level position, which means we will try to help someone just coming out of college to get used to what we do here."

Jerry Howard is the news director at KRTV in Great Falls, Montana, and has found over the years that the talented people he finds searching for work can come from big or small schools. "It's pretty even, I think, in the mix of tapes I get as far as skill level. I get good tapes from smaller places I haven't heard about and from the bigger schools."

WHAT THEY'RE LOOKING FOR

Howard gives us some insight on what hiring managers are looking for when they are watching and listening to tapes or reading résumés and cover letters. "I'm looking for initiative and ability to tell a story, and interpret, which are standards. I am looking for level of self-confidence, not arrogance, but someone who has the ability to go get the story."

Lee Anderson is an anchor and the news director of KTVZ News channel 21 in Bend, Oregon. He says that he looks "primarily for storytelling ability. I listen carefully for the writing skill, that's a tough one these days. The last few years I've seen a real lack of writing skills. I don't know if writing and storytelling are stressed enough in school."

Working at a small market station offers several great benefits to people just starting out. The pressure of getting ratings is not nearly as important as they are in big cities, and the jobs usually offer the opportunity to do and learn a variety of different things.

Steve McMurray, the news director at WKTV in Utica, New York, told us, "I need people who can come in and hit the ground running. People who can come up with a story idea that is turn-able for a show and set it up on their own. We can provide them guidance and some resources, but basically they have to provide their own destiny." When he's hiring, McMurray looks for someone who is versatile. He continues: "I think for small markets the day of specialization is gone. I need people who can wear many hats and be successful at many facets." McMurray goes into the process of hiring new talent with an open mind. "I know I'm not going to get someone who's a superstar anchor and producer and reporter, but they have to be good at all facets of the game."

Paul Swann is the program director at WVHU in Huntington, West Virginia. One of the main things he looks for in hiring is someone who is not lost when it comes to using the equipment. "The equipment is different from station to station, I understand that, but it's the basic concept they need to know. I'm really looking for people who can think on their feet because not every situation that pops up is something you have learned in a textbook." Another important element Swann looks for in hiring for an entry-level position is experience. He considers work done on the air at college stations as experience and says he can tell the students who took their classes seriously and those who did not. "You can tell the people who just went to the college program to spin CDs, play music, and hang out, and the people that really got involved in the program. They seem to be more aware and more alert to what's going on. I'm looking for people who have an understanding of the industry and who want to make a career out of it."

Jason Wentworth of KCOW agreed: "A lot of college radio stations, unfortunately, are a club more than a working training ground for commercial radio." Wentworth's advice is to "go to your college radio station and do everything. Do a shift on the air, do news, do sports, go out and do interviews, sell, come up with promotions. Everything your college station offers you, snap it up."

THE AUDITION PACKAGE

The hiring process at almost every radio and TV station for an on-air position begins with a cover letter, résumé, and audition tape. The key elements of putting a good all-around package together are:

1. Good writing. Writing for the eye on the cover letter and résumé, and writing for the ear on your audition tape/CD/mp3/DVD.

2. Good production value on the audition tape/CD/mp3/DVD.

3. Good voice and/or good appearance on the audition tape/CD/mp3/DVD.

4. A resume that points out all of the work, classes, projects, and community service you have done.

5. Good references.

The first thing hiring managers see is the envelope, so make sure it is clean and sharp. The next thing they see is the outside of the tape. Make it professional: something they want to watch or listen to. Program directors and news directors will then glance at the résumé to see if there is anything that impresses them. They will start to read the cover letter while putting the audition tape/CD/DVD into the machine. The cover letter is extremely important. It says a lot about you: not just about your writing, but who you are, your values, why you want the job, and why you think you should be considered. We will talk more about this later in the chapter.

THE MOMENT OF TRUTH

Unless your package is poor, the news director or program director will give your tape a quick glance or listen. That is the key moment. Jerry Howard of KRTV has a little trick that he thinks will get your television tapes watched a little longer. "News directors are so trained to see your face that if you don't start off with your stand-up montage, you will make them watch your package longer. They will watch it until they see you and they might actually get a minute or so of your work, where if you give them your stand-up up front and they don't like your look in ten seconds, you're done!"

News directors will make a snap judgment of your look, your voice, your writing, and your likeability within the first few seconds of seeing or hearing your audition tape. Jerry Howard relates some insight: "As soon as they give me that stand-up montage, I quickly determine their competence and it doesn't really change if I watch them for ten seconds or ten minutes. I have that person pegged. I don't think there has been a time yet after making my initial judgment that I kept watching the tape and thought, 'Wow, I was wrong.'"

The good news is that if you have talent, even if the talent is unrefined, these hiring managers at small market stations have become pretty good at spotting potential. Lee Anderson of KTVZ in Bend, Oregon, said, "You can see the diamonds. You can definitely see who has the talent and who doesn't, even when it's pretty raw."

Just as everybody has different taste in food, hiring managers have different taste in talent. Never underestimate the power of the little things, because the difference between being hired and a pass is frequently very slim. Howard said, "For me the number one measuring stick is the measure of character. When I get to my final handful of tapes, they all have the skill level. To me gender is not a factor so I'm looking at, if they all can do the job, who is the self-motivated one? Who is the honest one? Who has the most integrity? Whose tape reflects that? Whose tape is not hype, not a lot of 'look at me.' Whose tape is about stories that matter and showing the initiative to go get the story without making themselves the story."

Mr. Howard taught broadcast journalism at the University of Oklahoma and Central Oklahoma before taking on his current role as news director in Montana. As a teacher he found one thing very difficult to teach: "To do more than the basic minimum requirement. Minimum requirements are not even average—they are minimal! Getting students to do more than what the handout requires, to take the initiative to go out and hit some home runs instead of just getting on base. They would stand out so much in their crowd of peers. And believe me, you can see that on tape. Those are the ones I hire."

THE PERFECT RÉSUMÉ

Brad Karsh is the president of JobBound[1] and author of *Confessions of a Recruiting Director: The Insider's Guide to Landing Your First Job.*[2] He has seen tens of thousands of résumés and cover letters over the years and has some profound advice to offer someone looking for a job. On the subject of résumés, Karsh said, "A lot of times students put together a résumé from their perspective and not the perspective of the person who is going to be reading it; that is a big mistake. Students write what I call 'job description résumés,' where they describe what they've done, but that is just what everyone has done in that job. You need to focus on what you have specifically done that is better or unique from what anybody else has done. Get specific about what you have accomplished doing the job."

People doing the hiring already know job descriptions. They want to know what you accomplished in that position. Karsh has some easy tests to make sure your résumé will get noticed. "If what is written on your résumé can be written by the person who held the job before you or after you, then rip it up and start over. Focus on 'Scope' and 'Results': Scope is how many and how often. Results are what happened because you did something, even if you are not entirely responsible. I tell people if you don't have five to ten numbers in the descriptions of what you have done then you haven't done a good enough job on your résumé. It comes down to results, results, results."

Karsh gave us a couple of examples of a standard résumé, and a good résumé. These examples are listed below.

STANDARD RÉSUMÉ SAMPLE

Jennifer Howards
713 E. ORANGE STREET, APT 519
CHACKBAY, OK 12931
PHONE (819) 749-3278
E-MAIL Jennifer@OK.EDU

Objective To obtain an On-Air position with WIHN, 96.7 The Rock.

Education (8/99–6/03) Victor J. Andrew High School, Arlington, OK
(8/03–PRESENT) University of Oklahoma, Chackbay, OK

Broadcast Journalism
Senior Standing in the College of Communications, Broadcast Journalism Curriculum, Interdisciplinary Minor in Gender and Women's Studies

Work experience (8/04–PRESENT) Cochrane On Daniel's, Chackbay, OK

Head Bartender (4/05–PRESENT)
Responsible for customer service and maintenance of the establishment. Oversee staff members and train new staff members.

Party Booker (8/06–PRESENT)
Plan and book social events.
(4/05–present) WPGU, 107.1 The Planet, Champaign, OK

Promotional Director (4/05–PRESENT)
Plan and run all station promotional events.
Develop on-air promotional ideas.
Develop Promotions Department intern program.
Maintain high level of communication with Programming, Production, Sales, Marketing, Advertising, and full-time staff.
Develop new station image and re-launch agenda.

On-Air Personality Mid-Days (4/05–PRESENT)
Develop listener interactive show concepts.
Serve as an on-air talent.
(2/06–6/06) WILL–TV Urbana, OK

Volunteer
Run studio cameras.
Floor directing.

Extracurricular activities
Alpha Chi Omega Sorority, Vice President Chapter Relations and Standards

• Responsible for annual revision of chapter governing documents

• Responsible for discipline and regulation of all chapter members

University of Oklahoma Panhellenic Council 2006 Recruitment Counselor
The LaSalle Bank Chicago Marathon, Chicago, Illinois, October 12, 2005.

Honors
Alpha Lambda Delta Honor Society
Phi Eta Sigma Honor Society

BETTER RÉSUMÉ

Jennifer Howards
713 E. ORANGE STREET, APT. 519 • CHACKBAY, OK 72931
819.749.3278 • JENNIFER@OK.EDU

Education
University of Oklahoma, Chackbay, May 2007
Bachelor of Arts in Broadcast Journalism, Interdisciplinary Minor in Gender and Women's Studies
Phi Eta Sigma Honor Society, membership based on superior academics
Alpha Lambda Delta Honor Society, for outstanding GPA

Experience
Promotions Director
WPGU 107.1 FM, Chackbay, OK, April 2005–Present

- Revamped remote broadcast process overhauling on-site logistics and improving client experience for up to 20 remotes per month
- Member of 15-person executive committee relaunching station including format change, rebranding, image reinvigoration, and creation of "street team" to canvas local area
- Oversee integrated promotional programs for clients including FedEx, Budweiser, and Hardee's
- Created new client evaluation and promotional staff evaluation forms insuring overall quality and driving dramatically improved event execution
- Plan and execute "PGU Pre-game" tailgate party—station's largest event attended by more than 300 students and staffed by 75 station employees
- Launched department's internship program, enhancing training, evaluations, and work content for 20 interns
- Manage a staff of 20 for a 3,000-watt station covering 50 miles and targeting 70,000 18 to 34-year-olds
- Work 35–40 hours/week while maintaining a full course load

On-Air Personality
WPGU 107.1 FM, Champaign, OK, April 2005–Present

- Promoted to host Monday–Friday 9:00 AM to noon slot
- Handle weather, news reads, and listener calls
- Created a host of programs including *American Idol* spoof, guilty music pleasures, and rock star crush

Event Planner/Head Bartender
Cochrane On Daniel's, Chackbay, OK, April 2005–Present

- Partnered with six social committee chairs to sell and plan several key bar events
- Oversee a total staff of 50 student bartenders: 12–15/night
- Trained more than 50 new staff members, bartenders, and servers

Vice President, Chapter Relations/Standards
Alpha Chi Omega Sorority, Fall 2005–Fall 2006

- Led house finances from deficit to surplus by rewriting by-laws and overhauling financial operations
- Developed new house rules governing all activities for chapter with 155 members and 55 live-ins
- Chapter nominated as most improved out of 27 sororities on campus

Activities/Interests

- American Cancer Society, Relay for Life participant, 2005–2006
- OK Union Board Spring Musical, 2005
- Leukemia Team in Training, Mayor's Midnight Sun Marathon Runner, Anchorage, AK, 2004
- LaSalle Bank Chicago Marathon Runner, 2005
- Panhellenic Council Recruitment Counselor, 2006
- Interests include running, fitness, dancing, astrology

Which résumé do you think puts the applicant in a better position to get the job?

A GREAT COVER LETTER

Another key element in job-hunting is a good cover letter. Companies generally request a cover letter to make sure the applicant is applying for a specific position and not just applying to every job out there. Karsh says, "Cover letters are a tremendous opportunity to sell yourself, and yet each and every person writes the exact same cover letter. The first paragraph is how they heard about the job. The second paragraph is why they're interested in the job. The third paragraph is why they would be good at the job and the fourth paragraph is how they're going to follow up on the job."

Writing the standard cover letter will give you no advantage in getting the job. Try to use the cover letter as something that will spark the interest of the person doing the hiring and that will make you stick out in a positive way. Karsh says of cover letters, "They need to be a 'teaser ad' for your résumé, not your life's story, just enough to get them interested. They should be incredibly short and incredibly interesting and very personal. They should tell your story."

As a former recruiting director, Karsh has seen over ten thousand cover letters. Here are the first paragraphs of the best he's seen. This was a woman applying for a job in advertising:

✳   ✳   ✳

Ms. Smith,

Baby food.

Yes. Baby food got me interested in advertising.

I was a sophomore in college taking my first class in advertising when we had to compare Gerber and Beechnut. I loved everything about it. I loved the creativity, I loved the variety of the work, I loved the fact that I could impact human decision based on the words that I wrote. From that point on I knew I had to work in advertising.

✳   ✳   ✳

The cover letter is a great opportunity to make yourself a unique candidate for the job, to tell them why you are so interested in the field, and about your unique skills, facts, or experiences. You can also use the cover letter to address a concern that you think a hiring manager may have. You can turn a negative into a positive by answering a question in your cover letter. This was from a history major who decided he wanted to be a journalist:

✳   ✳   ✳

Mr. Smith,

Why would a history major want to be a broadcast journalist?

That is a question I have asked myself on several occasions. Let me tell you why . . . .

✳   ✳   ✳

The cover letter needs to intrigue the reader, but it does not have to be bizarre, weird, or strange to do that. Let it tell your unique story.

A GREAT JOB INTERVIEW

Job interviews are another key element in nailing down a position. Hiring managers have noted that students coming out of college tend to drop the ball quite often when it comes to interviews. In job interviews, there are basics, like showing up on time and dressing appropriately. You may lose a job the second you walk in the door if you are late or dressed poorly.

Brad Karsh has another key insight into having a good job interview. "A lot of students think that an interview is a battle of wits. Where the goal is to outguess or out-bluff the interviewer. They think, 'Every question that he asks me is clearly a trick question so if he asks me this then he wants me to say that so I'm going to think about it this way and answer it that way.'"

Thinking like that will only get you in trouble. When going into an interview, be prepared by practicing and answering questions to yourself that you think might be asked. You want to come off as relaxed and confident. The best way to do this is by actually being relaxed and confident. Do not try to outwit the interviewers. They have invited you there because they want to like you. They are not out to get you.

LITTLE THINGS MAKE A BIG DIFFERENCE

There are other little but very important details for students to remember when looking for a job. Little things like your e-mail address, the message on your phone answering machine, and what you are posting on the Internet.

In this day and age, a lot can be accomplished via e-mail, including sending cover letters and résumés. While having a cool and unusual e-mail address may be great between friends, it generally does not impress hiring directors in the same way.

Brad Karsh has a couple of perfect examples of e-mail addresses from actual students looking for jobs:

⚜ **spicychica2@....com.** "What really impressed me about Spicy Chica 2 was her perseverance. Obviously Spicy Chica and Spicy Chica 1 were both taken, so she held out for Spicy Chica 2."

⚜ **thedirthead@....com.** "I can just see them around the board room saying, 'Lets get the Dirt Head in here. I really want to hire the Dirt Head, he sounds nasty."

⚜ **imsodamntired@....com** "There's a guy who is going to move your company forward, assuming he can get to work before noon, Mr. I'm So Damn Tired."

Another thing that may diminish your chances of getting a job are the messages you leave on your answering machine. Again, what may be funny to your fellow students will not necessarily impress a program director.

An answering machine message like this has been heard by more than one program director contacting someone who has sent in a resume: "Hey, this is Chris. I'm probably hung over again so just leave a message and I'll call you when I'm sober." I can guarantee you that the program director will not be waiting for that call.

Internet social directories like Facebook[3] and Myspace[4] or Web search engines like Yahoo and Google offer hiring directors a great source of information on people too. Make sure the information you are putting on these sites is not something that will cost you a job. You also might want to do a Google or Yahoo search on yourself to see what people can find out about you. There is a good chance the person hiring you will do the same.

End Notes

[1] *www.jobbound.com*

[2] Karsh, Brad. *Confessions of a Recruiting Director: The Insiders Guide to Landing Your First Job*. Saddle River, NJ: Prentice Hall Press, 2006.

[3] *www.facebook.com*

[4] *www.myspace.com*

Crossing Over

You can also get started in the broadcast business by earning a name in a different occupation and turning that reputation into a job on the air. This usually involves former sports stars or coaches crossing over but also included actors, lawyers, former military generals, and politicians (see any cable news channel), as well as comedians who have all found second careers in broadcasting.

This is more noticeable on a national level, but it also happens frequently in local areas. For instance, a popular community politician or athlete may get a job hosting a talk show on a local radio or television station, a lawyer may do a segment on the local news station when there is a big case underway, or a comedian can step in as a regular side-kick on the wacky morning show. Name recognition in another field provides a great opportunity to get into broadcasting.

In this chapter, we will hear from people who have done exactly this and have worked their way into a successful second career. Troy Aikman, Harold Reynolds, Babe Laufenberg, and Danny Bonaduce all tell us how they made the transition, and their stories and advice may help you as well.

TROY AIKMAN

Troy Aikman played quarterback for the Dallas Cowboys for twelve seasons; he was the number one pick in the NFL draft in 1989 and retired after the 2000 season. In that time, he led "America's Team" to three Super Bowl titles and was named to six pro bowls (the NFL all-star game). Troy is now a part of Fox Sports' number one NFL play-by-play team working alongside Joe Buck.

Despite his success on the football field, Troy did not think he would get into broadcasting when his playing days were over. "No. No, I didn't at all. I know some guys they think that that's what they're going to get into as soon as they're done. For me, I wouldn't say that I never gave it any thought; I gave it some thought and felt that I would never do it."

Troy Aikman, NFL Hall of Famer.

Troy actually got his broadcasting career started a long way from home. "The NFL has a league over in Europe. In the off-season, they take guys over and let them do some broadcasting. It's a developmental league for players, and it's also become a developmental league for broadcasters. I had been asked to go over there a few times by Fox, but I just had no interest in doing it. Then I was talking to Brad Sham [play-by-play voice of the Cowboys] one evening on a plane ride after a game, going back to Dallas. He indicated that he would like to go because he had primarily done radio. I said, 'Hey, why don't we

go over together?' So I called Fox up and said, 'I'll go over and do some games but I want Brad Sham to be my play-by-play guy.' I did it just thinking I'd go over and spend a couple of weeks in Europe and vacation and then do a couple of games. That's how I viewed it. Once I got there I didn't want to embarrass myself and not do a good job so I ended up preparing more than what I had originally planned and did the game with Brad and really enjoyed it. Fox apparently liked what they heard. That's kind of how the whole thing got started."

Photos courtesy of Troy Aikman

Troy grew up in Oklahoma.

USE STAR POWER TO GET EXPERIENCE

Being a celebrity athlete prepared Troy for a career on the air more than he thought it would. He had many opportunities to practice as a guest on radio and television shows when still playing. "Every year that I've been in Dallas I had a radio show with Brad, whatever radio station he went with, that's who I did my show with. Brad taught me so much early on and I say all the time, if it weren't for Brad I wouldn't be doing this. There was tremendous comfort for me going over there to do the game because I knew that no matter how bad I could be, Brad could carry the whole thing by himself. In commercials, Brad would stop me and tell me what I was doing well and what I wasn't. It was great."

As for the things Troy had to learn in order to improve his skills on the air, he commented, "You know, there's a tendency to just tell viewers what they're watching, and I think the important thing is to avoid that. The big key is trying to tell the viewers what's happening and yet they're not really seeing. Trying to approach it from that standpoint helped me from the very beginning. The other thing is just the preparation, there's a lot more preparation to it than what I imagined going in. I guess it's whatever you want to get out of it. Some guys would probably say they can do it in less time, but for me to feel comfortable going in, and I think that's the real key, is you have to reach your comfort zone. For me to do that I have to put a lot of time into it."

Troy has also found a lot of similarities between improving as a quarterback and improving as a broadcaster. He said, "You know, as a player, everything that's done on a practice field is documented and filmed. So you go back and you watch it, so there was never a pass that I threw on the practice field or in a game that I didn't go back and watch. That's the way it's been for me in this. I review all the tapes. The most frustrating part of this business for me has been that I'm extremely competitive, and having grown up in sports in my whole life there's always been a scoreboard. In broadcasting, it's just a lot harder to define [a winner]. Early on, coming out of the booth after a game, it was a big letdown for me because I never knew how we did: If we did well, if we did poorly or, more importantly, if we won or if we lost. That has taken probably the most time, just becoming more and more comfortable with the fact that there is no scoreboard in this job. Some people like it, some people don't, and that's hard because the evaluation is so subjective."

Being behind the microphone has changed the way Troy watches games now. "I listen to games entirely different when I'm watching them as a fan. Now I'm listening to what the broadcasters are saying and why people like John Madden have been successful. What is it he does that is so good? I do that with all of them now."

KNOWING YOU ARE IMPROVING

Over time, Troy was able to recognize his improvement. "I could sense it when I was watching it. I was making points that weren't quite as obvious. I think all broadcasters early on have phrases that they use, and I think that it's often times used just to try to buy time. I found myself doing less of that. Then just getting more and more comfortable with the business of television and what's going on in the booth."

For most professional athletes, playing their game is natural and being on the air is not. Is broadcasting tougher for Troy than playing in the NFL? "I don't know if it's harder, it's a different challenge. For my whole career, if I was struggling with a particular pass, or if I didn't quite understand this defense, I was able to go in and study it or go out and throw that route over and over and over in practice until it became more and more comfortable for me. In this, there are no reps, you know, you don't get reps in the off season, you don't get reps during the week leading up to the game. You get live shots and that's it. The only thing you can really do is mentally study it and then just try to envision yourself doing it a little bit differently or this and that. I think you get better the more chances you get to get up there and get behind the mic and do it. In this profession, it's not like sports to where you go practice it. That's a little bit frustrating."

TROY'S BATTLE WITH THE MICROPHONE CORD

Troy has had his humorous moments in the booth, too. "Probably the funniest thing that's happened to me so far is at the end of halftime we come on and we do an 'on camera.' Kind of recap what happened in the first half, what each team needs to do in the second half, what have you. Every time we go to sit in these chairs to do the on-cameras the stage manager always wants to hide the [headphone] cords behind our backs so the people don't see them. Well, they never give us enough length on the cord to where I can really put my cord back behind my back. It's always pulling on me, and it never quite works. So, we're getting ready to come on the air and they are counting us down to like twenty to when we come on. I'm trying to get this cord behind my back and the tension is too tight, like it usually is. I was in somewhat of a surly mood that day and was just tired of going through this gymnastic every time. So I grabbed the cord and yanked it about as hard as I could, not even caring really if it came yanking out of the wall. I had a hold of the wrong cord. I had Dick's [Stockton] cord in my hand. So Dick's headset went flying off of his head, clear across the room (he laughs). They're scrambling to get us on the air; they're doing [the countdown], ten, nine. Dick's out of his chair running, trying to get his headset on, he finally gets it, he comes flying back in the chair, I mean literally right before we went on. Dick was laughing, fortunately, and I was laughing, so through the whole 'on camera,' I'm sure the audience is thinking, 'What in the world is going on?'

After winning three Super Bowls, Troy knows how important it is to be a part of a good team. "Working with Joe [Buck], I really equate it a lot to, and I think it's true in anything: you always need a good team. There are a lot of people that help put it together. I've got great teammates and that allows us to just go out and do our job."

TROY'S ADVICE FOR OTHER ATHLETES WANTING TO CROSS OVER

As for advice for other athletes thinking about a career in broadcasting, Troy said, "It's funny because I go down on the field before the games. I go down there to talk to these guys about what they're thinking for the game and what I can look for, what they think of the match-ups and different things like that will help me for the game. I've had a ton of guys come up to me in the last two years wanting to talk to me about how they can get into the business. The only thing I can really tell them is to try and get over to Europe. That was the path I took. If they can get over to Europe and then do games and be seen and heard, maybe they can spark interest in somebody."

Working on the other side of the microphone now, Troy has a more of an appreciation for broadcasters than when he was playing. "I really believe that if I were to go back and play, if I knew then what I know now, I think I would have been a lot different guy to interview. Because I understand it a little bit better now. When I was playing, I was just interested in playing. The interview part of it was just a part of the job, now, kind of seeing how it works, seeing why somebody, when they're candid to us and how that helps us, not that they have to say anything irresponsible. I would probably be a little bit more helpful for the media than what I probably was as a player."

Troy suggests current pro athletes and other professionals who have to deal with the media in their current jobs use candor to their advantage for a future career on the air. "The players that are being interviewed now, for those that want to get into this, if they are a little more candid and open themselves up a little bit more, I think TV executives see that and they generally have an idea of who they think will make a good broadcaster. Those guys generally get opportunities, that doesn't necessarily translate that they're going to be successful but the ones that are open and a little more candid they usually get an opportunity to at least see what they can do."

YOU DON'T HAVE TO BE A HALL OF FAMER

Babe Laufenberg has become one of the more successful all-around former athlete-turned-broadcasters in the nation, turning an average pro sports career into a wonderful profession on the air. Brandon "Babe" Laufenberg played quarterback for the NFL's Washington Redskins, New Orleans Saints, San Diego Chargers, and Dallas Cowboys. He was also a baseball star and was drafted by Major League Baseball's San Francisco Giants. Babe is now the number one sports anchor at CBS Channel 11 in Dallas, he hosts the Cowboys coaches show on television, and is also the color analyst on the Dallas Cowboys Radio Network play-by-play team. He was named the Texas Sportscaster of the Year in 2000.

Babe started thinking about a job in broadcasting early in his playing career. "I kind of observed what guys did, how they did it from the other side of the camera. I thought, you know, that kind of looked like it could be fun. . . I thought that could be a pretty cool job."

Babe played college football first at Stanford and then Indiana. He knew that his sports career would not last forever, so he spent time off the field trying to prepare for when his playing days would come to an end. "Every year I would do something in the off-season, or try to do something, to kind of point to the future, if you will. I took the L.S.A.T., Law School Admission Test. I got my real estate license in Virginia when I was playing for the Redskins. I never took an internship at a television station or something like that in the off-season, which is something I should have done, looking back." Even without the internship, Babe has done all right for himself.

Despite his interest in the broadcast business, Babe can chalk up his start in broadcasting to a bit of good fortune. "I was released [from the NFL] in '91. I had done something called the 'Two Minute Drill' at KVIL [the former Dallas Cowboys Network flagship station] when I was still playing. KVIL in 1990 did these two-minute interviews with the players. One day, I went down, and I did it at the studio and Ron Chapman [program director] was in the room just listening, and I guess, unbeknownst to me, he walked out and said, 'Hey, that guy is pretty good. We should keep him in mind if anything happens to him.' Well, lo and behold, the next year I get released and he asks me if I want to do the post-game show, you know, just take the call-ins. So I said, 'Well, sure.'"

Within a few weeks of the season, Babe was not just doing the post-game show, but the pre-game and halftime shows as well—not a bad start to his second career.

Despite the good fortune and quick start with getting on the air, Laufenberg had to work very hard to maintain, and then enhance, his position on the air.

"Once I said, 'Hey, this may be a profession for me,' then I really started to work at it. I went to a talent coach, worked on my speech, that type of thing."

OVERCOMING A SPEECH IMPEDIMENT

As for the lessons from the talent coach, Babe says he learned "just how to work with the camera, enunciation, inflection. I also had a lisp, which can be a relatively debilitating thing for a commentator, although there are people out there with lisps and I think sometimes you don't even realize it. I went to a speech pathologist and worked on that for about a year."

Babe can be a great source of inspiration for those with a lisp or some form of speech deficiency that must be overcome. "It's funny," he said. "You need to work at it. I was doing three times a day, 'Sally sips seashells by the seashore.' You know, there are exercises you can do and basically you kind of train your tongue like you train everything else, to speak a certain way. It's a muscle memory."

Laufenberg is not the only major talent to overcome a speech impediment; plenty of great names are on the list, such as: Winston Churchill, Jimmy Stewart, Julia Roberts, Bruce Willis, James Earl Jones, Carly Simon, and many others. If you have a speech impediment and want to work on the air, your task will be more difficult than usual, but in many cases you can overcome your problem and achieve your goals. I will provide more information on dealing with speech impediments in chapter 16.

As can be expected, Babe also had to overcome nerves the first several times on the air. "Part of my nervousness at first was thinking that the people around you were kind of judging you. When I first started here [at CBS 11] as the anchor, I would say, 'Are the other anchors looking at me, are they kind of feeling me out?' Then you realize, 'Hey, they really don't care, they're going to do their thing.' [He laughs.] You've got to forget that you're not talking to a thousand people or ten thousand, whatever's out there, you're just talking to one person who happens to be sitting right where the camera is and be conversational."

With all the different things that he has done, Laufenberg has most enjoyed doing the color commentary during the play-by-play radio broadcasts of Dallas Cowboys games the most. "I love the spontaneity of a game, of not knowing what's going to happen. I don't script what I'm going to say, but, you know, you write down notes and things on players and anecdotes and little tidbits and many times you leave a game and 90 percent of what you have going in never got used. You don't know what's going to come up, but you have to be prepared when it does."

DO ON-AIR WORK WHILE STILL PLAYING

Laufenberg has some advice for athletes who are interested in making the transition into broadcasting: "Just do everything, everything you can. Somebody asks you, 'Hey, you want to come in on a Sunday night for five minutes and join us?' Do it. A morning show, do it. Anything where you can get a feel for what's going on and put yourself in front of people making those decisions. You never know if you go down to a television station and do a little part on the morning show and one of the producers is looking at it and says, 'Boy, you know, that guy's got a little something to him, we should keep him in mind, we should get him worked in here.'

"The other thing is, I always tell guys, especially now: it'll never be worthwhile to you financially. Somebody is going to pay you two hundred or three hundred dollars to come in and do a Sunday night show. You are not going to make ten thousand dollars a show and if you're making a million dollars, you say, what do I need with another two hundred and fifty dollars a week. But it's not the money, it's the experience, because once they get done, and then they say, 'Hey, I'd like to get into it,' some people already have a head start on them."

Good air personalities make things look easy—sometimes too easy. So, does Babe think broadcasting is a good career for former athletes to get into, despite the fact that it's harder than it looks? "I think if they're in for the right reasons. I've had a number of players say, 'I can do what you do.' Not in a belittling way but they say, 'We played the game, it's easy.' Just because you played doesn't mean you will be good on the air, it's a whole different thing. And you see them, you see athletes who aren't very good. Joe Montana only lasted a year [on the air], maybe the greatest quarterback of all time."

Harold Reynolds played Major League baseball for the Seattle Mariners, Baltimore Orioles, and California Angels. He was voted an all-star at second base two times and represented the United States in Major League baseball's annual tour of games against Japan. Harold found a way to make the transition from being an all-star baseball player to an Emmy Award–winning broadcaster as part of ESPN's *Baseball Tonight* show.

Despite his success on the air, broadcasting did not cross his mind while he was still playing. When I asked him if he ever thought about a second career on the air, he said, "Never really did. I had a couple of local TV stations in Seattle ask me to come in during the post-season and break down a couple of pitchers that were going to be in the post-season or something like that. Even then it was the furthest thing from my mind, thinking about doing TV, because I was still in the player mode."

A chance meeting with some ESPN folks led to an audition for a job on the air, which Harold made the most of, beating out some impressive former athletes to get the coveted spot. The pressure of playing pro sports, coming through in the clutch and performing in front of fans is a good way to prepare for the strains of being on the air, he insists. "I think that's why I like *live* TV more so than I do the taping. Because live gives you that adrenaline and you have to concentrate like it is a ballgame. You know, that competitiveness of trying to make sure your comment comes out properly. Taping it, I mess up every time."

There are some parallels between playing baseball and being on the air, as making a mistake on the air is much like making an error on the field. Harold explains, "Yeah it is, once it's out there, it's out there. Live keeps you sharp. Live keeps you on your toes."

IMPROVING ON THE JOB

Harold had plenty of help improving in his early days on the air. "A lot of it came with watching a lot of shows, watching a lot of tape. Carl Ravech [ESPN anchor] was really instrumental in taking time with me and sitting down, going over my comments. He would say, 'Hey that's not going to work, you didn't tell me anything there.' And Jeff Snider who was the coordinating producer at the time, they both put a lot of time into me and sat down and talked with me."

Harold even gets plenty of advice from fans watching. "I get more people writing me, 'Well, you put more emphasis on the verb! You shouldn't have done that in that sentence.' I'm like, '*What!*'"

Being a natural athlete does not necessarily make for being a natural broadcaster. "The toughest transition is to verbalize what you do naturally. Because you don't think about it, you just do it. Now you're asked all the sudden to put those actions into words and make it clear."

For all his success on the air, Harold has had a lot of challenges. "I think the toughest time for me was trying to find myself and not worry about how I'm presenting things. Just like in anything that you do, until you're able find yourself and not worry about what everybody else is thinking, then you're on your way to doing some great things."

Meeting the challenge of being good on the air was tough for Harold; a lot of former athletes find broadcasting more difficult than playing their sport at the highest level. He tells us, "In baseball you figure it out, you go get it done, and your on-field performance lets you know what everybody's thinking, instantly. If I'm 0 for 20 [at the plate] they're booing me, I better fix my swing. If I'm struggling here [at ESPN], they may not tell me that, 'You know what, we're getting ready to get you off the show.'"

As a former athlete, its not surprising that he actually enjoys the pressure of having to be good night in and night out. "Yeah, I love that. I love that because you're not allowed to be complacent. I've always been driven to be better anyway so, that's a reality here."

It takes plenty of off-air work to be good on the air. "It's a constant thing. I find myself watching ball games or even watching TV shows or watching the news and seeing how somebody presents what they're saying. I'm constantly watching and learning, seeing how they're doing things."

The hardest part of being on the air every night may be a little surprising. "The toughest challenge is the season is so long that it can easily become redundant. Ok, lets talk about Sammy Sosa again. Hello. Lets break his swing down again, well, as I've said for the last two weeks. . . ."

HAROLD'S ADVICE FOR ATHLETES WANTING TO CROSS OVER

Harold has some advice for athletes that are thinking about getting into the broadcast business: "I think you've got to really be open; you've got to have an open personality. Very extroverted instead of introverted. I think the thing that helped me out was I did a lot of public speaking while I was playing ball so I was never really nervous getting in front of a camera and talking in front of a ton of people. That didn't bother me. The other thing is, I've learned so much about the game and about the inside scoop being in this arena because you worked your tail off. You think you might just go out there and sit down and talk, but you spend a lot of time doing homework. Watching a lot of games, talking to a lot of people, everybody having a lot of input on you."

Harold feels the trend of athletes getting into broadcasting has benefited the fans. "I think it's been good, particularly since I've been here the last six or seven years, they've really put an emphasis on, take us inside the game. What were you thinking, you know, the why. Why did he do that? Why are you swinging at that pitch? Why are you running there? The why's are being answered more so than anything else."

Only former players that have actually been there and done that can answer those inside questions, which is why former athletes are in a great position to get into the broadcasting business.

CHILD ACTOR TO BROADCASTING STAR

Danny Bonaduce had a slightly different transition to make. He transformed himself from a child actor into a broadcasting success. Just as star athletes can have an advantage breaking into the business, being a former acting star certainly helped Danny get his first radio job. When I asked him if his acting career helped him get his foot in the door, Danny said, "Oh, absolutely. I would not be a vastly overpaid disc jockey if I were not once Danny Partridge, absolutely."

Danny does not see many parallels in his transition into broadcasting and those of former athletes. "I don't see the similarity. What you're saying is, you are going from being an expert in one endeavor to being an expert in the same endeavor except for not having to do the hard part. In other words, you take a quarterback who's spent the last seven years getting smashed by linebackers, and now all he has to do is talk about other people getting smashed by linebackers. So, you know, it's not a big jump."

Danny started as a morning show sidekick in Philadelphia and went on to get his own show in Chicago a few years later, in 1991. He knows that unlike most of the people who get started working on the air, he can credit his early broadcasting fame to his fame in acting. He says, "I didn't work my way into it. Philadelphia is the number five market in the country. It takes people their whole careers to end up doing mornings in Philly and that's where I started. I'm one of the lucky ones. I'm probably the luckiest one."

Bonaduce has co-hosted syndicated TV talk shows with big-name stars like Dick Clark but likes doing radio a little more. He says, "I would have to say radio is more fun because there are almost no rules. I mean literally there are no holds barred. On a television show there's often things like segments that will get dumped because they were unacceptable to a sponsor, where that just doesn't happen on a radio show. If you have listeners, you have sponsors, the radio is more of a free-for-all."

MAKE A NAME FOR YOURSELF

The bottom line is that if you make a name for yourself in a profession other than broadcasting and you want a job on the air, your chances are better than most. If you are an athlete, you do not even have to have a great career to be a success on the air. Bob Ueker, for example was a rarely used catcher who is now in the Baseball Hall of Fame—not for anything he did as a player, but for being a broadcaster. Ueker currently does play-by-play for the Milwaukee Brewers but is also known for his work in television commercials for national products including Miller Lite and his roles in movies. In the movie *Major League*, he played Harry Doyle, the infamous radio voice of the Cleveland Indians. Ueker's one-liners, such as "Just a bit outside," have become a part of the American lexicon.

You do not have to have perfect grammar to be an announcer either; in fact, sometimes you are considered more colorful and entertaining if you don't. John Madden has made it big not only because of his wonderful insight as a former head coach of the Oakland Raiders, but also because he says, "boom" and, "bam," better than anyone else. America loves Madden's down-home way of speaking.

THEY ACTUALLY SAID IT

While athletes and coaches have wonderful insights and colorful ways of talking, sometimes what they say comes out just a bit wrong. These errors make them even more entertaining. Here are a few of the better quotes from athletes and coaches over the years, as chronicled by Ross and Kathryn Petra in their compilation of *365 Stupidest Things Ever Said* (Workman Publishing):[1]

* * *

"That was so complicated, folks, so let's have a replay for all you fans scoring in bed."
– Hockey announcer Bob Kelly

"Me and George and Billy are two of a kind."
– Baseball player Mickey Rivers, talking about his relationship with Billy Martin and George Steinbrenner.

"Three things are bad for you. I can't remember the first two, but doughnuts are the third."
– Florida State football coach Bill Petersen

Question: "Did Don Mattingly exceed your expectations?"
Yogi Berra: "No, but he did a lot better than I thought he would."

* * *

It is no wonder the world loves to hear former coaches and athletes talk on the air. What could be more entertaining than that?

End Note

[1] Petra, Ross, and Petra, Kathryn. *365 Stupidest Things Ever Said*. New York: Workman Publishing, 2000.

Buying Time on the Air

The eye of every station and network is always on the bottom line and nearly all cities have radio and television stations willing to sell their air-time for certain specialty shows, especially on the weekend. This can be a good way to get an on-air career started. Dallas program director Tyler Cox explains why stations sell blocks of air time on the weekends: "For news/talk radio the primary audience ratings day-part is Monday through Friday from six in the morning to seven at night. I understand general managers who, when faced with needing to hit a bottom line say, 'What if we sold that five PM hour on Saturday to some guy who wants to do a financial advice show?'"

BUYING TIME TO PROPEL YOUR BUSINESS

One reason to buy air time is that you own or are a part of a business that would benefit from an information talk show. These programs can show-case your business to the public and increase public awareness of your business and expertise. Buying air time for a business talk show can pay for itself with added business stimulated by the show. For instance, if you are a real estate broker and want to do a show to help people who are looking for a new home, the show might bring you a lot of new business to pay for the air time and even make a profit. This idea can work in many different areas, including financial advice, car sales, car repair, physical conditioning, health and diet, gardening, baseball cards, fantasy sports—the list of possibilities goes on and on.

As for the parameters for doing a business show like this, Cox says, "The parameters are as varied as there are radio stations. Certainly it's got to be a legal product, to begin with. It's got to be product that a station is going to be comfortable having on their air."

BUYING TIME TO START A CAREER ON THE AIR

You might want to buy air time to start your career as an on-air personality if you believe this is the best, or only, way to get your start. ESPN Radio general manager Bruce Gilbert says, "I've even told people who want to do talk shows: if you have to, find a way to buy the time so that you can pay for your way on the air. Buy the time to do a talk show; it will be worth the investment if that's what you really want to do so you can get some real tape, and you can really get a feel for what it's like to do live radio."

Tyler Cox agrees, "It can happen—it's hard, but it can happen. At least it's a way, if you can find a smaller station in a smaller community willing to sell you that time, you can start at least developing air checks to hone your craft."

This can be a good way for someone creative to get himself on the air, even if he has no experience at all. "That's right," Gilbert said, "I mean, some of the wackiest concepts in the world have made it on the air on the weekends now."

COST OF BUYING AIR TIME

The price that it costs to buy time on the air varies greatly depending on several factors. Tyler Cox tells us the price "depends on the market size and it depends on the radio station within the market. Some stations, because of higher ratings in the week, can demand higher dollars for a weekend show than another can."

Regarding cost, ESPN's Bruce Gilbert agrees: "I've heard everything. I know people that have bought shows for fifty bucks an hour in smaller towns, and I've heard people pay up to three grand an hour in large markets. Those are some of the ranges that I've heard. Its all over the board, depending on the time of day, obviously."

The factors that influence the cost of buying air time are the size of the market, the ratings of the station, the power of the radio station's signal, what time of day you want to buy, and how much time you purchase. Nights and weekends are generally less expensive. Buying larger blocks of air time, say three hours every week instead of one, or if you buy for an extended period of time, say for six months or a year, you should always be able to work out a discount.

Another factor in price includes how many of the station's commercials you will play in your show. If you buy an hour outright, not playing any of the stations commercials, it will cost you more. If you buy an hour but agree to play ten minutes of the stations commercials, it should cost you less.

There is even a way to get the air time for free. If you have a great idea that the station thinks its regular listeners will enjoy, you may be able to negotiate the air time for no cost, as long as the station can sell commercials to put in the show. If this is the case, you should be able to negotiate a certain amount of commercial time in the show where you can run your own commercials and make some money for yourself.

While the price of the air time can be negotiated, the station will probably want part or all of the money paid up front, whether that be for one hour for one weekend or twenty-four hours over six months. If you are serious about buying air time, the station is going to be serious about getting paid. Once you have been on the air for a while and you have built up a relationship with the station and staff, they will be more willing to work with you on a payment plan.

TAKING IT FROM IDEA TO REALITY

Let's assume that you have an idea for a show. Tyler Cox tells us who to talk to about getting it on the air: "Get with the radio station sales management and go over the concept. Find out if the price is right. See if there's a time slot available. See if you can work out a deal. I mean, it's that simple. That happens all the time on information-based radio stations all around the country."

A word of advice: do not set up a meeting with the radio station without having worked out a detailed plan. If you do not have a well thought out, serious idea for a show, the station's staff will not give you the time of day. You must decide before the meeting how long you want the show to be, one hour or two. What are you going to do on the show? Are you going to talk business and take phone calls from people with questions in your area of expertise? Are you going to play music and be a disc jockey? If so, what kind of music are you going to play? Will you supply the records or do you expect the radio station to do that? Do you want to do a sports talk show and take phone calls? What if nobody calls you? Will you be able to fill the time all by yourself? All of these things have to be figured out in advance.

The kind of program you do will ultimately be a combination of what you want to do and what the station will allow you to do. Many radio stations have set formats that they want to stick to every hour. For instance, some stations always run network news at the top of the hour and commercial breaks at certain times during the hour. At well-run radio stations you will have to conform your show around their basic programming.

Another thing to consider is who will be helping you while you are on the air. The amount of assistance the radio station offers you usually depends on the size of the market and what you negotiate. At smaller stations you may be expected to do everything yourself or supply your own help. Stations in larger cities usually have their own board operators running the control room, but you may have to answer your own phones or bring in someone who can do it for you. In these cases, the radio station is expected to train you and your assistants on what you need to know. For those wanting to start a show who have no previous experience, the station could demand that you hire a professional to co-host your show. This makes things much easier on you, but also makes it more expensive.

REAL EXPERIENCE OF BUYING AIR TIME

Ralph Russell currently hosts a successful financial talk show called *On The Money* at WGN Radio in Chicago. He gets paid to do the show now, but started his on-air career in 1987 by buying air time on a little station called WBBX in Highland Park (in Chicago).

Ralph wanted to be a broadcaster growing up in Cleveland and went to Ohio University—known for its broadcasting department. "I thought there must be a way to combine broadcasting with a second major, if you will, and that's why I decided to go to law school. When I went to law school to study broadcast law, it wasn't nearly as interesting to me as being behind a mic was. When my friend called about interviewing with Dean Witter, I thought that was when my broadcasting career was probably done, you know, when I got started with Dean Witter. Then a couple of years later it sort of dawned on me to, I had not heard of many investment radio shows, so I thought it would be worth a shot."

As it turned out, Ralph's on-air career was far from over. In fact, starting out by buying air time has probably allowed him to have a better career on the air than if he would have tried to make it a full time job from the start. "You know, like anything else, initially, unless you have some experience on the air, especially in a major market like Chicago, the major stations aren't going to even begin to talk to you. Luckily, when I started buying good air time and getting that experience, I opened up some other doors to doing some television work, you know, when major network weekend news shows would want some comments about the markets they would invite me down. I would do some things like Channel 9 WGN TV, which is a superstation, and MSNBC. I would do a lot of guest appearances on TV. As you know, those things usually last two or three minutes and then they move onto another topic, but at least that got more exposure for me, and that's what helped me, along with meeting one of the key people at WGN to get me in the door there."

Ralph had a leg up on many people considering buying air time because he had studied broadcasting in college. He still had to improve his sound on the air in order to make the most of his experience. "I listened to tapes, not all the time, I mean even now I probably listen to a tape maybe once a quarter [three months] just to hear the crutch words that every broadcaster uses that you don't realize that you're using. So occasionally I would go and listen to a tape but that's about the extent of it."

WHO CAN BUY AIR TIME?

The next big question for somebody interested in starting his or her broadcasting career by buying air time is who can actually buy air time? Is it something that anyone can do? Ralph said, "I think anybody can do it. Whether it is long term successful or not is another question. It takes a year, I think, to really build up any kind of listener response (if you are doing a business show), and that's a lot of money that you're throwing down the tubes without getting a response on, and typically like anyone making an investment you want to see a return on your money. If it takes a long time to get a return on the money, eventually some people get frustrated and quit."

If you feel like you are on the right track, do not give up too quickly. Ralph's investment paid off rather nicely. "There were years, probably, [that] it paid off four or six to one. And at those odds, who's not going to like that!"

Crossing his two favorite career interests has worked out very well for Ralph. He no longer has to buy his own air time; he gets paid to do his show now. "It's great. I could not ask for a better situation, I couldn't be happier with how it's all worked out. I hope I'm there [WGN] for many years to come."

The response for his day-to-day financial business is still good from listeners. "No doubt," he said. "It carries the business. No question, it's an awesome setup."

AMUSING MOMENTS

As anyone with much time invested in radio and television would expect, Ralph has had an amusing moment or two on the air. "One time when we were on WBBX, I had a partner at the time, and we were taking a listener's call. The host of the "German Music Hour" [another show on the station] was a popular German lady in town here, and we thought we had the caller on the line on the air, but evidently we had the wrong line, and we had her conversation on the phone with her, at then-time, fiancé and she was screaming at him in German for staying out all night the night before. This went on for like ten minutes. They were screaming at each other in German and swearing at each other, and this went live on the air. So the listeners thought it was hysterical, that was kind of embarrassing. We had so many calls on Monday about that, people laughing

Larry North helped start the fitness craze.

hysterically, but she didn't think it was that funny. That was probably the strangest one."

LARRY NORTH

Fitness guru Larry North does his own local radio show in the Dallas/Fort Worth area but never had to buy time on the radio. He has, however, been a part of some of the most lucrative infomercials on television. "I had the most successful weight-loss infomercial actually of all time. It was called the *Great North American Slimdown*, [it] ran from '95 to 2000 [and] did about one hundred and twenty million in sales. That was with an infomercial company; I had nothing to do with the media time or anything, but all good stuff, though."

Paid programs on both radio and television have produced staggering responses. North says, "My show alone, in its peak, during its four-and-a-half-year run averaged ten to fifteen million dollars in media buy each year. It paid off handsomely for the company; it paid off for me, too. I get a royalty. The show generated one hundred and twenty million in revenue off of fifty million in airtime, about forty-forty five million actually."

According to North, there are some major differences between television and radio paid programs. "When you're buying a thirty-

Photos courtesy of Larry North

Larry is still in great shape today!

minute spot on television, you've already tested your show. You're not going to buy air time unless you know your show is working. So anytime you see an infomercial on TV, you know that it's already been tested, and it's cash flow positive.

"With buying air time on a radio, it's the same situation [as television]. You're not going to pay for that advertising unless you're getting a return on your investment. Paid programming, though, for live [shows] is a big difference because it is live programming, it's not really scripted, and you are taking calls as if it's a regular radio show."

IS IT A REAL SHOW?

So is a talk show that has been paid for considered a real talk show or not? North responds, "It is, and it isn't. At the end of the day, if you listen, they are definitely promoting [their product]. And it's their right; they're paying a lot of money for the show. And I can promise you this, no one would continue doing it if it wasn't making money for them."

Ralph Russell is one of the most successful broadcasters in the country who starting out by buying his own air time. He shares some advice for those interested in taking the same path. "You know if they really, really, really want to go for it they should go to some kind of broadcasting school. Whether it's community college courses or something else, take a semester or two of courses. I would get experience doing that first because if you don't, and you try it without any experience at all, you're going to sound bad and you're going to be flustered being on the air, and the people listening to you are going to be like, what in the world is this?"

THERE WILL BE MISTAKES

No matter how much you prepare for your time on the air, you will still make mistakes. This is a part of moving up the ladder to success. Make sure you see the big picture—where you are going—and learn from your mistakes. Russell continues, "The only way to do it is to buy time, get some experience in the market, get your jitters out sitting in front of that microphone taking your listeners' calls. Then if you do get a good break then you're ready to go."

In the next chapter, we'll begin to take a look at how you can work to improve yourself on the air.

Being Good on the Air

While the biggest step in anyone's broadcasting career is breaking into the business, the process does not end there. The next step is learning the art and skill of your job. If you have been able to secure a position on the air, now the work of transforming your voice into an instrument begins. If you are serious about a successful career on the air, not just a job, you must dedicate yourself to doing several things to improve.

Here are some of the main things you must focus on if you plan to succeed:

‡ Make yourself available to the station and program director or news director to work as much on the air as possible. Take advantage of being on the air by recording air-checks of yourself. Constantly evaluate yourself and recognize what you are doing well and what needs improvement.

‡ Use your off-air time wisely by practicing.

‡ Study the air talent from the closest major market cities. Listen to them and learn what makes them good.

‡ Read autobiographies by people in the business to learn how they moved up. Read trade magazines and Web sites to keep up with the business. If you are a news reporter, read newspapers and magazines. If you are a sports reporter, keep up with sports magazines and Web sites. Be as knowledgeable as possible in your field of expertise. This knowledge will help you ad lib when you need to fill some time and ask better questions of guests on the air. Reading is also good food, keeping your mind sharp.

Each of these steps can bring you closer to your dreams of a career in radio.

GET AS MUCH WORK ON THE AIR AS POSSIBLE

We all need as much on-air experience as possible to improve our craft. This usually does not just fall in your lap. It will be up to you to do what is necessary to get more time behind the microphone.

When I got my first job on the air, I was given the worst shift possible, the overnight or graveyard shift on the weekend. I didn't care. I was in heaven every time I turned on the microphone. It was my bliss, pure joy.

At the first disc jockey meeting I attended, I was introduced to everyone at the station for the first time, and I made it a point to tell every air personality in the room that if they ever wanted to skip a shift, if they were sick or if they ever needed someone to work for them for any reason, I would be happy to fill in. They took me up on my offer, allowing me more on-air work and experience to learn and get better. Before long I was moving past all of the other part-timers on the depth chart, soon management started assigning me the prime-time weekend shifts, and I started getting the first call when one of the full-timers was out.

Not only will you gain experience by filling in for others, but you also give yourself more of a chance to air-check and hear how you sound on the air. Find a way to record yourself at least once a week so that you can see and hear what you are doing right and, of course, what you are doing wrong.

RECOGNIZE YOUR MISTAKES

Many times we say and do things on the air without realizing it until we review the recording. The most common early mistakes on the air are saying things like, "you know," "um," and "right now" too frequently. Inexperienced broadcasters also tend to mispronounce words, and say things like, "fer," instead of "for." You will find that you have certain pet phrases that you tend to get repeated again and again. We usually do not realize we are doing it until we hear it for ourselves.

We can fall into the same verbal traps on television, but being seen offers the added pitfall of using repetitive, meaningless mannerisms as well. For instance, you may see yourself blinking too much, or closing your eyes altogether, over-smiling so that you look ditzy or under-smiling so that you look like you are in pain. There are as many little quirks as there are people on the air. We can catch these pesky little habits just by looking at ourselves on tape. You may find out that you need to do your hair differently or add to or cut back on the amount of makeup you use (yes, guys wear makeup on television too). Air-checking is the best way to do quality control on yourself.

Rarely are we able to hear or see ourselves doing these things while we are on the air. If you are anything like I was when I first started on the air, you will think you are the second coming of Wolfman Jack. Obviously this was not the case, and I learned as much by reviewing my own tapes. Go back and check out your work. The only way to catch your mistakes is to either be told by someone else (always embarrassing and hard on the ego) or hearing it for yourself. It is just as important to recognize the things that you are doing right, so that you can keep doing them.

As valuable as it is to air-check, there is no need to do it everyday. You can be unnecessarily hard on yourself because you are your own worst critic. Listening back to your work on the air twice a week to start with and then once a week after a while should suffice.

IT TAKES A WHILE TO LIKE YOUR OWN VOICE

I have yet to talk to a single on-air personality who liked the sound of his or her own voice the first time that person heard it recorded. My parents were the first people who tape-recorded me—just for fun, of course. When I heard the tape, I seriously thought that it was someone else. Not only did my voice sound strange, it sounded bad. I was not nearly as smooth or as confident as I thought. This reaction is actually very common in the broadcast business; self-critique is a gift because it pushes you to get better all the time. Do not get depressed because you do not sound as great as you thought you would. You have a fine future ahead. Working on your voice is just a step in the process.

I remember listening to air-check tapes of myself in the production room after some of my early overnight shifts. I would be cringing as I listened. When one of the other jocks (disc jockeys) would walk into the room, I was so embarrassed that I would turn off the machine in shame. Even though I thought I was so horrible, my kindhearted coworkers would tell me that I sounded fine. I might have sounded fine to them, but my own ears told me I was horrible. What a great gift that is. While we can sound fine to others, we can hear for ourselves what we need to work on. It can also help to have a kind and honest coworker or boss that can give a good critique session once in a while.

MAKE TIME TO GET BETTER

Work is work, and for most people when the workday is over they hit the door running. If you are building a career in any field, you need to rethink your schedule in order to give yourself the best opportunity to advance. In the book *Managing Up!*, organizational development experts Michael and Deborah Dobson advise, "Sometimes, important elements of the job—especially those related to long-term goals—aren't being done because crisis and firefighting interfere. Try to set some time aside each day (even a little bit adds up over time) to work on any important projects. Use the 'Law of The Slight Edge' to your benefit: an hour a day, each workday, applied to long-range beneficial work, adds up to 200 hours, or 25 eight-hour workdays, per year! Imagine how much you could get done with 25 eight-hour workdays to devote to long-term valuable work—and then remember that an hour a day is about the only reliable strategy to get those days."[1]

While you are at the station, even if you are not on the air at any given time, you can still use the facilities there to get in even more voice work. In the production room you can practice by voicing commercials, promos, public service announcements (PSAs), and any other copy you can get your hands on. This kind of work helps you sound more natural and entertaining. At the same time, you can work on your timing. Get proficient at making thirty-second commercials exactly thirty seconds, get the feel of talking over the ten-second intro music of a song before the singing starts. Use production room sound effects to practice moving in and out different sound bites. Sound bites are short segments of pre-recorded sound that you use in your show. They can be short clips from movies to accentuate your point, funny or classic television moments, short pieces of a song, or the usual sound bites from athletes you hear during a sportscast or police and politicians in a newscast. When you use these various pieces of audio you want to flow into and out of them so that it all sounds seamless and natural. This takes practice. Become an expert at running a control board while talking in and out of songs or sound bites.

Practicing on station apparatus also allows you to become more familiar with how all the different equipment works. Offer to help others do their production work or work with the production director to learn from him or her. In television, learn how to work the editing and voice-over equipment and practice on it as much as you can in your off-hours. Get to where you can do things smoothly, quickly, and expertly so that when you get your chance to shine, you will.

PRACTICE OFF THE AIR

There is one main key to getting better on the air, and that is practice. We just talked about how you can practice at the radio station, but that is not going to be enough. You will need to work on your craft away from the station as well.

You can practice just about anywhere, in the shower, in the car, mowing the yard, or doing dishes. This off-air practice can consist of several elements. Talk to yourself as you would if you were on the air to find the tone and inflection that feel good to you. Read out loud. It is also helpful to think up interesting questions to ask a would-be guest in an imaginary interview. This all may seem silly, but it's not. You must practice your craft, just as an NBA player would practice shooting baskets on his home court, a baseball player would take batting practice, or a singer would do vocal exercises at home.

READING OUT LOUD

Reading out loud is valuable for several reasons. It makes you a better reader, and being a good reader is an extremely important part of being good on the air. Even if you are just reading your own writing, reading out loud helps you become more comfortable translating words from paper to sound. Learn how to do it so that it sounds and feels natural. Speaking naturally when you are reading is not as easy as it sounds; it is a skill that must be practiced and learned. Your goal is to sound like you are not reading at all but just talking off the top of your head.

Work on the inflection of your voice so that you sound entertaining as well as natural. Initial work on voice inflection can sound a little strange, so you may want to make sure no one else is around to hear. Talk with as much inflection as you possibly can, from very low to very high. Record this if you can and listen back. Yes, it will sound ridiculous, but you will also learn what the range of your voice is and how much range you have. You will want to sound natural on the air, so once you have found a comfortable range, practice using inflection in your conversation.

FINDING THE "VOICE TONE"

The hardest thing for me to find at this early stage of my career was a comfortable tone. I would have it on the air one night when I was in a groove, and everything I said came out smoothly. Another night I would be on the air and my voice just felt off, forced and unnatural. I practiced my voice tone in my car every day, trying to find that tone so that I could have it every time I turned on the mic. My tone came in small measures, and after some practice I noticed that I was in the groove two days a week, then three. After a while I found that I had it 100 percent of the time, and I didn't even have to think about it anymore. It was just there. The hard work had paid off.

LISTEN AND LEARN FROM MAJOR MARKET TALENT

When I got my first on-air job in Wyoming, the closet major market city was Denver, Colorado. I listened and watched as often as I could to the Denver stations to learn how these major market broadcasters performed. Then I copied them. Now, you do not want to build your career out of copying other talent, but you can certainly learn from them and use what you learn to fit your own style.

LEARN TO REACH THROUGH THE SPEAKERS

Speaking and communicating (they are not the same thing) are the keys to being successful in both radio and television. Speaking is talking and verbalizing. Communicating is the ability to reach through the radio or television and touch the person listening on the other end. Radio people can learn from television personalities, and vice versa. If you do not live near enough a big city to pick up its radio and television stations, check in on the local cable network broadcasts—many times you can get both radio and television stations from the nearest major markets. You can also buy air-check tapes of major market personalities in trade magazines. Listening and watching talent from larger cites and learning from them will take years off the time it takes you to learn the art of being on the air.

Top air personalities have moved up the ladder because they have figured some things out. You can learn these things the hard way, by yourself, or you can study these people closely and learn from them. You should pay attention to the following qualities: their breathing pattern when talking on the air; the inflection in their voice; the way they emphasize certain words when talking for effect; their transitions in and out of sound bites or songs. Great broadcasters make you feel like they are talking directly to you. If you listen closely, you can learn every time they open the mic.

LOCAL OR REGIONAL ACCENTS

Another element to be conscious of is sounding too local. To reach the top of the profession in either radio or television, you will need to have a fairly middle-of-the-road sound—no thick accents.

Having an accent is not always a bad thing. Speaking with a Boston accent in Boston is not necessarily a strike against you, and sometimes it will even help you, but only on the local level. In Dallas, we have a local talk show host with a thick Texas twang, and listeners love it. When I did talk shows in

Los Angeles and Chicago, I always asked my producer to try and book him on our show whenever there was a story out of Dallas, just because he added so much flavor to the story with his accent. However, if he were to try and get a radio show somewhere outside of Texas, he would probably run into some brick walls because of his drawl.

You go about getting rid of an accent the same way that you get better on the air. Listen and learn. Listen closely to and make tapes of those who speak with the non-accent sound that you are looking to acquire. Do the same thing that actors do when they are preparing for a role: learn how to change your speech pattern. I recently heard a movie star from Tennessee talking about how she worked from the age of fourteen to get rid of her southern drawl so that she would not be typecast. It worked, although she does admit that she falls back into some old speech patterns when she gets on the phone with her mother.

Do not go to the other extreme, either. If you want a job in the South, don't try to pull off a Southern accent to get a position. It doesn't matter how good you may be at faking it, you will eventually slip and be found out.

NEVER STOP IMPROVING

Keep listening, learning, and growing. You will find that none of us gets better overnight. Don't let that bother you. Like any other art form, getting better on the air takes time; it took me quite a few years to become a decent broadcaster. I worked every day to hone my voice to what I considered instrument quality. It takes work and practice to sound good on a regular basis. It will be frustrating at times, but you will get better with work and practice.

You may find it hard to believe now that big breaks will come your way and allow you to climb the ladder of success in the broadcast business, but it actually happens every day.

End Note

[1] Michael S. Dobson and Deborah Singer Dobson. *Managing Up!* AMACOM Div American Mgt Assn, 2002.

How Top Radio and Television Personalities Improved Themselves on the Air

In the last chapter I gave you some ideas on how you can get better on the air. No one makes it to the top of any industry without putting in a lot of hard work. Some broadcasters may seem lucky, but don't kid yourself: there are no exceptions in radio and television. In this chapter, I will show you how some of the top air personalities in the country worked to get better and climb the ladder.

It is the job of an air personality to make things look and sound easy, as if life is one big amusement park, but it takes a lot of work to do that. In order to get to the top of the broadcast business, you will need to work on the three key elements we talked about in the last chapter. The work you do to improve you voice, and how you learn to use your voice as an instrument, will be more important than anything else.

HONE YOUR VOICE

All the work you do off the air networking and marketing yourself is vital to advancing, but you must have something to sell, namely your voice and performance talent. You can work harder than everyone off the air promoting yourself, but if your delivery is not pleasing, enjoyable, and entertaining on the air, you will run into a lot of dead ends. It doesn't matter if you are Chris Berman, Bob Costas, E.D Hill, Rene Syler, or Larry King. In order to move up the ladder, you must hone your craft, the art of speaking on the air.

Larry King did not waste any time after securing his first air position and then getting over a case of the jitters. "Once I started, I just worked. I just loved working. I offered to do anything, if the all-night guy was sick, I'd work the all-night shift. I just wanted it. I really wanted it. I improved my talents by listening to radio a lot. I loved it, I had an ear for it."

Charlie Tuna followed a similar philosophy. "I worked hard, I think, writing, you know, lines, bits, and things like that. I owe a lot of credit for that to Larry Lujak, who I watched in Boston when we worked together. He always brought in his spiral notebook and was always making notes out of the paper and writing down things. I kind of adopted that philosophy to always start writing stuff down, just trying to remember things. Then it comes off on the air as spontaneous and you're given credit for 'gee he's so bright.' Well, I just did a little more homework than everybody else. Even my old boss at KHJ [in Los Angeles] said, 'You work harder than any other jocks I ever had, you always had a great work ethic.' I said, 'Well, I wanted to be where I wanted to be, so I worked hard.'"

Despite all his success, Charlie still works very hard today. "You really have to read a lot and watch a lot of stuff and listen to things because you kind of have to be like a sponge. When you come to the air you're kind of like a Renaissance person at that point, it's like cocktail party chatter and you have a lot to bring to the table. Hopefully people find it interesting enough to stay and listen to you."

LAMPLEY THROWN INTO THE FIRE
ON NATIONAL TELEVISION

For his first on-air job, Jim Lampley was thrown into the fire on national television. He remembers: "The play-by-play man is Keith Jackson, who is already a sort of hallowed presence in 1974. The expert commentator is Bud Wilkinson, chairman of the Presidents Council on Physical Fitness, and nobody said a word to me, by in [*sic*] large, about what to do or how to do it. It was sink or swim from the beginning. I had to sort of feel my way into understanding what it was that would get me on the air: what the producer might appreciate, how to do it without being so obtrusive that I would piss Keith off, or piss Bud off, or piss anybody else off around me. A lot of what the original concept had been went by the wayside as I just sort of pared it down to pursue the goal of survival. It was really trial and error from the beginning.

"I like to tell people, and it's almost true, that the only performance training I ever had came on the second day of my career, when I was in Knoxville, Tennessee, preparing for my very first college football game, UCLA against Tennessee, September 7, 1974, and I can see it like yesterday, I'm standing there on a rehearsal on Friday afternoon and I hear Andy Sadaris' [Director] voice in my ear saying, 'Jim are you standing on the sideline?' I said, 'Yes;' he says, 'Stand right there.' He comes running out of the truck about twenty seconds later, little roly-poly guy, rolls all the way out to me, grabs me by the shoulder and points up at the sun. He says, 'You see that?' I'm looking right at the sun. I said, 'Yeah, I see it.' He said, 'That's your key light.' He turned around and ran back to the truck. That was my on-air training."

PAINFUL EARLY AIR-CHECKS

Watching early air-checks of himself was not much fun for Lampley either. "It was painful. I was a little bit flabbergasted, a) at how young I looked, I looked like a child on the air, and b) how high and sort of reedy thin my voice sounded to me. But that's always the case for all of us, I mean, I guarantee you, the guys with the deepest pipes in the world, the first time they listened to themselves on the air they thought, 'Wow, do I really sound like that?' Because you never sound like you think you do. The bottom line is the first few of times I looked at myself on tape, I was so terrified by that I decided I better not look at those anymore, and I didn't. For years I didn't look at anything that I did."

LAMP'S KEYS

Lampley's key to being good on the air: "Be yourself. Point one is be yourself, but 1-A, almost right there with it would be, be a strong, confident, verbal communicator who never worries about your ability to complete a sentence under pressure. Be somebody for whom proper, effective, clear, confident use of the language is second nature. That's the single biggest asset you can have because at the end of the day this is about being able to communicate on your feet. Sooner or later you're going to have to be yourself and be smart on the air. So be sure you can be smart being yourself."

SYLER'S RISE

Rene Syler's meteoric rise from an intern in Sacramento to co-host of the *CBS Early Show* is nothing short of amazing. When I asked her how she improved, she told me, "I watched a lot of tape. I didn't really do a lot of practicing but I did time and grade [trial and error], there really is no substitute for that. It's like my husband and his golf game, the only way you get better is by doing it. I wasn't really one to take a newspaper and read in front of the mirror because newspaper copy is not the same as broadcast copy.

"I watched a lot of tape early on, and then I realized that sometimes watching too much tape is detrimental, so I stopped watching tape. I didn't like do the whole, you know, make faces in the mirror, raise your eyebrow, this, that, and the other. Here's the other piece of advice that I would give. Be yourself. Of all the things that I just told you I think that is the biggest one. It is exhausting to try and be someone you're not, and pretty soon someone will find out, and that camera with its unblinking eye can pick up on phonies. So I would just say be yourself. When I was starting out in the business people said, 'Oh, we hate her laugh or we hate this or we hate that,' well you know what, I wasn't about to change for any one person because you change for one and you make everyone else upset. It wasn't worth it! I really am a firm believer in just being yourself."

It can be tricky to know if you are actually getting better, and sometimes you can get too down on yourself for making mistakes. Rene says, "To me it's all really internal. I just felt a whole lot better about my performance and I was becoming more confident. I was handling interviews and breaking news situations better. That's how I gauged my progress, I would gauge it in terms of my confidence."

HOW COSTAS GOT BETTER

Bob Costas was one of the best at improving himself early in his career, and there is nothing surprising about his winning formula. He tells us: "I listened to my tapes and evaluated them and tried to focus on areas where I could improve. Just by doing it, the rough edges get smoothed out." According to Costas, it does not matter how long you have been in the business, or how much success you have had, the growth process never stops. "I'm still learning, it's just that the improvements are smaller, they are smaller by degree. I can look back at things I did five years ago and say, you know, here's how I could have done that better, let alone thirty years ago."

As for being unique, Costas discusses strategies of finding one's personal style and rhythm. "It is important, I think, to find a style that is comfortable for you and true for you and doesn't sound like it's forced or that it's copying somebody else. When you start out you're kind of searching for something. You turn down the sound on the television set and try to call the game, you've got a play-by-play running through your head, you're listening to other broadcasters while you're driving around in the car, and you're trying to think, what about this sounds good and what doesn't. Then after a while, once your style is established, you're not doing that as much."

KINGSLEY'S IMPROVEMENT PATH

Bob Kingsley's improvement strategy was pretty simple. "It was a matter of just staying after it, you know, just staying after it. Of course, the thing was always, 'Well, as soon as you get some experience come on back.' I said, 'If you don't give me the job how am I going to get the experience?' You know, the same old line. A lot of times [I would be] working other jobs so I could continue to do that. You just kind of learn as you go, kind of like life."

DETOURS CAN BE LEARNING TOOLS

E.D. Hill took a detour in her career after her second job on the air in Waco, Texas. She found out later that this detour was one of the best learning tools she could have ever hoped for. "VH1 was having a contest for a VJ [video jockey] to replace Don Imus. I sent in my tape. I always wanted to live in New York City and I figured what the heck. Well, I won this contest to be the new VJ. My agent told me I was crazy. She told me, 'If you get out of news, you will never get back in again.' It turned out that I didn't enjoy it. I didn't find it that interesting, but the benefit was that in being a VJ there was no script. I think the toughest thing for news people to learn to do is to just talk. To take information, remember it, and then just talk like a normal person. That's what I learned at VH1 and it made a huge difference in my career. I think it's very unnatural to talk into a camera and pretend like you're talking to your mother. There's nothing natural about that. Learning to just speak without a script at VH1 was a great asset to have."

BERMAN ON THE GROUND FLOOR

Chris Berman started at ESPN when it was a fledgling organization just getting off the ground. The all-sports network has since become a major power in the communication business, but when Chris first started, it was just a small cable sports station. He learned on the air in front of the nation. He says, "The early days were a little different. I can't say that I sat and listened ad nauseam to myself, or watched tapes of TV I did early on. I think becoming aware of everything that is going on around you—that is even more in your job. If I got to this tape a little better, if I wrote a little more concise, this would snap a little better and he [the producer] could roll this tape there. I think I got a little better by being observant, being honest with myself. Come to the realization that when you think you've done a really good broadcast, it's not that good. The good news is when you think you've really been horrible, its not that bad."

Plain and simple, time on the air was instrumental in Berman's impressive growth process. "I was, again, fortunate that we did an hour [on the air] every night. You could do local sports back then at six and eleven o'clock on TV and not have the time on the air in a week that I had in a day. And believe me, we didn't have a lot of tapes early on, so if you had a face for radio, which maybe I do (he says, chuckling) you're on there a lot. So you had to figure out a way to be informative yet entertaining. Not necessarily a slapsticker, but just however you would do it talking to a friend of yours.

"The hours on air that I logged, doing all those SportsCenters all those years more than anything else helped. We used to do two shows a night. I mean you're writing the whole thing, so like I said you're on a lot, in other words everything's in fast forward for you in time, which gave me about five years of experience in a year. And I was on at 2:30 in the morning, so if I was atrocious, ah, that's okay."

BERMAN: MR. NICE GUY

Berman is known as one of the nicest guys in the business. Former ESPN *Baseball Tonight* co-host Harold Reynolds knows that from firsthand experience. Reynolds says, "When I first signed [with ESPN], I came here [Bristol, Connecticut]. I get here and all the big shots, they send me to New York to see this speech coach. So I go to New York to go see this guy, and I come back and see Andrea Kirby [talent coach] and she's telling me, 'You have to sit this way, you have to pick up this camera, that camera'—whatever.

"As for the first show, per my instructions from the speech coach, Carl [Ravech] says, 'Hey we'd like to welcome our new baseball analyst Harold Reynolds,' and I'm like, '*Thank you very much!*' I'm sitting there stiff as a board looking into the camera, you know? After the show I said to myself, 'I'm done, I'm quitting, there's no way I can do this stuff, this doesn't work.' The next day I do a show with Berman and Chris says to me, thirty seconds before we go on the air he goes, 'Hey, that show yesterday, it sucked! Throw all that garbage out of your head. Look into that tube right there [the camera], and let's talk baseball. It's me, you and the boys in the bar.' Then he started talking about all his nicknames, I think I laughed through the whole show. Since then I've done a lot of growing, a lot of changing, and stuff like that, but I will always remember that intro into TV because it just wasn't getting it done the other way."

ESPN BOSS'S IMPROVEMENT ADVICE

There are a lot of important reasons why an air personality needs to improve his or her skills on the air. These reasons include feeling satisfied with yourself for doing a good job, making your listeners and viewers happy and building the size of the audience. The number one incentive for improvement for most is the desire to climb the ladder of success; most broadcasters want to move up and work in larger markets where both the audience and the paychecks are bigger.

In order to do this, you will have to impress some program directors and station managers along the way and convince them to hire you. ESPN Radio general manager Bruce Gilbert's advice for getting better on the air: "Live life like your listeners. Go out and do things. Pay attention to what's around you. If you are a sports talk host, don't just watch ESPN, I mean once in awhile you've got to watch some other things and find out what's going on."

You may wonder how to go about being so observant. Gilbert explained, "Always take notes, always carry a notebook, and even carry a small recorder if you can. Everything that happens to you in life could wind up on your show, so be sure you are constantly being observant and paying attention to everything around you."

COMMUNICATING ONE TO ONE

Another piece of advice that top programmers around the country will consistently give you: Our medium is all about being able to *communicate* with the listener or viewer, to make them think you are talking directly to them. Bruce Gilbert says, "The very basics of radio is one-to-one. I have a real pet peeve for people who say, 'Good morning everybody.' I mean, it's not everybody. The most powerful word you can use on the radio is the word 'you.' I think that the first word that every air talent should embrace is the word you. 'How are you,' should be the question not 'Hello everybody.' Just learning that it's a one-to-one medium."

You may wonder if there are any tricks or ideas you can use to remember that you are talking to just one person at a time. Gilbert suggests, "Consider the microphone an ear. I actually at one time, at a small station I worked at, I got a cutout of an ear and put it over the microphone to send the visual message to the air talent that this is one ear, one person that you're talking to."

Top Dallas program director Tyler Cox agrees, "Radio is the ultimate one-on-one medium. As a personality, whether you're in talk or in music, you have got to remember that you are talking to one person at a time. Whether it's that guy behind the wheel driving to work in the morning [or] mom in the car with the kids in the back seat heading off to daycare, you're communicating to one person."

Bruce Gilbert offers other methods of improvement: "Talking 'to' people, not 'at' people. Don't read stories, tell stories." Bruce has a simple suggestion for doing this. "Read the story out of the paper, then put the paper down and then turn on the microphone and tell people just as you would tell a friend if you bumped into them at the office."

Tyler Cox says all top personalities have one simple strategy to make their air work great. "They are doing show prep every waking minute of the day. As they go through their day they're kind of looking at things and saying, 'Gee that would be an interesting thing to talk about,' and not just whatever's on the front page above the fold on the morning paper."

IMPROVEMENT KEYS TO REMEMBER

Your improvement on the air depends upon how well you incorporate these ideas into your life and how you put them together to work for you. While everyone's road to the top is a little different, there are a few main points to remember: be yourself, listen to and watch yourself, and find a style with which you are comfortable. In order to actively work on all these things, you must watch, listen, and practice. Watch and listen to everyone you consider to be good on the air. Learn from them. Study what they are doing to find out what it is that makes them easy, fun, or compelling to listen to. If television is the focus, study the gestures of anchors and reporters to find out how they use their voices and their bodies to get their message across.

In order to make it to the top, you will need a big break. Don't worry. Big breaks are pretty common. Every major personality has had at least one, and most have had several. Your big break will come, but it will not be free—you will have to earn it. We will find out how some big breaks have come about in the next chapter.

The Big Break

One of the keys to a successful career in the broadcasting business is to make yourself the beneficiary of a big break or two. Big breaks are those events in your career that either allow you to leap forward to the next level or that put you in a position to move forward in the future.

In talking to people who want to be on the air, the big break is one of the main topics I am asked about. (Although popular, this question runs a distant second to "How do I get a job on the air?") In this chapter I will show you how I, along with some of the top personalities in the business, was able to make big breaks happen so that you can help make your own big breaks happen.

BIG BREAKS AND HUGE BREAKS

As I look back over my career I have enjoyed at least six or seven big breaks, which is not uncommon. While everyone needs these opportune moments in order to advance, there is an even higher level of break, a "huge" break that allows a person to really leap into the big-time. My huge break came in August of 1987 while I was working at my fourth radio station in Wyoming as a sportscaster. I had just resigned as the program director and afternoon drive disc jockey because the station could only afford to pay me "every once in awhile." I was married with one small child and another on the way, and we were desperately poor. We were so poor that I specifically remember the day that I emptied out the last of the coins I had saved in a tin can over the years to pay for baby formula.

My new job was paying me $800 a month, which was not a lot, but it was better than what I had been making at the other station. I was at home over the lunch hour one afternoon when the phone rang. It was John Adams, the News Director of the USA Radio Network in Dallas, Texas. I had sent John an audition tape six months earlier and had never heard back from him. I had actually given up hope on hearing back from him and had forgotten all about the job until he called. The network flew me out for a job interview and offered me a position as sportscaster for $18,000 a year. The money was horrible, but a lot better than $800 a month. Even more important than the money was the opportunity to make the jump from a small market to a major market in one fell swoop.

If it had not been for that forgotten tape and résumé I had sent out, a surprising phone call over a lunch hour, and the willingness to uproot my family and move to Dallas for $18,000 a year, my career would have been completely different. I doubt seriously that I would have been able to work in places like Los Angeles, London, Chicago, and Dallas, or with the wonderful people that I have been blessed to meet. I certainly would not be writing this book right now, and none of it would have happened if it were not for that one phone call. Now that is what you call a huge break.

In one form or another, every major market talent can pinpoint at least one of these big or huge breaks that propelled them to the heights they reached.

BONADUCE'S HUGE BREAK

Danny Bonaduce's huge break came at a shopping mall in Philadelphia. After his child-star days as a member of the *Partridge Family*, Danny found himself in pretty bad shape. "What happened was, I was a completely washed up ex-child star, all of thirty years old, penniless, homeless, and I went to live with my mom in Philadelphia. Literally washed up, strung out, it couldn't be a worse situation for either of us. I was at a shopping mall in Philadelphia and some disc jockey invited me on his show and I happened to be sober that day. I did what I guess was a very good job and the general manager and program director hired me before I even left the building to be the wacky sidekick on the morning show."

Danny also had to clean himself up in order to take advantage of his opportunity. He says he did exactly that, and a wonderful career behind the microphone was born.

TUNA'S HUGE BREAK

Charlie Tuna's huge break came compliments of another legend of the radio business, Larry Lujak. Tuna had left Kearney, Nebraska, just two years earlier and was on the air at KOMA in Oklahoma City when lightning struck, metaphorically speaking. Charlie recalled the way it happened: "Larry Lujak, who wound up at WLS in Chicago, was driving across the country from Seattle to his new job in Boston at that time. He heard me on the radio [while driving] in

Charlie Tuna, a kid from Nebraska in the '70s.

Wyoming, he said, on KOMA. He got to Boston, and Larry was impressed enough to recommend me to them: they were looking for a guy and I went to Boston. After a couple of months in Boston, Bill Drake was in town one night; they were starting up their new station, their new boss radio format on WRKO. They heard me and they needed a guy at KHJ [in Los Angeles] and so they offered me the job. I got to Los Angeles less than three years after I left Kearney, so it was kind of whirlwind."

His trip to the top was a whirlwind indeed. Charlie's is the kind of story that Hollywood scripts are made of, but his true-life script that has allowed him to earn a star on the Hollywood Walk of Fame. While it may seem like success happened overnight for Charlie Tuna, it really didn't. Remember he had been practicing in his room since he was five years old for just this moment, and his hard work paid off.

KING'S RISE TO GREATNESS

Larry King remembers the origins of his unprecedented rise very well. He recalls: "First big break was getting a job hosting a radio station talk show at a local restaurant. Pumperniks was a restaurant in Miami Beach, Florida, and the

Photos courtesy of Charlie Tuna

Tuna now has his own star on the Hollywood Walk of Fame.

[station] owner liked me and he said, 'Do you want to be a disc jockey all your life or do you want to do some talk too? Do you want to interview people?' They didn't even call it a talk show, just the Larry King Show. So I did my disc jockey show in the morning and then I did a mid-morning show at Pumperniks—and one day Bobby Darin walked in and then another day Jimmy Hoffa came, and I had no idea they were coming 'cause Miami Beach was that kind of town. I interviewed them and that was my big break—to get that chance—the opportunity to interview people in a public setting on a widely heard radio station. That led to doing a nightly show at Surfside 6, it led to my beginning of having my own television show in 1960 and then more shows throughout the sixties and seventies."

You can see a theme building here now with the ways big breaks happen. There is a lot of work involved in getting to the point to where you get discovered and things start happening. This is generally referred to in the business as paying your dues. Big breaks seem to come out of nowhere and magically happen—but only after a lot of hard work and putting yourself in a position where you can be rewarded.

COSTAS: THE WONDER KID

Bob Costas' career took a big leap forward when he got his second job out of college. He remembers, "I guess going from Syracuse to KMOX [in St. Louis] at age twenty-two, using, as my audition tape, a tape of a game between Syracuse and Rutgers that I had done as a sophomore or junior on the campus radio station. Just kind of sending it out on a flyer and getting hired to do the Spirits of St. Louis [American Basketball Association]. The Spirits only lasted two years but my connection to KMOX lasted a long time and I was at KMOX when I wound up at NBC. Even more so than the first breakthrough in television, that was a quantum leap to go from Syracuse to St. Louis especially then, you know, pre-cable TV, pre-ESPN, and all the rest."

HELP MAKE YOUR BREAKS

You have to play your part in making your big break happen. You have to be good on the air, and you must represent yourself well during the interview process. Usually before making the final decision to hire you, a program director or station manager will want to meet you face to face. As you might imagine, Bob's interview for the job in St. Louis was nerve-wracking. "Oh, I was very nervous. I really thought that my youth would work against me but I think it actually helped me because they figured that maybe I had some precocious talent and that there was a higher upside with me than in hiring a thirty-five-year-old guy that might have, actually, at that point, been better than me but maybe didn't have the same amount of potential."

It looks like they may have been right.

"Well, maybe they lucked out," he concedes.

SYLER, INTERN TO NATIONAL STAR

Rene Syler, former co-host of the *CBS Early Show*, went from an internship in Sacramento to being a part of a major television network morning show so fast that it is hard to differentiate the big breaks. She says, "You know what, I don't think any of them has been bigger or smaller than any of the others. When I was on my way to Reno, I thought that was my big break, and when I was on my way to Birmingham, that was my big break, and then I went to Dallas, and that was my big break. You just have to make the most of every opportunity."

Big breaks happen, and they happen quite often, but seldom do they happen without having worked hard to make it happen. Sometimes when opportune moments like this come along, other people in the business get nasty towards you because you got lucky. Most of the time jealousy is the motivation behind their negative comments, and you have to remember that you earned your big break. Rene Syler knows how best to handle it: "People say to me, 'Oh, you're so lucky,' and I think, 'You know, luck really didn't have a lot to do with it, I worked my butt off to get here.' You know, I gave up more holidays than I care to talk about because I was willing to work, and I volunteered to work. I did a lot of breaking news stories where there was no glamour involved—glamour was far, far, far away, because I was interested in honing my craft and being credible. Luck is when opportunity meets hard work, you gotta to make the most of your opportunities. So I don't really think I had any one big break."

While there may not have been a certain break that sticks out for Rene, the most memorable moment may have come when she found out she had been hired to be a part of the CBS *Early Show*. "All my other jobs have been kind of like, 'Oh well, that's great, I can't wait,' but you know what, when I got this job it really was kind of like, 'Whoa!' This was a big, big, BIG job. When I got this, I did, I screamed in my office, 'Oh my gosh, I can't believe this,' you know? Because this was, of all the things and all the jobs that I've had and opportunities that I've had, I look back on now and I can see they were all priming me for an opportunity like this. All of the things that I went through, all of the times that I had to handle breaking news situations on the set or the times when tapes didn't roll or the times that I got a chance to do lighter news and lighter features and show my personality. All of those things, what you see now is a sum total of all that. So that was all, you know, none of it was a waste of time."

YOU NEVER KNOW WHO'S WATCHING

Chris Berman has not had a whole lot of big breaks, because he has only needed a couple of them. "ESPN is my fourth job; I've been here for twenty-four years. I began at ESPN October 1, 1979, but while I was doing the radio, I got a job doing the weekend sports in Hartford on channel 30, which is NBC. They didn't have a full-time second sportscaster at the time, so I got paid $23 on Saturday night and $23 on Sunday night. But I had a chance to go on TV. Long hair and mustache and everything, I did it."

Most of us would think getting a job on the air in a top 30 market doing weekend sports is a big break, and it is, but Chris knew that he had to continue to work hard to take advantage of his good fortune, which he did.

Berman continues, "You never know who's watching, and you never know who's listening. So when ESPN was starting, or about to start, I said, 'Well, instead of me sending you a tape, why don't you tune in on the weekends. It's live, you know, it's not me showing you the best of my work, here's where I am, I've only been on a couple of months.' And they watched and I guess I wasn't atrocious—I certainly wasn't too polished. You never know, you never know who's out there. I got hired at ESPN after three months there at channel 30."

SOMETIMES YOU HAVE TO TAKE A CHANCE

ESPN at the time was not the massive entity that it is now. It was a startup all-sports cable channel. Most experts did not think it would last very long. What turned out to be a big break for Berman was actually a great risk at the time. "The circumstances were unique. ESPN was just starting, so they frankly needed a few of us who would cost them nothing, who could speak in complete sentences, had knowledge of the subject and were eager and young. I was twenty-four, I had no family, so I wasn't gambling leaving a good situation. Let's say I was the main guy in Hartford at channel 30, and I was thirty-two with a two-year-old. Would I have gone to a cable thing like that? We don't even know if it's going to make it. We don't even know what cable TV is. Well maybe not, but it was a no-brainer for me. I can't say I was so smart for taking a gamble; I was twenty-four, why not? Even though that was four jobs in three years, I've now done twenty-four years in one. ESPN could have been a parking lot after two years, but it wasn't."

As Berman's story indicates, sometimes you really don't know when a huge break is sitting on your doorstep. How was he to know that ESPN was going to turn into what it is now? He didn't, of course, but remember, Chris Berman was part of the formula that would help ESPN survive the early years and become the sports broadcasting giant that it is today.

TRAGEDY INTO TRIUMPH

Big breaks come in a lot of different forms, sometimes, as unbelievable as it may seem at the time, something you view as tragic can actually be a big break. Take Jim Lampley, for example. "I've been fired three times, every time I made money from it and every time I wound up with a better job. So, you know, I'd have to say that my firings were spectacular lucky breaks, although of course, I didn't recognize them as such at the time. . . . I'd say I've had an unbelievable run of good breaks because I'm still alive and well twenty-eight years into this business."

Big breaks don't just happen for career broadcasters, they also happen for those people trying to cross over from other occupations. Making the move from being a Major League Baseball player into broadcasting was the last thing on Harold Reynolds' mind when his big break came. He remembers, "I was at the World Series in '95 and I was shopping at Hugo Boss Warehouse and ran into Carl Ravech and Bob Roucher [ESPN producer at the time]. I had no idea who they were because I never saw the show [*Baseball Tonight*]. Now it's on all the time, but when I was playing it was once a week, it was a half-hour show and I was on the West Coast so you never saw it I was always playing. My brother, who was with me, Larry, he knew who Carl was, he goes, 'Hey, that's the guy from *Baseball Tonight*!' I go, 'What? What show is that?' So we gave them a ride back to the hotel and then they came back here that fall, they were looking to audition to people. They said, 'Hey let's talk to Harold Reynolds, see if he's interested. They gave me a call and I ended up audition-ing and it worked out."

While meeting the host and producer of *Baseball Tonight* was a huge break, Harold still had to beat out a few big-name former athletes to land the job. How many other applicants were there? "A lot, because that's when it was just starting to take off. Dave Winfield, Steve Lyons, I mean almost every baseball analyst, Ozzie Smith, you name it."

BIG BREAKS COME IN ALL SIZES

Most big breaks are obvious, like Danny Bonaduce's discovery in a mall, or landing a job on the *CBS Early Show* like Rene Syler. Be prepared for the breaks that are not so obvious as well, the ones that you play a vital role in making happen, like the risk Chris Berman took in helping a startup cable channel. You will usually find that when one door gets slammed in your face, another opportunity is opening up somewhere else; take advantage of the situation, like Jim Lampley was able to do.

The one common denominator of all these big breaks is that they were earned. All of these people worked hard, not only to help make the big break happen in the first place, but then to make their break a success.

The single most important factor in making breaks happen in your career is diligence: working professionally every day, every week, and every year. This will build the foundation for your success.

Did They Really Say That?

The radio and television business is notorious for attracting very intense and creative people. These talents can result in delightfully entertaining personalities but sometimes make for some strange and amazing stories. Unlike the rest of this book, this chapter does not advise you on how best to move your career forward, but it does give you an idea of the kind of people you will need to be able to work with and the type of situations you will need to be able to handle. Climbing the ladder of success takes more than talent; it also requires understanding the people you work with and the knowledge that even the greatest people in the business have made the same mistakes you will make. There will be that terrible moment, milliseconds after you have committed a stupid error, when your blood runs cold and you think you may have just done the most stupid thing in the history of broadcasting. At that moment, take heart, remembering from this chapter that we all make mistakes, and we all bounce back.

Some of these crazy stories center around disc jockeys trying to make their cohorts laugh while on the air, some are unfortunate slips of the tongue, and some, like many of mine, you can credit to just plain stupidity. All of these were, in their own way, hilarious when they happened, so I will try to do them justice. Again, remember—you are not the only one who has ever made a mistake.

SCHOOL SLIPS

There are some great stories from journalism schools, as Kent Collins from the University of Missouri relates. "Live shots tend to be the comedy hour around here because they [the students] have precious little experience both in the newsroom and the microwave remote setting. So, we get real tongue-tied out here, and we say things like, 'At the university fundraiser there was an eating contest where the participants ate each other under the table.'

"We had a weekend student anchor who read a story about a drowning at the resort lake here called Lake of the Ozarks, a report on how a man fell out of his boat, hit his head, and drowned. The next story's lead line was 'The Lake of the Ozarks is filling up with tourists this holiday weekend.' Our viewers [of KOMU-TV] have long been patient with us."

COSTAS BLOWS IT

Even the best, most respected talents in the business have had their embarrassing moments on the air, like Bob Costas. He recalls, "The second game that I ever did for the Spirits of St. Louis. I'm a twenty-two-year-old kid, very wet behind the ears, very nervous about whether I can fit in at KMOX, but excited about the opportunity. I do the first game, it was on a Friday night, and the Spirits led the game by five points with about a minute to go and they lost it in regulation on their home court, they blew a five-point lead in the last minute. The next game was two nights later, on a Sunday night, and they led that game, also a home game, they led the game by seven with about two minutes to go, and they called a time out. The guy who was doing the color commentary on the broadcast with me was a guy name Bill Wilkerson and I looked at Bill and I said, 'Bill, the Spirits apparently have this well in hand, but coach Bob McKinnon is taking no chances, because the last thing he wants is a repeat of Friday night's blowjob."

"Oh, no!" I said.

"Oh yeah. Yeah, and you know, this isn't now, where certain things, you know, almost anything goes on cable TV, I mean, this is KMOX in 1974 in a conservative community and the most established radio station you can imagine. Obviously what I was trying to say was that they didn't want to blow another game and the thing came out entirely wrong!

"Wilkerson and the engineer, whose name was Tom Barton, both looked at me as if the Hindenberg had just crashed or something. Their eyes are wide and they can't believe it. I remember Barton just giving me a signal, the rotating finger signal, like just keep on going, act like it didn't happen, so I just kept on going, and I finished the broadcast. I thought maybe the next day I would be fired."

Obviously Bob was not fired, but the tape would live in infamy.

"It was saved forever on a blooper reel at KMOX and it is semi-legendary. People in the years following sometimes upon first meeting me would say, 'Oh my God, I was driving down the road that night, and I almost drove into a ditch.'"

Some of these things will stick with you awhile, no matter how big you become in the industry. Just ask Bob. "It was over thirty years ago—and there you go."

MY LITTLE SLIP

Sooner or later, we will all have a slip of the tongue on the air. I, for instance, during the Texas Rangers post game show, *Rangers Replay*, called some of the team's power hitters, "power shitters." While my producer, board op, and listeners thought this was the funniest thing in the world, I was more than a little embarrassed.

BERMAN CAUGHT WITH HIS PANTS DOWN

Chris Berman saw his young radio life pass before his eyes working at a little station called WERI in Westerly, Rhode Island, when he was running the control board for a Boston Red Sox game being played out on the West Coast.

Berman remembers, "You're the only one in the station, I mean, I'm talking one in the morning, okay. The bases are loaded, the manager goes to the mound, he doesn't make the pitching change, there's one out and I've got to go to the bathroom, and I mean number two. The bathroom, which is all the way at the other end of the building, and I'm alone in the thing and here's my shot, you know what I mean! And so I run down to the bathroom and I get in there, but I crank the sound up high, you know, so that I can hear. Here I am, sitting on the toilet, and I hear, 'First pitch *lined to third, da—da—double play, and they're out of it!*' It's like, oh my gosh! And you know they're going to the break for a commercial and I've got my pants at my ankles! I guess we heard ads for Boston in Westerly, Rhode Island. I couldn't, not even I, at twenty-one, could get there."

BERMAN MET HIS WIFE ON THE JOB

A personality as big as Berman could not have just one great story, though. Another of his early jobs, before ESPN, was doing traffic reports in a beat-up old station wagon. He says, "You learn to speak in complete sentences when you are driving at sixty-five miles an hour, and you're on the air. So you're on the radio, and people do listen, you know, and a truck is playing cat-and-mouse with you. You've got one hand on this mobile phone, which was much more crude than today's phones and one hand on the wheel and he is playing cat-and-mouse with you! Your life is at stake and you're on the radio trying to say,

'Hey Route 8 today has a slight little tie-up at exit twenty-seven.' That was quite interesting.

"However, I did meet my wife as a result of driving the traffic car. I saw her come past the good side of town, of which there was only one of the four sides that I checked, every day at about eight o'clock. She was a blond in a silver Firebird. So after a couple of weeks, I got enough guts to follow where she was going and it was an elementary school. I parked my car, followed her into school and introduced myself and ask if she'd like to have coffee the next morning and she did. This summer we'll be married twenty years. So, you know, to say that doing traffic reports was a waste, well, it changed my life, literally."

THE FLYING SKIRT

E.D. Hill's most memorable moment came when she was on the air at the Fox News Channel, in front of hundreds of thousands of viewers. "I happened to be wearing a skirt one day and we had folks from one of the zoos in. They gave me this lovely python to hold. It was a very pretty snake but, uh, deadly. They assured me, 'Just don't flinch and it'll be no problem.' So, I'm holding this python and all of the sudden it drops down and starts sliding up my skirt. It circled my leg and kept going all the way up my dress. I stood there with my, you know, deer in the headlights look because I thought, 'I can't jump and I can't grab this thing and pull it off, but I'm getting really nervous!' [She chuckles.] Finally, the snake handler comes over and coaxes this snake out from under my skirt and takes him off of me. We have that video, in fact we've got still shots that I think we used on our calendar one year."

Larry King's run-in with a legend helped make his career. "No one believed I could get Frank Sinatra to do a local radio show for three hours in Miami. Frank showed up, and the whole city was shocked. The first question I asked him on the air was, 'Why are you here?' He said he was sick a few years earlier, he was working in a nightclub, and he asked Jackie Gleason to sit in for him, and Jackie came and did a show; Frank had laryngitis. When Frank came to Miami, Gleason called him and said, 'Remember the favor you said you owed me? This is it.' So he called a favor and I got Sinatra."

Why would Jackie Gleason do that for Larry? "He liked me. If Gleason liked you, you were a lucky person, and Gleason liked me. He would come on my radio show, he would come on my television show. He changed the set of my television show, he didn't like the chairs, he brought in new chairs. Jackie was a wild guy, and a control freak."

KINGSLEY'S ACE IN THE HOLE

An early slip of the tongue nearly got Bob Kingsley thrown off of the air and out of the business before he even got started, when he was still in the service. "I can remember when I was overseas, you know, inside the station the guys are talking and saying stuff. There was a pop music segment on Armed Forces Radio and everybody always referred to the *Four Aces* as the *Four Asses.* Well, I said that once on the air! It came out of my mouth and it took the colonel about three seconds to get down there and bust open the door. I was off the air and demoted to television!"

PULLING THE CHAIR OUT

While Kingsley's slip of the tongue got him in trouble, I can only blame my own stupidity for what nearly cost me my career early on. I had been working in radio for about a month when I pulled this stunt. I was the new kid, just hired to do the weekend overnight shift. The regular Monday through Friday on-air crew started coming in at about five o'clock to get ready for their shift one Monday morning. The news director at the station was a guy named Ken, who eventually became a great friend of mine, but I barely knew him at that time. Ken has since lost about two hundred pounds, but back then was a short and large man, about five foot seven inches tall and 350 pounds or so. He came running into the studio just before six o'clock one morning to do a top-of-the-hour newscast, and his arms were full of papers and carts. The papers were his script for the newscast, and the carts were the sound bites he planned to use, stacked in the order he needed to play them. When big Ken went to sit down in the chair in front of the microphone, for some unknown reason that hit me at the spur of the moment, I decided to pull the chair out from under him.

Ken, along with his scripts and carts, went flying in every different direction possible. I think I remember the ground shaking when he landed. It happened so fast that I had not really considered the consequences of my actions, but it began to dawn on me that I may have just ended my entire broadcasting career, the career that I knew in my heart I had been born to do.

This huge guy, now sprawled on the floor thanks to me, had the power to end it all. I laughed nervously as Ken shook off the effects of my juvenile prank and glared up at me from the studio carpet.

"You little shit!" he finally screamed after realizing what had happened.

That was all I needed to hear. I left the studio, now 100 percent sure that I had just accomplished the dumbest act of my life. The unlikely scene kept replaying in my head, and as hard as I tried and as scared as I was, I still could not help but laugh. I left the building before Ken got done with his newscast, figuring I could save my life and dignity if not my job. To this day, I am not sure what he did on the air that morning, or if he had been able to gather his information and wits in time to sound coherent or not.

I did not return to the radio station until my air-shift the next weekend. I was extremely relieved to find out that I still had a job. I apologized profusely to Ken when I saw him. Thankfully, he had had enough time to get past his anger and we had a good laugh. In the years to come we would spend many hours on the road together doing play-by-play for local sports teams. He is one of the kindest people I have ever known; he would have to be for allowing me to get away with that one.

AN INCONSPICUOUS STAR

One of the great gifts of being a radio celebrity is that you can be a star and still have a private life, because not many people know what you look like (unless you are Howard Stern or Don Imus). For instance, more people know Bob Kingsley's voice than his face now that he is heard every week around the world. "It's an amazing thing sometimes, because there is a great anonymity in radio, which I dearly love. I was in the market the other day, at the Kroger down here this last week. I was talking to the clerk and she said, 'Anybody ever tell you that you sound like Bob Kingsley?' I said, 'You know what, I've heard that.' She said, 'Don't you just hate that?' I just started laughing and I thought, should I say something? I didn't, I just left."

SHAKE AND BAKE

One of the qualities that makes Charlie Tuna so great is his ability to find humor in even the toughest of situations. "The main thing has been just going through all the major earthquakes here. In '71 I was at KHJ, getting signed on just forty seconds before the big Silmar [California] earthquake hit back then. Funny, the record was *Rare Earth* and over the intro of the song just before the earthquake hit I said, 'I feel a little shaky this morning,' and then there it is!

"In '73, I guess, when I had a major aftershock, I was working at K-Rock [doing the morning show], I thought, well, I've got to have another line ready for the next quake. So, this major aftershock, five-something on the Richter scale hit. I waited about ten, fifteen seconds after the shaking finally stopped and I cracked the mic (he remembers with a chuckle) and I just said, 'All right, if you don't get up, I'll do it again!'"

SNOW DAYS AND HOT COPY

Before ESPN G.M. Bruce Gilbert made the switch from being on the air into management, he took part in his share of radio hijinks. "Practical jokes, you know, small market radio is famous for it. We had a couple of great ones when I was on the air and still in my late teens in Wisconsin. Obviously, in Wisconsin you have a lot of school closings because of snow. We had an afternoon air personality who wasn't that bright; nice guy, but not that bright. One Friday afternoon it was just snowing to beat the band, one of those big-time Wisconsin winter storms. The forecast was for eight to twelve inches; again, keep in mind this is Friday afternoon. So we decide that we're going to type up a bogus list of school closings for the next day and pass them along to the afternoon guy. He was so excited to have breaking school closing news that he went on the air Friday afternoon and said all these schools would be closed tomorrow. Well, obviously tomorrow was Saturday. We got a kick out of that."

Apparently the cold Wisconsin weather had Bruce and his friends constantly thinking about fire as well. "Back in those days, everybody smoked inside a radio station. I never met a disc jockey that didn't smoke because what would happen is, you would start your record, you would queue up your next record, you'd think about what you were going to say and you'd have two minutes left in the song so what did you do? You fired up a cigarette. You know, everybody smoked. So there was plenty of fire around a radio station and it was always fun, back then, for whatever reason, to light people's copy on fire. Whether they were in the middle of a live spot or reading weather, someone would sneak in while they were live on the air and put their Bic lighter underneath the weather forecast. That was always great fun, you know, cause some scrambling and some fun on the air."

WHAT ARE FRIENDS FOR?

Much like Bruce and his early radio friends, during my first few years on the air in Wyoming, the group of part-time disc jockeys that I worked with were pretty good friends. We made it an ongoing game to try and make each other break up laughing while on the air. There were a lot of ways we went about doing this; making weird noises in the background was a common tactic. The sounds we used most often were some combination of flatulence, tropical birds, and sultry women. Sometimes we would also position ourselves within view of whomever was on the air and make funny faces or dance a strange jig. Seldom did the antics work, but early one morning I hit the mother lode.

A friend of mine named Greg had come in to relieve me from my overnight shift at six in the morning. Greg was very focused on his career, working hard to become a news anchor. He aspired to become the next Dan Rather or Peter Jennings. In order to get a little extra practice, he offered to do a newscast that I was scheduled to do at 6 AM. I eagerly agreed, happy to get out of doing a little more work at the end of my shift so that I could go home and sleep.

Just as Greg opened the microphone to start his very serious newscast, I started zipping and unzipping my pants a few feet behind him. I had pulled this stunt several times before to no effect, but for some reason on this particular morning the sound struck Greg as very funny. He spent the next four minutes on the air trying to talk through, and catch his breath in between, laughing fits. He never could quite get a grip on himself though. If you have ever gotten a case of the giggles in a situation where it is prohibited, you know how tough it is to stop. It did not help that I was laughing hysterically behind him the entire time.

With my stomach sore and my lungs out of breath, I finally had mercy on Greg and left the studio about three minutes into his newscast. I proceeded to howl with laughter as I listened to him struggle through his final minute on the air. He played a record when his cast was finally over and came bursting out of the studio in a combination of laughter and fury. He punched me in the arm a few times, but couldn't really be that angry because, in the past, he had tried to do the same thing to me. I just happened to get the better of him that time.

HUMOR IS GOOD

Even at the helm of a huge entity like ESPN Radio, Bruce Gilbert has not lost track of the importance of the funny side of broadcasting. "I think that humor is one of the things that makes radio so valuable to people. I've been a part of a lot of different shows on the air; at one time I did a team show with a buddy of mine, it was a pretty racy show, we would get blue [dirty] at times. We would actually get letters from people who would say they had lost a friend in a traffic accident or they had a family tragedy or something, and if it had not been for the humor we provided, they don't think they would have been able to get through it. That is amazing! It makes you feel so wonderful that you're able to help people through things just by being yourself and by having a good time and that that fun is contagious and helps people to get through. You know, that's what we all do it for! What we do it for is that rush we get when a listener says we actually touched them. When you get those kind of e-mails or letters from people, that they were touched or that you helped them through something, that's when you know that radio is what we teach people. It's a one-on-one medium, it's me talking to you, one on one. That's what radio is all about."

Gilbert continues, "As long as the listener isn't given false information that could be damaging, I'm not going to get in the way of that. I think it's all part of the fun of working and I think people who work in other fields in other offices have practical jokes and have fun like that too. You know, you should encourage that stuff. If you can't have fun working in the radio business then you don't belong in it. It's hard, hard work and we put in a lot of hours; if you can't have a good time, you should be doing something else."

EQUIPMENT MALFUNCTION

Sometimes equipment malfunctions make for some interesting anecdotes. Rene Syler has experienced that. "One of the things under the title of 'learn how to keep your cool' is, I was doing an intro to a piece and a light bulb exploded over my head. It sounded like a gunshot. You know, you have to learn not to scream, but I was just like, oh-my-gosh! It's the worst. I thought someone was firing at us! I just kept on reading. One of the keys is you just have to roll with the punches."

JUST PLAIN WEIRD

Good air personalities tend to be very creative, high-strung folk, with notorious egos. While sometimes that makes us quirky and a little hard to tolerate (just ask our husbands and wives), the combination usually makes for some pretty good fun. However, every once in a while, the quirkiness becomes too much to handle.

I once worked with a gentleman who was a little over the edge. He was our evening disc jockey, working the seven to midnight shift, and was a bit odd, to say the least. He wore rubber galoshes everywhere he went, both on the air and out in public. A bunch of us disc jockeys would get together and go out for a drink on occasion, and, of course, this guy would want to come with us. So there we all were, in the bar, dancing, drinking, picking up girls, and he was right there with us in his floppy rubber boots. We certainly got some strange looks. He was afraid to talk to the ladies, and considering his stylish footwear, they weren't beating down his door. He didn't get in the way

too much, but he certainly was a piece of work. He was also afraid of own-
ing a car for some reason, so he would either have to get a ride from one of
us to go to work or take a taxi. The last I heard, he had voluntarily checked
himself into a mental hospital and was doing fine.

CREATIVE, AND PROUD OF IT

While broadcasting personalities can be a bit unusual sometimes, most of us
would not have it any other way. It adds a spice to life that is priceless.
Bob Kingsley explains, "I think anytime you are in involved with creative
people there's always going to be a certain amount of weirdness involved.
I think that's applicable to just kind of the way the creative mind works, the
really creative mind. Those are the people that I love. So, it's not so weird.
I think people on the outside may think they're acting weird or sound weird
but it sounds good to me."

As fun and amusing as the broadcast business can be, broadcasters go
through hard times too, just like professionals in any field. Some of the best in
the business have survived some hard times and lived to tell the tale, as we hear
in the next chapter.

The Ups and the Downs

We live in a sophisticated and free society in which our freedom allows us to choose what we want to do with our lives. This freedom to decide forces us to accept the ups and downs that go along with these decisions. Tough times find all of us; it does not matter what business we ultimately decide to pursue. The radio and television industry is no different. Many of the broadcasting industry's top personalities have had to deal with challenging stretches of their careers and have used the lessons they learned during these stretches to make themselves stronger and better.

In this chapter, I will tell you about some of the trials our big-star friends had to endure on their way to the top, so that when you find yourself fighting through troubled times, you will know that it is just a part of the road to success. When you are going through these tough times you may see no light at the end of the tunnel, and you may be uncertain whether you can survive. During those times, remember that you are not alone, and that every air personality's journey includes plenty of strife.

Sometimes the best way to view difficult stretches in our careers is to look at them as necessary evils that will teach us something we need to learn to advance to the next level. In the book *An Unshakeable Mind*, author Ryuho Okawa, founder of the Institute for Research in Human Happiness, advises us to deal with hard times like this: "I have no intention of worshiping difficulties or distress, but it is an undeniable fact that these challenges work as catalysts for increasing human stature. If your life is merely ordinary, you will have no chances to grow. On the other hand, if you feel you are being torn apart by suffering, you will gain tremendous self-confidence by overcoming these struggles."[1]

NEAR-DEATH EYE-OPENER

E.D. Hill graduated from the University of Texas and took graduate studies at Harvard. Millions, if not billions, of people have seen her on television over the years. Despite all her successes, it took a near-death experience to put things in perspective. She tells us, "I was pregnant with my third child and I got sick. I was very, very, very close to death. I survived, miraculously; seriously, they used it as one of the case studies for freak diseases. The only thing I could think about when I was sick was who in the world would raise my kids. That scared me to death, not knowing who that would be. It brought so many things into focus for me. I realized I didn't miss the job. I didn't miss the news. I realized that I had my priorities totally screwed up. When my kids were sick I would pretend I was sick so that I could stay home and take them to the doctor because I was afraid if I called in and said, 'My child is sick,' they would think I was a weenie. Because it was just so 'girlie' to say, 'I want to take them to the first day of kindergarten.' It was when I was ill that I knew that's what matters in life. If an employer doesn't value that same thing, that's not the right place for me."

E.D. now has eight children. She takes the younger kids to work with her where Fox News pays for a babysitter when she's on the air. She offers her advice for other women in the business trying to balance family and career: "Honestly, I think you have to be up very up front with wherever you are going to work or wherever you are working now. You just have to go in and have that heart-to-heart. I know other women who have done that, in big markets. There was one person in particular I saw do this, and they started treating her better, clearly respecting her more than a lot of the other women there who probably wanted the exact same thing but didn't have the guts to go up and talk to them about it. If you're honest about what the priorities are in your life, any smart manager will respect that and any smart company will work with you."

MONEY PROBLEMS FOR THE KING

Larry King started the format of national talk shows with his legendary overnight show on the Mutual Radio Network. He has been a fixture on CNN since June of 1985, but even Larry King had to overcome hard times. "The hardest career stretch was when I was out of work for awhile. The station I worked for had switched to an urban, all-black network, and I was off the air for, like, six months. That was a killer. Then I went back to another station and that worked. Being off the air was hard."

Larry encountered another tough time during a four-year stretch of money problems. Those led to legal trouble in the early 1970s, and Larry found himself an outcast in Miami. He was forced to go to places as far away as Louisiana to find a job on the air. With grit and hard work, however, he fought his way back and was eventually offered to host his former show again at WIOD in Miami.

The broadcasting business can be volatile, so you must be prepared to stay tough when the hard times come. Battling through these hard times never made Larry question his calling in broadcasting. When I asked him if doubt ever got the best of him, he said, "No, no, no. I never thought it would be over. I knew I would come back. I have a lot of faith in myself. I don't have that much faith in myself in social situations. I'm not a hit at a cocktail party. I tend to be bored by them and I don't like to make the social whirls. I'm uptight in traffic jams and I don't handle being late well; I'm very much on time. But once I'm on the air, I'm home."

KINGSLEY BACK WITH THE PARENTS

Bob Kingsley's career took some difficult twists and turns early on that had to be endured as well. "I heard about a job in Vegas, so I just climbed in the car. I was working weekends in Palmdale, California. I think I gave them a week's notice and they said, 'You don't need to do that,' so I was gone that night. Showed up in Vegas and got a job at a station called KORK, which I believe is now history. It was at the Thunderbird Hotel, and it was pretty exciting stuff. I think I was making almost $75 a week. From there I went to Tijuana [Mexico], where I worked at XEAK for almost a year. They had convinced me what a fine opportunity that was and said that everything would be great about that except the pay. I was back to making $56 a week. This was not working out too well [he chuckles]. I was living off the gas card and, you know, I think I had to get out and go back to live with my parents for a while to get out of debt."

As for how Kingsley pulled things back together to get his career back on track, he said "I went and got a first-class radio license. From there it was all uphill. I could go out and work at a transmitter and some pretty decent places. It was great."

Remember that when you start moving up the ladder, working in bigger markets and making better money, the trials don't end. For instance, even after Bob Kingsley started doing the American Country Countdown, he still faced some stressful times. "There was one point where Tom Rounds, 'TR' at Watermark, wanted to cancel the Countdown, the Country

Countdown—because we didn't have any top 100 stations, that was real nerve-racking and it went on for a while. Sometimes in negotiations, you know, when the contract comes up, that can put you in not a good place. I had a couple of divorces, that'll put you in a bad mood [more laughter]. Career-wise it's been a pretty happy state of mind."

Right after we talked, Bob Kingsley was replaced on the American Country Countdown. Rather than get down about it, he started his own program, Bob Kingsley's Top 40 Countdown. His new show is quickly gaining a devoted following across the country.

All of the hard work and tough times have paid off for Bob. He has won Billboard, CMA, and Country Music Hall of Fame awards, and he has been recognized as one of the best radio show hosts in the world.

PACKING UP AND MOVING ON

I went through a divorce myself in the early 1990s. I was working at the USA Radio Network in Dallas as sports director. I had a friend who lived in Los Angeles, and since I was no longer tied down by family obligations, I figured I should make the most of my opportunity and try to make another huge break happen in my career. I packed up all my belongings, threw them in my car, and drove to Los Angeles. I told all my friends back in Dallas that I already had a job lined up, but I really had nothing at all. I was relying on faith. When I got to Los Angeles, I called program directors and dropped off audition tapes at every station I could find. One week went by, then two. The PDs were nice but had no jobs to offer me. After about five weeks, I finally had to break down and find an off-air job to start paying the bills.

My first job entailed helping people on and off the trams at Universal Studios. It was kind of nice to see how everything worked behind the scenes, but it definitely was not what I wanted to do with my life. I especially had a hard time stacking the baby strollers. I still have nightmares about those strollers.

After having my fill of being a tram loader and baby-stroller stacker, I took a job as a waiter at Hamburger Hamlet in Westwood right by UCLA. I found that I was even worse at waiting tables than I had been at loading trams.

While doing all this, I continued to call program directors and to try to make appointments to meet them in person. Using all the courage that I could muster, I dropped by a certain station without an appointment one afternoon. I sat in the lobby for over two hours while the PD sat in his office and refused to see me. I finally left, and he left a message on my home answering machine telling me how much he did not appreciate how I had rudely dropped by without an appointment.

I was really beginning to wonder if my big gamble had been a mistake when Len Weiner, program director of KMPC, the new all-sports station in Los Angeles, called to offer me a part-time job. In my typical cocky way, I told him that I would be happy to take the job but that I thought he was making a mistake by not putting me on full-time. Despite my attitude, he still hired me.

I continued to wait tables at Hamburger Hamlet while working part-time at KMPC for about a month, when Len called me into his office and actually told me that I had been right. He told me that he had made a mistake, and he offered me a full-time job! My big gamble had turned into a massive career jump.

At KMPC I had the great honor of working with people like Len Weiner, now at ESPN, along with Charlie Tuna, Jim Lampley, and many other great broadcasters. I would have stayed at KMPC for the rest of my career had the station not been sold in 1994. This sale broke my heart. It was the best radio station I had ever worked for, and during my time there I had met some magnificent people.

Stations being sold and formats being changed are two of the most common ways people lose their jobs in the broadcast industry, and there is not much you can do about it. As with everything else in life, it helps to take a philosophical perspective; everything happens for a reason. When one door closes, start looking for the door that is opening.

PASSED OVER FOR THE PERFECT JOB

Losing out on jobs that you know would have been just perfect for you is always painful too. When I was still very young, about nineteen or so, I had the opportunity to work as the weatherman on a local television station in Wyoming. I auditioned and did very well. The general manager told me that I did great, looked fantastic, and was definitely a finalist for the job. A few weeks later the news director called and told me I did not get the job because I looked too young on camera.

I remembered this about five years later while doing TV in Dallas. I was afraid I still looked too young, so I grew a mustache in an attempt to look older. The mustache did not fill in very well and I looked like a strawberry blond Charlie Chaplin. The general manager called me in to his office one day and told me to shave it off. While I was in his office, he told me a story about

Bob Costas going through a similar situation when he was younger, so I asked Bob about it. Here's what he told me.

"When I started at NBC, Don Ohlmeyer, who was then the president of NBC Sports, calls me into his office and he says, 'You know, we like your work, you have potential. Let me ask you something, how old are you?'

"I said, 'I'm twenty-eight.'

"He says, 'God-damn-it, you look like you're fourteen!' And he says, 'How much older do you think you would look if you grow a beard?'"

"I said, 'Oh, five years at least.'

"He said, 'Five years, really?'

"I said, 'Yeah, because that's how long it would take me to grow it.'"

DEALING WITH CRITICS

Bob's career has done just fine without any facial hair, but, like any public figure, he has had to deal with criticism now and then. "You could go out and do the best job anyone has ever done and you would still receive a certain amount of criticism because it's just the nature of the position. You're just out there and some people will take pot shots at you. There's no way to please the entire audience, there's no way to satisfy everyone in the audience at any given moment."

Despite a few critics here and there, he has never been fired from a job.

Not a bad career, Bob!

"Yeah, so far," he said.

Bob's advice is dead-on. You will never be able to make everybody happy, no matter how good you are or how hard you try. There will always be listeners, bosses, and colleagues who find something wrong with what you are doing. Your best response is to listen to what they are saying, learn what you can, and filter out what is only meant to hurt you.

THEY SAID, "YOU'RE NEVER GOING TO MAKE IT"

Rene Syler experienced tough times when her career was just getting started, but she had the strength to battle through it. "Early on in my career, I can remember having a teacher say, 'You probably are never going to make it as an anchor because there are so few anchor spots at a TV station. You really ought to go for being a reporter.' Well, I believe good anchors have to know what good news is. Sometimes you have to be a reporter to know that. Being out in the field helps you learn what good news is. So I never let his dire picture have an impact on me. I knew that, yeah, it was going to be rough and there would be some people who said, 'You're not cut out for

Danny Bonaduce, Child TV star in the '70s.

this,' and on and on, but I knew in my heart of hearts that I could do it."

IT'S NOT ABOUT THE GLAMOUR

When you are just starting your career, remember that nothing is as glamorous when you are working on the inside as it looks from the outside. Being a big-time Hollywood actor looks easy, but you do not see the actor working twenty-hour days in miserable conditions to make the movie when you are watching from the balcony with a bucket of popcorn on your lap. The same principle holds true in our business: what you are doing on the air looks and sounds enchanting to those listening and watching, but for you it is work. Rene Syler offered her thoughts, "I think a lot of people look at the anchors and think, 'Oh, that's what I want to do, it's so glamorous.' Early on in my career, there was nothing glamorous about it. When I had to produce and report and anchor the show and edit all the video tape. Trust me, there is nothing glamorous about that."

We can all expect to have ups and downs in our careers, but Danny Bonaduce may have cornered the market on the highs and lows for one career. He went from being on top of the world as a child star to being down and out, strung out, without a job and living at home, and then back on top again.

Danny does not take himself, or the ups and downs of the job, too seriously, though. "You know, it's hard to have a crowning achievement when what you do for a

Danny now with his wife Gretchen.

Photos courtesy of Danny Bonaduce

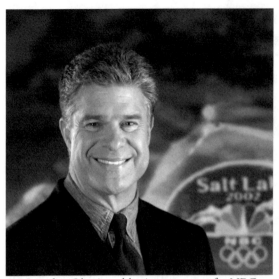

Jim Lampley, Olymic and boxing announcer for NBC and HBO.

living is, almost by definition, trivial. I just kid around for a living."

Danny does take great pride, however, in what he has been able to give back. "I get a lot of letters from people who got sober because they saw me get sober. I like that. That makes me very proud."

KEY ADVICE TO MAKE IT THROUGH

People who have survived major triumphs and disappointments in their careers can offer very important advice on how to build a successful career. Jim Lampley says, "Part of your job is to properly attribute and thank all the people who make it possible for you to be the lucky one. Step one in that is don't inconvenience them. Don't show up five minutes late, or ten minutes late, when they are there on time. Don't make them feel that you care less about them than you do about yourself. They aren't worth naming, but I could name for you a half dozen people who became, at some point, major broadcasting figures, who ultimately tumbled into obscurity precisely because of that piece of negligence. If you screw the anonymous people consistently enough over a long period of time, they'll find a way to cut you off. And they should. They deserve that you care for them and about them.

Photos courtesy of Jim Lampley

Jim's career started by winning a talent contest.

"That's step one. Step two would be don't take yourself too seriously. You're not the only one. When your feelings get hurt, when somebody betrays you, when the subjective opinions of your masters don't go your way, you're not the first person to whom that's happened. Your job is to dust yourself off and move on. But it's tough to remember."

SOME OF MY MORE CHALLENGING MOMENTS

Those "subjective opinions of your masters," as Jim calls them, are hard to swallow sometimes. I have had some general managers and program directors do things that have stunned me several times.

I was the top disc jockey at a Top 40 radio station doing the morning show when we had a new general manager take over. He called individual meetings with everyone on his first day. I felt pretty good about my position at the station, knowing that I was the station's top personality. When he called me into his office, he told me that I had a choice: I could either stay on as a part-timer working on the weekends or be fired. It caught me so off guard that I sat stunned for a few seconds, and then (at the ripe old age of twenty) told him that he could stick it up his ass! I walked right out of his office, out the front door of the radio station, and went home unemployed.

Before I even got home there was a message on my answering machine from Bruce, the new G.M. He had apparently talked to the program director after I had left and found out that he had gotten people mixed up and fired the wrong person. In his message he asked me to come back to the station so that we could work it out. I decided that I did not need to work with someone so completely out of touch, and I moved to another station across town, into my first full-time sports job. It all worked out for the best.

Strange decisions are made even at the best stations, in the biggest markets. I was working at a station in a top five market a few years ago, and our sports director left. After a job interview, our program director told me that I was the most qualified for the job and that my promotion to sports director would be made official the next week.

When the next week came, I was informed, to my shock, that the job was not mine, but was instead being offered to a young producer who had absolutely no experience for the position. In fact, she had never even been on the air before! I was outraged, not to mention a little embarrassed. I was now working for someone who was half my age and who had no experience in the business!

I found out later the move was made because another executive at the station had solicited sexual favors from this young producer, and offering her the job was the station's way of keeping her quiet. Needless to say, it was a disaster. This young woman was thrown into an impossible situation. She was trying to lead people who had been in the business longer than she had been alive. During this period, there were some hard times, hard feelings, and a lot of jokes made at the station's expense. Eventually the situation was rectified when a new program director was hired.

Decisions like this happen all too often. When they affect you, you will need to decide to either make the situation work or to move to a different station.

In another instance, also at a station in a top five market, a new program director was brought in to our station from another in the company chain. He had been thrown out of his last position for being too belligerent. He proceeded to rule through fear and intimidation, just as he had done in his previous position. He berated everyone who crossed his path. Soon staff morale was at an all-time low, and nobody could do anything about him because he had friends in very high places in the corporation. This was one of the hardest times of my career because this man constantly made me feel worthless. The only way I got through was by faith. I had to choose to believe that I was doing a good job, despite the constant verbal whippings. I made a pact with myself that I would always do the best job possible, and I would always try to maintain my integrity despite this man's awful behavior. As anyone who has ever been in an abusive situation like this would know this is easier said than done. There were times I was ready to quit and other times I wanted to fight. Happily, he was forced to move to yet another station after a while.

Disagreements with station management happen all too often, even with those who are considered superstars in the business. In his book *Private Parts*, Howard Stern shares how he and cohort Robin Quivers were treated by a program director they worked for in New York, a guy he nicknamed Pig Virus. He writes, "Pig Virus had issued his edict. I was fucked. My show was like nothing anyone was doing and they were trying to make me sound like everyone else.

"Besides all this, Robin told me that Pig Virus tried to undermine our relationship. He called Robin into his office and, out of nowhere, he told her that he didn't have any money to give her because 'Howard has taken it all.' Luckily, Robin is an intelligent woman who didn't fall for that."[2]

PATIENCE AND FAITH INSTEAD OF CRYING
AND WHINING

You will face challenges with bosses and colleagues during your career. Do not give into the passions of the moment and make a bad decision. Just because someone else is an ass does not mean that you have to make an ass of yourself. Rise above them, and have faith things will work out.

The most important single factor that has gotten me through these tough times is faith. If you know that you are doing what you are supposed to be doing in life, then things will work out. I have found that many other of the stars featured in this book share this sentiment.

Charlie Tuna: "It just seems like a destiny. I think I'm doing what I'm supposed to be doing. I have that feeling about my life, I always have."

Danny Bonaduce: "Yes, this is absolutely what I was meant to do."

E.D. Hill: "I think that things are destined for us. I think God watches over everybody. I also fully believe that the setbacks that we have in life are the greatest things sometimes that ever happen to us."

When challenges come your way, you have to gain some perspective and remember what Jim Lampley advised: you are not the first person who has faced conflict, adversity, or betrayal. Dust yourself off and move on with your life. The only other option is to whine and cry (which I have been known to do from time to time). As satisfying as it feels sometimes, this tactic does not help your situation much.

End Notes

[1] Okawa, Ryuho. *An Unshakeable Mind*. New York: Lantern Books, 2003.

[2] Stern, Howard. *Private Parts*. New York: Simon & Schuster, 1997.

Trouble Shooting

It is impossible to foresee all the pitfalls in any line of work, including broadcasting. There are situations that arise on a regular basis, however, that you can prepare for.

BE CAREFUL WHAT YOU SAY AROUND THE MICROPHONE

This is rule number one when you first start working on the air. Whenever you are around a microphone, whether in the studio, production room, or out at a remote location, you must act as if the microphone is live and you are on the air. All it takes to turn any microphone on is the flick of a switch or the push of a button. You can accidentally turn on a microphone yourself without even knowing it, or someone else could turn it on by accident or for a joke. That person does not even have to be in the same room, but if that mic is turned on, you are responsible for what you say on the air. Your job and your career may be in jeopardy if the wrong thing goes out over the air.

In the early part of my career, back in Wyoming, one of the disc jockeys at the radio station was goofing around while recording some commercials in the production room. When the mic was on, and the tape was rolling, he joked about the program director's wife having a little extra room on her backside. Not only did he say this with the microphone hot *and* in record mode, but he failed to erase what he had said when he was done.

The program director went into the production room to do some work a little later. He happened to turn the tape on to make sure that he was not recording over something important and heard the comments. The disc jockey was fired that very day.

Another similar situation happened at a Dallas station. A sports reporter was covering an event with a mobile broadcast unit and was not aware of the fact that when the unit itself came in contact with a piece of metal, it would automatically turn itself on. When he went to the restroom he took the unit in the stall with him. The unit touched the metal sidewall and turned itself on. The reporter then proceeded to serenade himself while using the facilities at the same time he was broadcasting back to the station. Fortunately for him, he was not live on the air, but everybody back at the station was monitoring what he was saying and doing. He never lived it down.

Whenever you are around a microphone, whether you think it is on or not, do not say anything that could come back to haunt you.

BE PREPARED AHEAD OF TIME

When you work on the air, you have to remember that you are doing more than representing the station you work for; you are also representing yourself. If you make a mistake, or if you miss something, it reflects poorly on you. Always prepare for your shift, so that when things pop up that catch you off guard, you can handle the situation with confidence.

If you are a disc jockey and your company hasn't yet installed a computerized system to play music and commercials, pull your music and your commercials before you go on the air. Do not live on the edge by pulling your next song ten seconds before it's supposed to start. This is just asking for trouble. Pulling music means organizing the songs that you are going to play. Years ago, that meant stacking up records (hence the term disc jockey). Records were followed by "carts" (they looked like eight track tapes), then came CDs. Now most stations are computerized. Depending on the station format and how rigid they are about their playlist (a list of songs the station is playing at any given time), songs are usually logged to play in a certain order at certain times of the hour to keep people listening longer. In the old days, vinyl records—albums and singles—were kept in filing cabinets and on shelves. Carts were kept in cart racks hung on the wall, and CDs were filed in similar racks.

If you are a news anchor or sports anchor, be prepared for the next newscast because you never know what is going to happen in between broadcasts. In my job as a sportscaster, I have several things happening at once. I write sportscasts, edit sound, take off a feed of sound bites, interview people on the phone, and many other small tasks, all basically at the same time. If something should go wrong or take longer than expected, then my schedule will be off and, if I am not prepared ahead of time, my upcoming broadcast will suffer.

Do not be caught unprepared. You have to be ready for interruptions of all kinds.

REMOTE BROADCASTS

At some point you will have to do broadcasts away from the station either because a client has paid money for the broadcast or because the station is doing a promotion. These broadcasts are called "remotes." Some stations do these almost every day, others just every now and then, but all stations do remotes. When you are scheduled to do a remote, there are several things you can do to make things easier on yourself.

Make sure you have the right address, phone number, and the contact person of where you are going. I know this sounds too obvious, but it happens all the time: someone forgets to bring the information and shows up late to the site. Give yourself extra time to get there if you do not know where you are going. If you get lost, or cannot find the place, you will be able to call the contact person for help if you remembered to bring the contact information.

Another sure way of getting yourself in trouble is showing up late. Tardiness is never good, but it is especially terrible in a remote broadcast situation where you are representing the station and people are relying on you to be there. If you get to the remote site early, this will give you extra time to prepare, get to know the people you will be working with, get more information on what you are doing, and get comfortable with the surroundings.

Go to every remote-site broadcast with the understanding that there will be a glitch or two. That should prepare you to handle adverse situations when they pop up.

BREAKING NEWS REPORTS

Breaking news reports are a staple in both radio and television, and at some point you are going to be required to do a live report from someplace other than the radio or television station. These reports are different from remotes. In remotes, a station event has been planned and you know about it in advance. In on-site reports, breaking news needs to be covered and a reporter is sent out with the mobile unit, or his own car, to cover it. This is a situation that allows talented people to shine. It is an unplanned event happening right then and there, and the on-air person has a chance to be great.

Depending on how much time the reporter has, he can either write a script on scene before going on the air or write bullet points to remind him of what he needs to talk about when he is on the air. If you are good at ad-lib, bullet points should be enough. If you are not comfortable ad-libbing, it is better to write a script for yourself.

A helpful hint: if you are not comfortable with ad-libbing on the air, you need to develop that skill. Being great on the air means you can speak on your feet, describe events, and communicate to the listener what is happening as it happens.

SETTING UP AND RECORDING INTERVIEWS

Depending on your job, you may be required to set up and conduct interviews with newsmakers and celebrities. Always treat the people you are interviewing with respect. If you do not, you may never have them, or anyone they know, on the air again.

If you set up the interview through an assistant, treat the assistant with as much respect as you would the guest. This is easy to do if it is a fun, entertaining type of an interview. It is a little more complicated if the interview is contentious, or if you have to ask serious and hard questions. If this is the case, you can still do your job with professionalism and respect.

Save your contact numbers for future use. You may want to have that guest on the air again in the future.

MAKING MISTAKES ON THE AIR

It does not matter how talented you are, you are going to make mistakes on the air. The question is, how big is the mistake, and how do you handle it.

Different stations and shows have different ideas about how to handle mistakes. If you are working at a place that likes to have fun and that encourages the personalities to rib each other and have a good time, then mistakes can be treated as an interesting and flavorful part of the show. Fun-loving stations will even encourage their people to record these mistakes and play them back later because listeners feel like they get to know the personalities better this way— and it is entertaining.

More serious stations or shows might not handle mistakes in the same way. For example, a news show dealing with serious subjects and important people will not want to have too much fun with a mistake. Usually the best way to handle mistakes at times like this is to correct yourself, if needed, and move on as if nothing happened. If you do not make a big deal out of it, odds are nobody else will either.

In my career, I have made too many mistakes on the air to count, but there are a couple in particular that stick out. When I was sixteen and working in Wyoming, I was doing a "live read" of a public service announcement for the Peace Corps. The Peace Corps fights hunger, disease, and poverty and is pronounced "Peace Core." Well, when I said the "Peace Corps," the "p" was not silent. A caller phoned into my show laughing to tell me I had renamed them the "peaceful dead." I was too embarrassed to mention it again to anybody.

Mistakes are a part of life and a part of the job. They happen to everyone.

LAUGHING

There are going to be times when something makes you laugh on the air. I do not mean a chuckle—I mean the kind of laugh where you get a case of the giggles and just cannot stop. This is one of the hardest things to handle as an air personality because you lose all control of yourself.

The best way of dealing with uncontrollable laughter on the air depends, once again, on what kind of station you are working for. If the management there likes you to have a good time, then it may not be a big deal. You will laugh, your fellow on-air team will have some entertaining fun at your expense, and you will move on.

If, however, you are working for a serious station that frowns on this sort of behavior, or if the laughter comes at an inappropriate time, you need to deal with it quickly. The best thing to do when the giggles are coming on is to wrap up what you are doing and get off the air. Go to a commercial or a song and get control of yourself.

Something to remember is that this happens to everybody. A friend of mine was working at an all-news station in Dallas many years ago, and he was doing a very sad story about a deceased baby found in a dumpster. He read the story very seriously, but then hit the wrong sound bite. The next thing on the air was a hot dog vender screaming, "Hottttt Dogggggg." My friend started giggling, but, of course, giggling during a story like this is inappropriate. He did the right thing and immediately went to a commercial so that no more damage was done. The moment was saved on a bloopers reel, however, and it is still played at the station every now and then.

PLAY-BY-PLAY

One of the most fun and most pure forms of being on the air is calling play-by-play of a sporting event. It is pure because you are describing what is happening right in front of you and what happens is just as new to you as it is to the listener. You are painting a picture for the listener on radio. On television, you are describing what people are seeing.

As I mentioned in the section on remote broadcasts, give yourself time to find where you need to be go beforehand. For road games, this usually means going to a town or city that you are not familiar with and it is easy to get lost.

At networks and bigger stations, you have assistants who drive you or meet you at the airport. There are engineers who are responsible for transporting and setting up the equipment. However, the play-by-play personality still has to do his or her homework, knowing the players, memorizing the numbers, and knowing what the teams, the coaches, and the players like to do.

It's even more work for the small station play-by-play voice. At smaller stations usually the play-by-play person is responsible for driving himself to the event. He is responsible for getting all the equipment there, setting it up, and making sure that it is broadcasting back to the station clearly. If some piece of equipment is missing or not working, it is his responsibility to find a place to buy the replacement part quickly. This all has to be done before going on the air and calling the game.

There are several things to remember about road trips, whether they are for play-by-play or any remote broadcast. Check the weather forecast for where you are going and bring the appropriate clothes. As an example of what not to do, I will tell you the story of when I was covering the Texas Rangers/New York Yankees playoff series in October 1999. The first two games of the series were scheduled for New York. When I left Dallas the temperatures were in the upper nineties. When I got to New York, fall had set in and it was getting down into the thirties at night. I had not thought ahead, and I neglected to bring a coat. The only coat I had was my sports jacket, and I froze. When I returned home I caught one of the worst colds of my life and missed three days of work. Check the weather forecast and pack accordingly.

OUT OF BREATH

Running out of breath is one of the worst things you can experience on the air. This usually happens because a broadcaster has to run into the studio from doing something else and finds himself out of breath. If he has to go on the air immediately, he is breathing heavily and trying to talk at the same time. This is nearly impossible to do. If he does not catch his breath right away, it can get worse and spiral out of control if he starts to panic.

Do not panic. The best thing to do is to go to a commercial or song as quickly and as painlessly as possible. If you are working with a team, have your co-anchors talk for a few moments while you turn off your mic and take a few deep breaths until you can talk normally again. If it is not possible to do this, then you have to be honest with the viewers or listeners. Tell them that you will be right back, turn your mic off, and quickly get your wind back.

The best way to avoid this situation is to never be caught off-guard. Do not run into the control room to go on the air at the last second. Be prepared and give yourself time. That being said, there will be situations, through no fault of your own, when breaking news happens or a mistake has been made, causing you to run into the studio and go on the air out of breath. Remember that it has happened to everyone and get through it calmly.

SNEEZING

Having to sneeze while on the air is another one of those situations you will have to deal with sooner or later. The best way to handle an oncoming sneeze when you know you have to go on the air is to force the sneeze to come sooner. Have some tissues handy. Rub your nose, tickle your nose, or whatever you have to do to get the sneeze out before you turn the microphone on.

Sometimes the sneeze just will not come before you have to go on the air. The best thing to do in radio is to turn the microphone off and sneeze. Then come back as quickly as possible and, if necessary, explain your absence. For example, you can say, "Please excuse me for that, I had to sneeze."

In television, you need to explain your situation to the director before you go on camera. Tell him he may have to cut away quickly because you may have to sneeze. This entire problem is much easier to handle if you are a part of a team where one of the other members of the show can take over while you sneeze in the background.

If you do not have time to turn the mic or camera off before sneezing, turn away so that the listener or viewer is somewhat shielded from the sound or picture.

HICCUPS

"Surprisingly enough—given how common hiccups are—no one really knows what causes them. But we're all hiccup prone, even fetuses in the womb. Something prompts your diaphragm to contract, suddenly and involuntarily producing a spasm that gets released as sometimes an embarrassing 'hic' noise. Irritating food can cause those contractions. So can swallowing air—when you get excited for instance, or chug down carbonated soda."[1]

Having the hiccups and being on the air do not go well together. If you have a history of getting the hiccups, avoid doing things that may set them off several hours before you go on the air. If you get a case of the hiccups while you are on the air, you need to do what you can to cut down the amount of mic or camera time you have. There is no way to make hiccups look good on the air. They can be a funny and interesting topic, but hiccups lose their charm quickly.

Several years ago, I listened as a national sports anchor went on the air with a terrible case of the hiccups. I thought it was funny during the first sportscast I heard that day, but six hours later I decided that the national radio network that still had him on the air was the least professional organization I had ever encountered. The station didn't do anything to get a replacement or allow the man to get off the air.

If you get the hiccups and you know they will be around for a while, call your program director or news director, explain what is happening and leave the decision to him. He can bring in a replacement for you, or he can leave you on the air. Either way, it is his decision.

HOW TO SLEEP WHEN WORKING EARLY OR LATE DAY PARTS

Our job on the air is to serve those who listen or watch us at all times of the day and night. I work the morning shift, which means I start recording my first sportscasts at 4 AM. In order to be at work on time and prepared, I am up at 2:45 every weekday morning.

The morning shift is difficult, and the graveyard shift, 12 midnight to 5 AM, is tough, too. Sometimes it seems like you are asleep when the rest of the world is awake, and vice versa.

What are the best ways to set up your sleep schedule when you are working these shifts? A lot of that answer depends on you. Determine when it is easiest for you to sleep and how you can live a full life despite the odd work schedule.

I have found that it is best if I can stay up all day, go to bed around 8 PM and get up at 2:45 AM. It is easier for me to fall asleep at night that way. I love taking naps during the day, but when I nap, I find it hard to get to sleep at night.

How much sleep you need? Dr. Sudhansu Chokroverty, Professor of Neurology at New York Medical College, addresses this subject in her book, *100 Questions and Answers About Sleep and Sleep Disorders*: "Human sleep requirements vary depending on a person's age. The average requirement for a normal adult man or woman is approximately eight hours. Sleep requirements, just like many behavioral functions and requirements assume a bell-shaped curve, however. Thus some people require less than the average amount of sleep and some require more sleep to function adequately during waking hours. Some individuals can get by with six to seven hours of sleep (or less); others require nine to ten hours of sleep at night. The basic sleep requirement is defined by heredity, rather than by any environmental influence." [2]

There does seem to be a constant when it comes to sleeping after an air shift. Generally people have a hard time going to bed right after they get off the air because they are still too keyed up. Sometimes you have to give yourself at least an hour or two to relax before going to bed.

Sleeping schedules for the mid-day, afternoon, and evening shifts are generally easier. You can stay up fairly late, and sleep in until a reasonable hour.

Working the early morning or late-night shifts can cause you to miss a lot of things that those on the nine-to-five shift experience. However, I have found that recording my favorite television shows that come on after I go to bed helps me feel like I am not missing out on what the rest of the world is experiencing.

SPEECH IMPEDIMENTS

We read in chapter 9 how Babe Laufenberg overcame a lisp to become one of the more accomplished athletes-turned-broadcasters in the nation. If you have a speech impediment, it will make your journey to be on the air more difficult, but not necessarily impossible.

Lisps and stutters are the most commonly known speech impediments. "A lisp results from improper placement of the tongue for /s/ and /z/. A frontal lisp produces a 'th' sound for /s/ and /z/. Instead of 'Suzy sat in the swing,' a frontal lisper would say, 'Thuzy that in the thwing.' Pulling the tongue back will usually alleviate the problem of a frontal lisp. A bilateral lisp is a harder problem to describe and correct." [3]

"Stuttering is a communication disorder in which the flow of speech is broken by repetitions (li-li-like this), prolongations (lllllike this), or abnormal stoppages (no sound) of sounds and syllables. There may also be unusual facial and body movements associated with the effort to speak." [4]

Speech impediments are more common than most people think, according to the Stuttering Foundation. Three million Americans, or one percent of the US population, stutter, and "Out of a class of eight to ten people, it's not surprising to find at least two or three with a 'labial lisp.'" [5]

Experts say there are a variety of treatments for speech impediments, in both children and adults. In order to find the right treatment, experts advise seeing a qualified clinician. In fact, some forms of stuttering go away when the person takes the stage or steps in front of a microphone. "Remember that many people who stutter, such as James Earl Jones, John Stossel, and Bruce Willis, are often fluent when they speak before an audience. But all three have overcome significant stuttering problems."[6] Country singer Mel Tillis is another famous person who stutters but sings fluently when on stage.

BE CLASSY COMPETITION

It does not matter where you go, how good you get, or how big of a market you ascend to; there will always be competition, both for your station and your job. Competition is an essential aspect of this business, and it forces everyone in the business to constantly improve. We push each other to be great. One of the keys to having a long and successful career is to take on the challenge of competition and be as good as you can be. It is also important to always carry yourself with class and style.

Instead of making an enemy of your competition, make friends. You can strive to win, give everything you have got, and still be friendly to the competition. You always want to have friends in the industry.

BE CONSIDERATE OF OTHERS

The radio and television industry is notorious for its confined working spaces. On-air studios are fairly small rooms, as are production rooms, news booths, control rooms, producer's booths, and editing stations. Not only are these spaces small and cramped, but several people generally share these rooms. Be considerate about how you use and leave these common work areas. If people cannot stand to work around you in close quarters, you will have difficulty moving up the ladder.

BE READY FOR DISASTER

Being on the air comes with responsibilities. You are there to provide a service. Most of the time that means just having a good time and being entertaining, but there are times when the job entails more. All parts of the country face disaster situations sooner or later, and it will be your job to keep your viewer informed and safe in a calm manner. When something important is going on, recognize its importance and step up to the challenge. Inform the public of what is going on, and do it in a way that does not cause more harm. For example, if there is a tornado approaching your town and you panic on the air, it will only cause your listeners to panic, too. But if you remain calm, relaying the important information with an air of confidence, you can help them avoid panic and increase their chances of survival.

You can either accept the advice given in this chapter, or you can learn the hard way through trial and error. It is always easier to learn from somebody else's mistakes than from your own. In the next chapter, we will deal with a couple of other major problems that arise when working on the air: the common cold and allergies.

End Notes

[1] "1,801 Home Remedies by the editor's of *Reader's Digest*," 2004.

[2] Chokroverty, Sudhansu. *100 Questions and Answers about Sleep and Sleep Disorders.* New York: Blackwell Publishing, 2001.

[3] Utterback, Ann S. *Broadcast Voice Handbook.* Bonus Books, Inc., 2000.

[4] *www.stutteringhelp.org*

[5] Jacks, G. Robert. *Getting the Word Across.* Wm. B. Eerdmans Publishing, 1996.

[6] Barry Guitar, Ph.D. professor of communication sciences at the University of Vermont, quoted in article by The Stuttering Foundation.

Dealing with Allergies and the Common Cold

Coming down with a cold and dealing with allergies are two very serious problems when your job requires you to use your voice. Both affect your voice and the way you sound. In this chapter, we will take a look at how to work around allergies and colds, and we will get expert advice from the "Doctor of the Stars," also known as Dr. Wayne Kirkham.

WHAT IS AN ALLERGY?

"An allergy is an adverse reaction involving the immune system which follows contact with a substance that is normally harmless. In many types of allergies the symptoms occur very rapidly and usually involve the part of the body that has been in contact with the 'harmless' substance. Most allergic reactions occur in the mouth, nose, lungs, digestive tract, or skin. So in hay fever, for example, contact with grass pollen causes a discharge from the nose and eyes, frequent sneezing and an itchy feeling in the eyes, nose, roof of the mouth and even the ears.

"The symptoms occur when the immune system, for reasons we do not understand, overreacts to a substance from which it believes the body needs protection."[1]

Allergies are a terrible affliction for anyone but especially difficult for someone who works in broadcasting. They make you sneeze, and we have already discussed how difficult sneezes can be. Allergies can dramatically affect your voice and, since your voice is a key instrument in your work, your work can suffer. Allergies can also make us look bad—a red nose and watery eyes certainly do not help our appearance on camera.

The best way to deal with allergies is to take some form of allergy medication. Depending on the severity of your allergies, this medication can be over-the-counter or prescription.

My allergies seem to be getting worse as I get older. They used to affect me once or twice a year, but a few years ago they got so bad that I started sounding sick for several days at a time. The allergies would go away and then come back again a few weeks later. Sometimes it would make my voice a little hoarse or less sharp than usual. Other times it made me sound deathly ill. It got bad enough that I had to do something about it. I consulted a specialist and he prescribed an allergy nose spray. I have not had major a problem with allergies since.

If you are working on the air, you cannot afford to have something like allergies affect your job performance. If allergies create a problem, do something about it. If you do nothing, you may be looking for a job soon.

THE COMMON COLD

"The common cold has had a remarkably long and successful career, meeting for the most part with a resigned acceptance and little opposition to its progress. Unpleasant but seemingly inevitable, most people have learnt to live with its troublesome symptoms and wait patiently for its passing."[2]

Allergies can be preempted by medicine, but they still have not found the cause or the cure for the common cold. Everyone who works on the air is going to have to deal with a cold sooner or later. Sixty-two million Americans come down with a cold every year, costing the US economy around forty billion dollars.

It happened to Dallas Cowboy Radio analyst Babe Laufenberg in the middle of a game. "I remember I lost my voice and we were getting all sorts of calls into the press box and people calling the station, the radio station. They heard my voice, you know, you could hear my voice going. Finally I just had to drop out basically. So I was getting all of these home remedies, somebody said, 'Sip beer,' so I go into the press box and I'm sipping beer. It did nothing for my voice but it gave me a little buzz. I think it just makes you feel better. I said, 'I feel pretty good but I just can't talk.'"

THINGS TO HELP A COLD

There are some things you can do to help yourself through a cold. First of all, if you are anything like me, you feel guilty whenever you have to call in sick. I would rather just go in and work than call in sick. While that may be the way we feel, it is not very smart for several reasons. If you have a cold you are probably not going to sound very good anyway, so the station might prefer to go on without you. If you do go to work, you will be spreading your germs through the microphones that are used by several people. Going to work will also increase your recovery time. Usually it is better for everyone if you just stay home.

I have found a couple of tricks over the years that help me get through a cold. Number one: make sure you have several tissues with you at all times. There have been times when I have been on the air and had to stuff the tissues up my nostrils while I continued to do the talk show. This would allow me to talk and keep my hands free to punch phone calls, work the computer, and shuffle through my papers. I know it's not sexy, but it works, and it's better than nothing.

I also find cough drops to be amazingly helpful. They keep my throat wet, they partially clear up my nose, and they help soothe the pain of a sore throat. I always try to keep a bag of these on hand just in case. Hot tea or hot water helps the voice stay fairly wet and clear as well. For me, ibuprofen for fever or body aches is always good, too.

If your cold brings a cough with it, obviously you do not want to be coughing on the air. If you have to cough, try to do it before you go on the air, and hold it back until you are done (easier said than done, I know). Cough drops are good for this, too. If you have to cough while you are on the air, turn your microphone off. Many mic's have a cough button that mutes your mic while you cough (or sneeze).

PHLEGM

You do not have to have a cold or allergies to have phlegm build up in your throat. Of course, you do not want phlegm when you are talking on the air. It can get in the way, make you sound hoarse, make you cough, or cause you to lose your voice in the middle of a sentence. You can deal with phlegm in a lot of the same ways you deal with a cold: hot tea or hot water with honey and lemon if possible and cough drops. I have found that I have phlegm problems the most either when I am tired or when I am just getting over a cold or allergy attack.

Whenever you clear your throat to get rid of the phlegm, do it gently. If you do it too vigorously, you can damage your throat and your vocal cords. This is not a great career decision. When you clear your throat, for whatever reason, do it as gently as possible.

TIPS TO AVOID GETTING SICK FROM "THE DOCTOR OF THE STARS"

Now that we have taken a look at how best to work around allergies and the common cold, we will discuss several things you can do to avoid getting sick in the first place. To help guide us through these things, I turned to

Dr. Wayne Kirkham, "Doctor of the Stars."

Dr. Wayne R. Kirkham MD, a physician based in Dallas.

Dr. Kirkham is an otolaryngologist, which is the big, long word for an ear, nose, and throat doctor, and an ear, nose, throat, head, and neck surgeon. He is known as "The Doctor of the Stars" because his patients include celebrities such as Celine Dion, Sting, Prince, Mick Jagger, Bono, Ozzy Osborn, Stevie Nicks, LeAnn Rimes, and opera stars such as Cecilia Bartoli and Fredericka Van Staade. He also works with many professionals in radio and television.

One of the best ways to avoid major voice problems is very simple, according to Dr. Kirkham. "There are a few basics in voice care that are there whether you are in radio, TV, a recording artist, or teacher. You want to drink plenty of fluids. Your voice is not going to do well with a dry respiratory tract."

Dr. Kirkham warns us not to drink or eat too late at night because of another ailment that can cause your voice harm. "The drinking should be done during the daytime, when you are up and around, not in the middle of the night. If you drink a lot of fluids late at night it increases the chances of reflux of acid up from your stomach and that can interfere with the voice. Don't eat or drink stuff late at night."

DOS AND DON'TS IN COLD COPING

In dealing with allergies and colds, there are some key dos and don'ts that we need to remember, especially regarding the kinds of medication we take to get through it. Doctor Kirkham warns anyone who uses their voice as an instrument against taking antihistamines (read the label on your medication). He says, "Antihistamines get thrown around like water and they are not without side effects. If a person is going to be a voice user they need to stay away from all antihistamines. Oral antihistamines get more voices in trouble than you can imagine." The problem with these antihistamines, according to Dr. Kirkham, is that they dry out your system too much, causing your voice even more damage.

There is an alternative to using antihistamines to deal with allergies and colds. Dr. Kirkham tells us, "Number one, you need to see a doctor that can put you on medicines that we would spray in the nose. Those are going to be prescription if indeed it's a real allergy. If somebody tries to be their own doctor, generally they don't do so well."

The doctor's alternative to antihistamines is decongestants. "Decongestants [like Sudafed] are fine with allergies, with colds and with flu. They are fine with a real sinus infection, a bacterial infection. Antihistamines should be avoided basically with everything."

There are a lot of similarities between allergies and the common cold, and sometimes it is hard for us to tell what we have. According to Dr. Kirkham, there are ways to tell them apart so that you will know how best to treat them. "Allergies aren't going to give you a fever. They will make you stuffy, congested, itch, and sneeze. Colds are going to make you feel sick, not necessarily totally wiped out like the flu. With a cold you will have congestion and you will tend to run a fever."

Another big difference between having a cold and suffering through allergies is that doctors can treat allergies, but there is no treatment for the common cold. While allergies can be treated, they cannot be cured. If you suffer from allergies, you will have to stay on top of treatments for them throughout your entire career on the air. For allergies, doctors can prescribe medications that will allow you to breathe through your nose and that will not dry out your throat. As for the common cold, according to Dr. Kirkham, "If you get it, you get it."

OLD WIVES' TALES

There are some false ideas that have become prevalent in the industry the last few years relating to cold and allergy prevention. A couple of these false ideas include taking high doses of vitamin C or using specific herbal medicines. Dr. Kirkham says, "It has been clearly shown, with good research published in reputable journals, that that does not change a thing. There is no benefit by taking high doses of vitamin C in treating a cold or preventing a cold."

One of the studies Dr. Kirkham refers to was published June 28, 2005. "Vitamin C May Not Fight the Common Cold—Finding Based on Review of Studies Done Since 1940. Vitamin C's reputation for fighting the common cold may not be justified, say researchers. They say they checked the best studies done on the topic in the last sixty-five years. Their findings appear in *Public Library of Science Medicine*. Researchers working on the review included Robert Douglas, MD, of the Australian National University. They found hints of possible benefits in some conditions. Those areas should be studied further, say Douglas and colleagues. But overall, they say they didn't find proof that vitamin C thwarts colds."[3]

THE DOCTOR'S ADVICE

While we have learned in this chapter that we can deal with allergies, it is inevitable that we will come down with a common cold every now and then. So what is the best way to get through a cold? Dr. Kirkham advises, "You want to maintain hydration, you should take a decongestant, like Sudafed, stay away from antihistamines. You can use original twelve-hour Afrin nasal spray, using it twice a day for three or four days. If you use it like that you are not going to get hooked on it." Dr. Kirkham warns not to use the Afrin spray for longer than four days at a time because it can cause other problems in the long run.

There are things you can do to try and keep from catching a cold. Dr. Kirkham says, "Number one, wash your hands frequently. Not to the point of obsessive-compulsive behavior, but wash them frequently and do not touch the inside of your nose with your finger and do not touch your eye with your finger because that will self-contaminate you. There are viruses and bacteria everywhere and your hands are going to have them on it. If your eye itches don't take your finger and scratch it, you can rub your eye with the back of your hand."

There are also times of the year when it is easier to catch a cold, but you can take preventative measures. Dr. Kirkham says, "During the wintertime people tend to get colds more often. The heat comes on in your house or apartment. Heat dries out the air in the home no matter what the humidity is outside and that dry air dries out the nose. Dry nose and dry throat make it easier for you to get sick. So during the cold time of the year, when the heater is on, you will do better if you take steam showers rather than baths and run a humidifier or vaporizer in your room at night."

Dr. Kirkham has a lot of his star singers sleep with a humidifier on in their hotel room when they are on concert tours in cold weather. The doctor cannot stress enough how important it is to keep your throat moisturized to prevent getting sick and to keep your voice strong.

Another situation that puts us at higher risk to catch a cold is air travel. Dr. Kirkham tells us, "When you fly, the humidity drops like a stone. Studies have shown that humidity will drop to 5 percent in the airplane. Well, there's 20 percent humidity out in the Mojave Desert, 5 percent in that airplane. So that means it is just going to suck the moisture out of everybody in the plane. So if your flying somewhere to cover a story or an event and you're dried out and the guy next to you is coughing or spitting or snorting or who knows what, you've just invited an infection to come and take root.

"When you fly even short distances you should be moisturizing your nose with a saline spray. There are various brands you can use. If you can keep your nose from getting too dry, your nose is going to humidify the air that you are breathing. If your nose gets super dry then it can't humidify the air as it gets down into your throat." The doctor recommends keeping your moisturizing saline spray close by and spraying your nose every fifteen to twenty minutes. He also recommends not talking much on the plane as talking with a dry throat can cause damage to your voice.

A pro athlete who does not take care of his body is not going to perform as well as he could. He will not live up to his potential if he is always injured and will not be offered the multi-million dollar contract. The same rule applies to us in the broadcasting business. If you do not take care of your voice and you are constantly getting sick, you are not going to live up to your potential. Your career will not go as far as you want it to. So take Dr. Kirkham's advice and keep your voice strong.

End Notes

[1] Scott-Moncrieff, Christina. *Overcoming Allergies.* New York: Sterling Publishing Company, Inc., 2002.

[2] Tyrrell, David and Michael Fielder. *Cold Wars: The Fight Against the Common Cold.* New York: Oxford University Press Inc., 2002.

[3] Hitti, Miranda. "Vitamin C May Not Fight Colds." *WebMD Medical News.* June 28, 2005.

Final Advice

As you go off on your path to success, I want to leave you with some final advice. The first piece of advice, is this: always be open to *good* advice because every little bit helps. The more wise counsel you absorb, the easier the climb toward your goals, and the fewer painful mistakes you will make. You will inevitably make friends and find mentors along your path that will provide you with more wisdom.

BERMAN'S ADVICE

Chris Berman has seen many great on-air talents come through ESPN in his years there and has some words of encouragement for those who dream to achieve a career like his. "I am now one of the older ones here at ESPN. I never thought I would see that day. I'm inspired by the energy of the kids in their twenties who are following a dream and a passion. It almost sounds too good to be true, but I think if you are good, you're going to get there. I would give that advice to kids. It may not be in the timetable that you want, but I would go for it. If it doesn't work out it doesn't work out, but boy, you'll never know if you don't go for it."

MISTAKES ARE GOING TO HAPPEN

You can count on your path to success being littered with mistakes. Everyone makes countless mistakes, and unfortunately there is no getting around it. Bob Kingsley reminds us, "You've got to make all those mistakes and do all those stupid things. Whenever anybody asks me, particularly a young person, how to go about it, there's only one way to go about it, and that is just go do it." Chris Berman agrees, "Live TV or radio, we all screw up. It's on its way to Pluto, don't worry about it, it's gone."

SYLER SUGGESTIONS

In order to be successful in this business you are going to have to be tough, focused, and committed to success. Rene Syler tells us how you can best do that. "Don't take 'no' for an answer. Don't let anyone try to dissuade you from what you want to do. The other thing I would say is you better steel yourself for rejection. Steel yourself for the fact that time and time again you're going to be told no. You may have ninety-nine doors shut in your face but it's the one hundredth one that opens. That's all you've got to do [she chuckles] is take advantage of the one hundredth one that opens up and make the most of your opportunity!"

That one hundredth door is just as important as the first door, she insists. "It doesn't matter where in the order it is, just as long as one of them opens."

E.D. Hill offered a story on how persistence pays off. "When I was hired in Pittsburgh, I didn't tell the news director there that he had already turned me down three other times for jobs in other markets. It was only after I signed the contract that I walked into his office with all the other rejection letters he had sent me over the years! I said, 'I just want to let you know that I wasn't good enough for you in those smaller markets, but for some reason you hired me here.' To that end, I believe the setbacks that we have in life are the greatest things that ever happen to us sometimes."

We can always count on these three things in our careers: mistakes, difficulties, and opportunities. When those magical moments of opportunity come along, you have to take advantage of them. Rene Syler described how to best go about it. "Be yourself. Because when you're trying to be the 'anchor man,' people see through that and this is a communication business. You have to communicate on the most basic level, and I think part of that means you have to make yourself somewhat vulnerable and make people comfortable when they're watching you. If you are not comfortable with what you're doing on TV then they're not going to be comfortable watching you. How can you be comfortable if you're not being you, because you're trying to live this lie? That's why I think it's so critical to be yourself."

HAVE FUN

I mentioned earlier that you will get a lot of advice in your career; you have to sift through the bad to get to the good. Danny Bonaduce remembered some words of wisdom thrown his way several years ago: "When I first got into radio, I got a rather big lecture from the program director that hired me. It went on for hours, and I really just glazed over, but the last thing he said to me was, 'Remember this, if you're having fun, they're having fun [the listeners].' That's the only thing that stuck with me, and it's true. To do radio, to be honest, in my opinion, if you're interviewing a bunch of people and they're telling you how hard it is, it's just because they're trying to somehow justify their outlandish paychecks. It's easy."

Jonathan Liebman, president and CEO of the Specs Howard School of Broadcast Arts, has dished out huge amounts of advice to his students over the years. He has boiled all this advice down to some pretty impressive gems. "This industry is not going to love you; you have to love this industry. Just get in there and give it everything you've got. Do more than you have to. Show up early. Stay late. Find out how you can contribute to your company, your radio station or TV station. Just eat it up. Don't burn any bridges, do the best job that you can, make as many friends as you can and stay at it because cream rises to the top."

How you define success is up to you. Success for you may be working in a small town, or it may mean moving up the market ladder to a big city. Either way, remember that relocating is, many times, essential to getting started and to moving up. Jerry Anderson is the director of the American School of Broadcast in Spokane, Washington, and he says, "There are ten thousand radio stations out there, you know. There are places to go. We try to encourage them [the students] to start in a small market. Move out of town, go to a one or two station market because they pay livable wages to start. You will learn a lot and work your way up. What you put into this is what you're going to get out of it."

GILBERT'S GRAPES OF WISDOM

Another key to success, not just in the broadcast business but any business, is learning from those around you. That has been one of the keys to ESPN's Bruce Gilbert's successful climb. "There is no way I would be able to achieve what I have achieved if it hadn't been for all the people I have worked with. I mean that, everybody. Board operators, producers, talk show hosts, on-air talents, sales people, managers, co-workers, and assistants."

Bruce has some advice for people who want not only to be good on the air, but are interested in getting into management as well. "If you create the right kind of environment where everybody is free and open to be creative and honest about what they believe will help the station, it is amazing how much you can learn. The experience part of this, and my ability to move up in the business, comes totally from just being a sponge and absorbing little traits from people that are far more talented than I am. I respect the people who give their heart and soul to this business every day because that's how I've learned."

As for how an on-air leader or manager gets his people to buy into the all-for-one attitude, he says, "It's a team effort. That sounds corny, and everyone talks about team stuff and it's a cliché, but when you work for a place where it really is successful you'll find there is teamwork. You can't force it, you can't make it happen, you can't go into a damned environment and make teamwork happen, but where it does happen is where you'll find winning."

INTANGIBLES

There were times in my career, and in the careers of all of the other great personalities we have heard from in this book, when I did not know if I would ever get out of that small town and go where I wanted to go. So much in this business happens because you are in the right place at the right time. You can definitely help yourself to be in the right place at the right time by working hard and networking, but there are the intangibles as well.

The intangibles are the things that you can not explain, they are the happenings that come from nowhere, out of the blue, that you can only credit to fate or providence. If you are doing what you are supposed to be doing in life, things will work out.

It is also important that you believe in yourself. It certainly helps to have friends or family that believe in you too, but ultimately you have to believe in yourself. This will come with a little time. You do not have to believe from day one that you are the greatest air talent in the world, but believe that you can get to that point.

You will be asked to prove yourself on occasion. You will have to sound good on the air, keep your cool under pressure, and handle mistakes with class and dignity. That is all a part of being a professional. Have the belief in yourself that you can handle these challenges when they come around, and you will.

You have joined a wonderful profession full of great and talented people. Welcome to the club.

Appendix A:
Further Information on
University and Career Schools

Limitations on space make it impossible to give you all the information on good universities and career schools around the country with good broadcasting, journalism and Radio/TV/film departments. This appendix is a good place to start. All of these institutions were mentioned in chapter 5. They are listed in alphabetical order.

UNIVERSITIES

Bowling Green University, 110 McFall Center, Bowling Green, OH 43403, phone (866) CHOOSEBGSU. Closest major city is Toledo. Founded in 1910, state-supported, 1230-acre campus in small town. Coed, around 16,000 students, 93 percent full-time, 55 percent women, 45 percent men, fairly demanding entrance level with 90 percent of applicants admitted. See Web site at www.bgsu.edu

Brigham Young University, A-153 ASB, Provo, UT 84602, phone (801) 422-2507. Closest major city is Salt Lake City. Founded in 1875, independent university, affiliated with the Church of Jesus Christ of Latter-Day Saints, 557-acre campus in small town. Coed, just under 31,000 undergraduate students, 81 percent full-time, 51 percent men, 49 percent women, fairly demanding entrance level with 76 percent of applicants admitted. See Web site at www.byu.edu

Brown University, Providence, RI 02912, phone (401) 863-1000. Closest major city is Boston. Founded in 1764, independent, 140-acre campus in urban area. Coed, just over 6,000 undergraduate students, 95 percent full-time,

54 percent women, 46 percent men, extremely demanding entrance level with only 17 percent of applicants admitted. See Web site at www. brown.edu

Columbia University, 2960 Broadway, New York, NY 10027-6902, phone (212) 854-1754. Founded in 1754, independent school, thirty-five acre campus in the middle of New York City. Coed, just over 4,000 undergraduate students, 100 percent full-time, 50 percent men, 50 percent women. Extremely demanding entrance level with only 11 percent of applicants admitted. See Web site at www.columbia.edu

University of Florida, Gainesville, FL 32611, phone (352) 392-3261. Closest major city is Jacksonville. Founded in 1853, state-supported, 2,000-acre campus located outside populated areas. Coed, just under 34,000 undergraduate students, 92 percent full-time, 53 percent women, 47 percent men, demanding entrance level with 52 percent of applicants admitted. See Web site at www.ufl.edu

University of Georgia, Athens, GA 30602, phone (706) 542-3000. Closest major city is Atlanta. Founded in 1785, state-supported, 1289-acre campus in suburban area. Coed, just over 25,000 undergraduate students, 90 percent full-time, 57 percent women, 43 percent men, fairly demanding entrance level with 62 percent of applicants admitted. See Web site at www.uga.edu

University of Maryland, College Park, MD 20742, phone (301) 405-1000. Close to both Baltimore and Washington, D.C. Founded in 1856, state-supported, 3688-acre campus. Coed, over 25,000 undergraduate students, 91 percent full time, 51 percent men, 49 percent women, fairly demanding entrance level with 43 percent of applicants admitted. See Web site at www.umd.edu

University of Missouri, 230 Jesse Hall, University of Missouri-Columbia, Columbia, MO 65211, phone (573) 882-7786 or (800) 225-6075 (toll-free in Missouri, Illinois and Kansas). Founded in 1839, first public university west of the Mississippi River, 1360-acre campus located in smaller town. Coed, 22,000 undergraduate students, 94 percent full-time, 51 percent women, 49 percent men, fairly demanding entrance level with 89 percent of applicants admitted. See Web site at www.missouri.edu

University of Nebraska, Lincoln, NE 68588, phone (402) 472-7211. Located 50 miles south of Omaha. Founded in 1869, state-supported, 623 acre campus in urban area. Coed, just over 17,000 undergraduate students, 92 percent full-time, 53 percent men, 47 percent women, fairly demanding entrance level with 74 percent of applicants admitted. See Web site at www.unl.edu

University of North Texas, Chestnut Avenue, Denton, TX 76203-1277, phone (940) 565-2681 or (800) UNT-8211. Located 30 miles north of Dallas/Fort Worth. Founded in 1890, state-supported, 744-acre campus in suburban area, over 24,000 undergraduate students, 78 percent full-time, 55 percent women, 45 percent men, fairly demanding entrance level with 71 percent of applicants admitted. See Web site at http://unt.edu-degrees

Northwestern University, 1801 Hinman Avenue, Evanston, IL 60208, phone (847) 491-3741, Chicago number (312) 503-8649. Founded in 1851, independent university, 250-acre campus located just outside of Chicago. Coed, 8,031 undergraduate students, 98 percent full-time, 53 percent women, 47 percent men. Extremely demanding entrance level, only 30 percent of applicants admitted. See Web site at www.northwestern.edu

Ohio University, Athens, OH 45701, phone (740) 593-1000. Located in the southeast corner of Ohio. Founded in 1804, state-supported, 1700-acre campus in small town. Coed, around 17,000 undergraduate students, 94 percent full-time, 53 percent women, 47 percent men, fairly demanding entrance level with 86 percent of applicants admitted. See Web site at www.ohio.edu

Syracuse University, Syracuse, NY 13244, phone (315) 443-1870. Founded in 1870, independent university, urban 200-acre campus. Coed, just under 11,000 undergraduate students, 99 percent full-time, 56 percent women, 44 percent men, fairly demanding entrance level with 59 percent of applicants admitted. See Web site at www.syr.edu

University of Texas, 1 University Station, Austin, Texas 78712, phone (512) 475-7348. Founded in 1883, state-sponsored, urban 350-acre campus. Coed, just over 37,000 undergraduate students, 91 percent full-time, 52 percent women, 48 percent men, demanding entrance level with 51 percent of applicants admitted. See Web site at www.utexas.edu

Washington State University, PO Box 641067, Pullman, WA 99164-1067, phone (888) 468-6978. Located on the far eastern edge of Washington State, near Idaho. Founded in 1890, state-sponsored, rural 620-acre campus. Coed, just over 19,000 students, 86 percent full-time, 53 percent women, 47 percent men, fairly demanding entrance level with 75 percent of applicants accepted. See Web site at www.wsu.edu

CAREER SCHOOLS

American School of Broadcasting, four campuses:

Oklahoma City Campus, 4511 Southeast 29th Street, Oklahoma City, OK 73115, phone (405) 672-6511.
Tulsa Campus, 2843 East 51st Street, Tulsa, OK 74105, phone (918) 293-9100.
Arlington, TX, Campus, 712 North Watson Road, Arlington, TX 76011, phone (817) 695-2474.
Garland, TX, Campus, 1914 Pendleton Drive, Garland, TX 75041, phone (972) 682-5500. See Web site for all four campuses at www.radioschool.com

Brown College, 1440 Northland Drive, Mendota Heights, MN 55120, phone (651) 905-3400. Founded in 1946, 20-acre campus close to Minneapolis Saint Paul. Coed, 2250 undergraduate students. See Web site at www.browncollege.edu

Columbia College Hollywood, 18618 Oxnard Street, Tarzana, CA 91356, phone (800) 785-0585. Founded in 1952, one-acre campus close to Los Angeles. Coed, close to 200 undergraduate students, 100 percent full-time, 72 percent men, 28 percent women. See Web site at www.columbiacollege.edu

Ohio and Illinois Center for Broadcasting, four campuses:

Chicago Campus, 55 West 22nd Street, Suite 240, Lombard, IL 60148, phone (630) 916-1700.
Colorado Campus, 1310 Wadsworth Blvd. Suite 100, Lakewood, CO 80214, phone (303) 937-7070.
Cincinnati Campus, 6703 Madison Road, Cincinnati, OH 45227, phone (513) 271-6060.
Cleveland Campus, 9000 Sweet Valley Drive, Valley View, OH 44125, phone (216) 447-9117. See Web site for all four campuses at www.beonair.com

New England School of Communications, One College Circle, Bangor, ME 04401, phone (207) 941-7176. Founded in 1981, 200-acre campus in small town. Coed, under 300 undergraduate students, 99 percent full-time, 74 percent men, 26 percent women. See Web site at www.nescom.edu

Specs Howard School of Broadcast Arts, 19900 West Nine Mile Road, Southfield, MI 48075, phone (248) 358-9000. Founded in 1970, campus located in Detroit metropolitan area. Coed. See Web site at www.specshoward.edu

OTHER ACCSCT AND ACCET ACCREDITED CAREER SCHOOLS OFFERING BROADCASTING OR AUDIO/VIDEO CLASSES

Broadcasting Institute of Maryland, 7200 Harford Road, Baltimore, MD 21234-7765. Contact John C. Jeppi, Sr.

Ex'pression college for Digital Arts, 6601 Shellmound St., Emeryville, CA 94608. Contact Kirk Engel.

Full Sail Real World Education, 3300 University Boulevard, Winter Park, FL 32792-7429. Contact Edward E. Haddock, Jr.

Institute of Audio Research, 64 University Place, New York, NY 10003-4595. Contact Muriel Adler.

International College of Broadcasting, 6 South Smithville Road, Dayton, OH 45431-1833. Contact Michael LeMaster.

Liberty Training Institute, 2706 Wilshire Boulevard, 2nd Floor, Los Angeles, CA 90057. Contact Julio Betbeder.

Los Angeles Film School, 6363 Sunset Boulevard, Suite 400, Hollywood, CA 90028. Contact Diana Derycz-Kessler.

Madison Media Institute, 2702 Agriculture Drive, Madison, WI 53718. Contact Chris Hutchings.

National Conservatory of Dramatic Arts, 1556 Wisconsin Avenue NW, Washington, DC 20007-2758. Contact Dennis A. Dulmage.

Northwest College of Art, 16301 Creative Drive N.E., Poulsbo, WA 98370. Contact Craig Freeman.

Omega Studio's School of Applied Recording Arts and Sciences, 5609 Fishers Lane, Rockville, MD 20852. Contact Bob Yesbek.

Platt College, Several Campuses

Los Angeles area:
7755 Center Avenue, Huntington Beach, CA 92647. Contact Brian Lahorqoue. 1000 South Freemont Avenue, Los Angeles, CA 91803. Contact Manfred Rodriquez.

San Diego:
6250 El Cajon Boulevard, San Diego, CA 92115-3919. Contact Meg Leiker.

SAE Institute of Technology, Nashville, 7 Music Circle North, Nashville, TN 37203. Contact Keith Sensing.

SAE Institute of Technology, New York, Herald Center, 1293 Broadway, 9th Floor, New York, NY 10001. Contact Udo Hoppenworth.

The Art Institute of Las Vegas, 2350 Corporate Circle, Henderson, NV 89074. Contact Steven Brooks.

The Illinois Institute of Art, 1000 Plaza Drive, Suite 100, Schaumburg, IL 60173-4990. Contact David W. Ray.

The Illinois Institute of Art—Chicago, 350 N. Orleans Street, Suite 136, Chicago, IL 60654. Contact Charles Restivo.

The New School of Radio and Television, 50 Colvin Avenue, Albany, NY 12206-1106. Contact Thomas Brownlie, III.

Westwood College—Anaheim, 1551 S. Douglas Road, Anaheim, CA 92806. Contact John Hanson.

Academy of Radio and Television Broadcasting, 16052 Beach Boulevard, Suite 263-N, Huntington Beach, CA 92647. Web address: www.arbradio.com

Broadcast Center, 2360 Hampton Avenue, St. Louis, MO 63139. Web address: www.broadcastcenterinfo.com

ACCREDITING WEB SITES

ACCSC (Accrediting Commission of Career Schools and Colleges of Technology) at www.accsct.org

ACCET (Accrediting Council for Continuing Education & Training) at www.accet.org

A great resource for information when researching universities and career schools around the country is http://education.yahoo.com/college/facts.

Appendix B:
Examples of Teaching Tools
Used at Top University Programs

THE JOURNALIST'S CREED

I believe that the public journal is a public trust; that all connected with it are, to the full measure of their responsibility, trustees for the public; that acceptance of a lesser service than the public service is betrayal of this trust.

I believe that clear thinking and clear statement, accuracy, and fairness are fundamental to good journalism.

I believe that a journalist should write only what he holds in his heart to be true.

I believe that suppression of the news, for any consideration other than the welfare of society, is indefensible.

I believe that no one should write as a journalist what he would not say as a gentleman; that bribery by one's own pocketbook is as much to be avoided as bribery by the pocketbook of another, that individual responsibility may not be escaped by pleading another's instructions or another's dividends.

I believe that advertising, news and editorial columns should alike serve the best interests of readers; that a single standard of helpful truth and cleanness should prevail for all; that the supreme test of good journalism is the measure of its public service.

I believe that the journalism which succeeds best—and best deserves success—fears god and honors man; is stoutly independent, unmoved by pride of opinion or greed of power, constructive, tolerant but never careless, self-controlled, patient, always respectful of its readers but always unafraid; is quickly indignant at injustice; is unswayed by the appeal of privilege or the clamor of the mob; seeks to give every man a chance, and, as far as law and honest wage and recognition of human brotherhood can make it so, an equal chance; is profoundly patriotic while sincerely promoting international good will and cementing world-comradeship; is a journalism of humanity, of and for today's world.

Walter Williams, Dean, School of Journalism, University of Missouri, 1908–1935

VOCABULARY—COURTESY OF UNIVERSITY OF MARYLAND

Actuality/ack/sound bite/bite
Audio recording (or audio portion of a video recording) of an interview

Incue (often written as "IC")
First 3–4 words of a sound bite (helps to identify the correct bite)

Outcue (often written as "OC" or "Q")
Last 3–4 words of a sound bite (lets a reporter/anchor know when the bite is ending)

Pronouncer
Phonetic spelling of a word in a broadcast news story...it is usually broken into syllables and placed next to the word in question; e.g., "The meeting of OPEC (PRON: Oh'-peck) ministers in Riyadh (PRON: Ree'-yad). . . ."

Slug
Heading on the script...in the upper left-hand side...includes a 2–3 word story name, writer's last name, date of the story and TST (total story time...definition elsewhere)

Background/ambient/NAT sound
Recorded sound from/for a story...not a sound bite. Examples: crowd noise, plane taking off/landing, opening a can, mowing a lawn, lighting a fire, hitting a golf ball, etc.

De-brief
An anchor or other person talks with a reporter in the field (or who has returned to the station) about the story they are covering. This can be live and/or pre-recorded. When recorded, the de-brief is cut into smaller segments to run in newscasts.

TRT
Total running time—refers to the length of a sound bite.

TST
Total story time—refers to the entire length of a story incorporating the sound bite and *the copy (this is usually noted in the slug)*

Reader
Copy for a newscast…a brief story (usually under 20 seconds) with no sound bite. This is also sometimes referred to as a copy story.

Voicer
Self-contained recording filed by a reporter on a story (either in the field or in the newsroom). It contains no sound bite.

ROSR
Stands for "radio/reporter on scene report." This is a voicer filed by a reporter from the scene of a story. It should include ambient sound (if appropriate) throughout the entire report.

Scener
Similar to a voicer and ROSR. This is also filed by a reporter on location…the reporter uses this field report to describe the "scene" at the story and, essentially, sets the stage for what's to come at the news event.

Wrap/wrap-around/package
Filed by a reporter (either in the field or from the newsroom) and includes at least one sound bite (and possibly other nat sound).

Lockout
The reporter's name, station's call letters and locater (where the reporter is filing the report). The lockout is voiced by the reporter and is included at the end of every recorded report. Example: "Sue Kopen, WBAL News, Bethesda."

Phoner
An interview conducted over the telephone or when a reporter files a story from the field via the telephone.

Lead-in
Used to introduce a voicer, package or other correspondent's report. The lead-in is used to set up the either the recorded or live portion of the reporter's story. It should never repeat or duplicate what the reporter says.

Backgrounder
Story that provides history, perspective.

React/Reax
Short for reaction. This is used to describe both a story and a piece of tape/soundbite which is a reaction to an earlier report/story.

Remote
Stories that are brought to the listener live from a reporter's location in the field. This applies to both radio and TV.

Rundown/line-up
Applies to both radio and TV. This is the story order for a newscast...as determined by a variety of factors including timeliness of the story and proximity to the listening/viewing audience.

Backtime
Method used to count DOWN the time so that a newscast ends precisely on time. For example, if you have a 10 minute newscast you subtract the time each story runs from the 10 minutes to determine how much time you have left to fill the newscast. This is done both BEFORE the newscast (to make certain you have sufficient stories to fill the newscast) and during the newscast to make certain you hit the 10 minute mark and are out on time.

Breaking news
An unexpected, suddenly occurring news event.

Segue
Transition from one story to another. The writer finds a way to make this switch by tying one story into another.

MOS/POS (also referred to as Vox Pop for vox populi or "voice of the people")
MOS stands for "man on the street"; POS stands for "person/people on the street". This is a collection of QUICK soundbites from the general public usually reacting to a story.

Back-to-back/montage
A production technique in which soundbites are edited one after the other with no narration in-between...often used for MOS/POS (no id's required of the soundbites for this).

Tag
A very short line used after a soundbite to end a story.

HFR/Embargo

HFR stands for "hold for release"…embargo means the same thing. This can be attached to a story and designates a time/day when a story can be released. Stories that are HFR are not to be released unless someone breaks the embargo, but most news organizations abide by the request to withhold the story until the designated time.

REPORTER'S CHECKLIST—U. MISSOURI

I. WHAT IS MY FOCUS?

1. Why will the viewers want to know about this story?

2. Why do they need to know about it?

3. Exactly how will viewers be affected?

II. HOW CAN I BEST TELL THE STORY?

1. How can I tell viewers how they're affected?

2. How can I visually show them?

3. How can I best "boil" the information down?

4. How can I find the people who are or will be affected?

5. How can I best interview on-camera the people affected?

6. What are the best questions I can ask them to show how they feel?

7. How can I best use natural sound segments?

III. HOW WILL THE LEAD BEST GRAB VIEWER'S ATTENTION?

IV. HOW WILL THE OPENING GRAB VIEWER'S ATTENTION?

1. Opening video?

2. Opening audio?

V. HOW CAN INTEREST BE SUSTAINED THROUGHOUT THE STORY?

What can I do that most other reporters would not think of?

VI. HOW CAN THE REPORT BE MADE DISTINCTIVE?

VII. WHAT ELSE CAN I DO WITH THE STORY?

1. How can I make my standup exciting for the viewer?

2. Does it need graphics?

VIII. HOW WILL CLOSE WRAP-UP STORY/MAKE MEMORABLE?

IX. HOW CAN I FOLLOW-UP ON THE STORY?

MAKEUP 101: "BETH MALICKI'S MAKEUP AND MAKEOVERS FOR BROADCAST"

Purpose: To make reporter/anchor look professional, credible, and attractive.

Requirements: Meet with faculty member/consultant to assess need; purchase necessary makeup and tools for applying makeup; maintain professional haircut and tools for achieving hair look; wear professional clothing from head to toe; critique on-air look with faculty member/ consultant and make adjustments as needed; update look every six months to a year.

MEN

There are dozens of brands of makeup to choose from. Many on-air personalities prefer MAC makeup, which is not available in all cities. Others swear by Merle Norman and still others with sensitive skin prefer Clinique. Lancome and Bobbi Brown are trustworthy lines also. Makeup, skin cleansers and moisturizers, haircuts, and hair products can be expensive, so try to negotiate that into your contract and look for sales. When you purchase your on-air makeup, try to take a TV news veteran with you whose look you admire. Don't let the salesperson talk you into items you don't need that will make you look unprofessional. Also, ask about returns and exchanges in case the colors don't work under your studio's lights or out in the field.

Foundation: Find a shade as close to your natural skin color as possible. If you're dark skinned, apply a thin layer. If you have 5 o'clock shadow, dark circles under eyes, freckles, moles or blemishes, apply a heavier layer. Apply with cosmetic wedge or foundation brush. You should not have to put makeup on your neck if your foundation is the right color. If your neck and ears turn red when you're on-camera, you might need to apply some makeup on those areas. Many men have to change the colors of makeup they wear when seasons change: darker foundation and powder for spring and summer and slightly lighter shades for the fall and winter.

Concealer. Needed to cover darkness under eyes or for some blemishes or birthmarks. Most men fund success with a thick, lipstick-shaped concealer, not liquid. Apply liberally and gently pat with fingertips to blend. You'll want a color one shade lighter than your foundation.

Powder. Use a shade close to your natural color or slightly darker. Apply with brush or puff. I prefer pressed powder because it isn't as messy and travels better.

Bronzer. Adds "warmth" and dimension to your face giving you a sun-kissed glow. Bronzer is great for lighter to medium skin tones. Apply lightly and ONLY to cheekbones, chin, forehead, and the end of the nose. Bronzer looks best when applied with a large blush brush.

Chapstick. When you're nervous you lick your lips, leaving them susceptible to unattractive chapping. Also, having a slight gleam to your lips makes them look healthy overall while on-air. Opt for chapstick with NO color—you don't want to look like its lipstick.

Cleansing wipes. Makes it simple to clean off makeup while out in the field. I recommend Pond's Cleansing Cloths Travel Pack because you can keep it in your bag with your makeup.

Clothing. The right fit means everything. Buy suits off the rack that are on sale—but spend a lot of money on tailoring. A well-tailored suit makes you look more professional. For most GA reporters there is a basic minimum wardrobe you'll need for the job:

- Three pair of (ironed) slacks. These pants will go through a lot and you'll probably need to replace them every few months—especially if you're one-man-banding.

- Two jackets (single-breasted compliment most men while only thin men should wear double-breasted. Never button the bottom button if your jacket has more than one button.)

- Four dress shirts with no buttons on the collars. Opt for white, light yellow, light gray, light green, or blue. Dark colors are too trendy and are sometimes OK for sports reporters but generally a bad idea for news personalities.

- Five ties that compliment the color scheme of the jacket and shirt you will wear with each.

- An "interview suit" that you'll wear for job interviews and stories where you know you won't get dirty. This should be a dark-colored suit that is more expensive and tailored perfectly.

- Casual clothes: nice jeans (no holes), button-down shirt (flannel or solid-colored, preferably with station's logo), and polo shirts for coverage of storm damage, heat waves, agriculture stories, etc.

- Clothes for extreme weather: long johns, gloves, hat, scarf, parka, rain coat, sturdy umbrella, wool socks, etc. Remember in the most extreme weather conditions you'll probably be required to be IN them—telling viewers to take cover.

Please be sure the pattern on your jackets and ties will not "jump" on the air. Tight patterns of highly contrasting colors (like herringbone) will "move" on the air and are inappropriate.

Tips to looking your best for men:

- Know your beard. Men who can skip a day of shaving might be able to use an electric razor. Those who have a five o'clock shadow by noon need to invest in a high-quality gel and a new blade with each shave. This can get very expensive, but stubble looks terrible on TV.

- Get into a skin-maintenance routine: always wash your face at the end of the day with a gentle soap and then moisturize. Inexpensive cleansers like Cetaphil work nicely.

- Stop tanning! Avoid sun exposure, use an SPF 30 every day on your face, neck, ears, and hands. Wrinkles are not good for your career.

- Avoid middle parts for your hair—they don't look flattering on TV. Find a stylist you trust and keep your hair maintained with a professional cut every two to three weeks. Spiky and trendy styles don't usually add to your credibility. Sports reporters have more freedom in this area than their news counterparts.

- Have your eyebrows evaluated and waxed if necessary. Uni-brows and bushy brows make men look angry on air.

- If you drink a lot of coffee, cranberry juice, or red wine, check your teeth. Crest Whitestrips are pretty good for getting out stains, although more severe yellowing may require a treatment from a dentist.

- Live a healthy lifestyle. Drink lots of water, eat a balanced diet, sleep a decent amount, exercise regularly, don't smoke, and lay off the alcohol. Maintain a healthy weight—not doing so is dangerous to your health and your efforts for on-air employment.

WOMEN

There are dozens of brands of makeup to choose from. Many on-air personalities prefer MAC makeup, which is not available in all cities. Others swear by Merle Norman and still others with sensitive skin prefer Clinique. Lancome and Bobbi Brown are trustworthy lines also. Makeup, skin cleansers and moisturizers, haircuts, and hair products can be expensive, so try to negotiate that into your contract and look for sales. When you purchase your on-air makeup, try to take a TV news veteran with you whose look you admire. Don't let the sales person talk you into items you don't need or know will make you look unprofessional. Also, ask about returns and exchanges in case the colors don't work under your studio's lights.

Foundation. Find a shade as close to your natural skin color as possible. If you are dark-skinned, apply a thin layer. If you have dark circles under eyes, freckles, moles, or blemishes, apply up to three layers. Apply with cosmetic wedge or foundation brush. You should not have to put makeup on your neck if your foundation is the right color. If your neck and ears turn red when you're on camera, you might have to apply makeup on those areas until you get over the jitters. Many women have to change the colors of makeup they wear when seasons change: darker foundation and powder for spring and summer and slightly lighter shades for the fall and winter.

Concealer. Needed to cover darkness under eyes. Use thick, lipstick, shaped concealer, not liquid. Apply liberally and gently pat with fingertips to blend. Darkness under the eyes will be greatly exaggerated by studio lights, so be sure the skin is evenly covered.

Powder. Any powder close to your skin tone will work.

Bronzer. Only recommended for women with light to medium-light skin color. Do not use contouring techniques—it ends up looking dirty on the air.

Blush. Rather than applying it to the hollows of the cheeks, put blush on the apples of the cheeks—directly below your eyes. Sweep up along cheekbone. Stay away from bright pink tones, choose plums, rose, and dark reddish brown.

Eyes. Find colors that complement your coloring and make your eyes stand out under harsh studio lights without looking overdone. Finding eyeshadow colors and applications that work for you will take trial and error. Some women wear eyeliner on the top and bottom of their eyelids and look fantastic, others end up looking beady-eyed. All women should wear two coats of black mascara on curled lashes and none on the bottom lashes. Avoid sparkly or shimmery shadow—it looks unprofessional on air. Most liquid liners and pencil liners look too harsh. A moistened angled brush dipped in a dark eyeshadow creates the most natural frame around the eyes.

Lipstick. Apply lipstick last and see if it overpowers your face or matches it. Bold colors can work for some on-air personalities, but it ends up looking overdone for others. Neutral shades never work on-air, but beware of bright reds or pinks. Finding a color that looks professional and attractive might take some hunting. If you have small lips, line them slightly larger than they are, use a bolder color, and top with a bit of gloss. If you have naturally full lips, consider yourself lucky as you can wear almost anything you want on your lips except for the boldest colors. Light-colored women should avoid brown and deep red lipsticks. Line your lips in a color as close to your lipstick as possible. Purple, light pink, bright orange, and matte colored lipsticks generally do not look good on camera.

Jewelry. Earrings are a must—they complete your look. Big hoops and long chandelier earrings, while popular, are not professional and should not be worn on air. The perfect earring size is between a dime and a nickel and should match or complement your necklace. Speaking of necklaces, chokers are not good for TV, nor are scarves (unless they're the winter kind and you're doing an outdoor live shot). Turtlenecks are not flattering on the air either.

Clothes. The right fit means everything. Buy suits off the rack that are on sale—but spend a lot of money on tailoring. A well-tailored suit makes you look more professional. Women can wear either pant or skirt suits—depending on the nature of the story, their personal comfort, and the weather. For most GA reporters there is a basic minimum wardrobe you'll need for the job:

• Ten suit jackets that complement your coloring and fit you perfectly. Avoid white and bright yellow—they don't work with many cameras. Have bold jewel tones and at least one black suit jacket. Avoid neutral colors because you won't "pop" on the air. Avoid highly seasonal jackets until you've built your wardrobe to more than twenty jackets that are all-season.

• Ten ironed blouses that contrast your suit jackets and still work with your coloring.

• Slacks (black goes with everything and covers stains from carrying gear). Skirts are permitted but can hinder reporting. If you choose to wear a skirt you'll probably have to wear nylons (nude or black, white hose are for nurses and brides). Be sure your slacks are tailored for the shoes you'll wear on the job.

• High-heeled pumps do not work for reporting, but tennis shoes are not appropriate either. Comfortable shoes that look professional are your best bet but have a spare pair of comfortable shoes in your desk for days you'll be walking a lot or wading through mud.

• Casual clothes: nice jeans (no holes), button-down shirts, polo shirts for coverage of storm damage, heat waves, agriculture stories, etc.

• Clothes for extreme weather: long johns, gloves, hat, scarf, parka, rain coat, sturdy umbrella, wool socks, etc. Remember that in the most extreme weather conditions, you'll probably be required to be in them—telling viewers to take cover.

Please be sure the pattern on your jackets and blouses will not "jump" on the air. Tight patterns of highly contrasting colors (like herringbone) will "move" on the air and are inappropriate.

Tips to looking your best for women:

• Get up early before your shift and make your hair and makeup perfect. This will save you lots of time in the field when shooting stand-ups and you will look fabulous with just a touch up. On ridiculously hot days, forget this advice—your face will melt before you finish your first interview—but at least try to get your hair taken care of.

- Buy suits that look great even when you're sitting down. Single button jackets tend to gape at the chest when you're sitting— not a good look. Avoid linen suits—they look wrinkled on the air no matter how recently you ironed them. Be honest about your body type and size and buy suits that fit both—then get then tailored to fit you to a T.

- Stop tanning! Avoid sun exposure and use an SPF 30 every day on your face, neck, ears, and hands. Wrinkles are not good for your career.

- Take care of your skin. Wash your face every night before you go to sleep and apply a moisturizer. An inexpensive option is Cetaphil face wash and lotion, which you can buy at Target, Wal-Mart, or Walgreens.

- Part your hair on the side—middle parts usually do not look as good on TV. Have all the products you need to achieve your look: styling crème, hairspray, pomade, etc. Get your hair cut every 4–6 weeks to keep the look maintained. If you color your hair, be sure to get it taken care of before roots are noticeable.

- Have your eyebrows evaluated and waxed if necessary. Schedule a waxing every time your get your hair cut or more often if necessary. Check for other facial hair that might need bleaching or removing. Have this maintained often.

- If you drink a lot of coffee, cranberry juice, or red wine, check your teeth. Crest Whitestrips are pretty good for getting out stains, although more severe yellowing may require a treatment from a dentist.

- Live a healthy lifestyle! Drink lots of water, eat a balanced diet, sleep a decent amount, exercise regularly, don't smoke, and lay off the alcohol. Maintain a healthy weight—not doing so is dangerous for you health and on air career.

In Closing: You do not have to be "hot" to find success in TV, you just have to be *warm*. Being too thin, too confident with your looks, and banking on your face to get you a job will be detrimental to your career in TV news. Working hard at reporting, writing, and polishing your look will ensure success beyond anything else.

STORY SCORE SHEET—U. MISSOURI

This form lists the criteria Greeley uses to evaluate and grade your Broadcast II story assignments.

Editorial Points	*Possible Scored*
Acceptable story idea	10
Multiple sources on camera	10
Humanized approach	5
Today angle	5
Hard facts present in story	5
Active voice/verb use	5
Beginning, middle, end (writing)	5
Writing to video/audio	5
Natural sound open	5
Natural sound bridges	5
Camera close to subjects	5
Sequences used	5
Opening/closing shots	5
People active in video	5
Interview framing	5
Involved standup/performance	5
Follow-up info recorded	5
Extra effort	5
Editorial Points	**100**

Penalties	
Unusable video (dark, shaky, soft)	−15
Unusable audio (wrong mic, too low)	−15
Scripting problems (times, tags, etc.)	−5
Grammatical error(s)	−10
Factual error(s)	−25
Editorial Points	**100**
Total Penalties	**−70**

BEAT REPORTING—OHIO UNIVERSITY

| *ATHENS* | *MIDDAY* | *WINTER* |

Beat Reports

PURPOSE: The goal of the beat reports is to generate **original**, newsworthy **local** stories—**not** to simply copy the news stories that you find in the local newspapers or from WOUB. Being able to develop original, quality news stories is an important skill for good reporters to have. News directors want to hire reporters who have the skills to come up with their own newsworthy story ideas without depending on an assignment editor to hand them stories.

ASSIGNMENT: Each **JOUR 458** student will be assigned a beat to cover and provide updates every day he/she works. The news producer and assignment editor will review every report each day, looking for strong local stories for the newscast. *Beat reports on stories not for TODAY also should be filed in the futures file!!*

BACKGROUND RESEARCH: Develop a list of sources with phone numbers—*that list should be at the bottom of your beat report file by Friday 1/7 (worth 10 points in beat report grade).* Find out if there are regular meetings that pertain to your beat. Find ways to get on any relevant mailing list for agendas, news releases, and other information pertaining to your beat. Find ways to localize national stories as they relate to your beat. Make phone calls; talk to your sources. HINT: Research for your beat report begins BEFORE it is due—NOT the morning it's due.

SOURCING: *EVERY beat report must be sourced!!* If the story was originally printed in the newspaper, or from a Web site or television news source—indicate that. If the story originally came from another source, your report must indicate how to take the story forward or localize it. Who are the local contacts? If the story is completely enterprise, indicate where the idea came from—who did you talk to?! *Taking a story idea from another source and not crediting that source is plagiarism and will be handled as such.*

FORMAT: *All beat reports must be submitted no later than 9:00 am MONDAY THRU THURSDAY.* Beat reports should be submitted in the **Hold Beats** file under the Scripps News Rover in ENPS. Each beat report should follow this format:

- today's date
- three-to-four sentences providing *details* of your story idea
- date/time and location of story event
- story development—who to interview, what video to shoot, how to personalize the story
- the name of at least one good/credible source with a phone number (even if it's on your source list)

GRADING: *Beat reports are a major part of your final grade.* Each beat report is worth 0–5 points.

5: original enterprise story idea with complete information, sources and ideas for story development
3/4: story idea from another source, but good information on how to follow-up and move story forward—full listing of local sources and ideas for story development.
2: good story idea, but missing sources or story development.
1: story copied from another source but not taken forward; missing basic information to follow-through.
0: wrong information; no beat report submitted by 9:00 am.

BEATS
CAMPUS
• OU Board of Trustees • Student Senate; Faculty Senate; Administrative Senate; • list of members and their phone numbers; schedule of regular meetings • agenda for Board of Trustees meeting • Greek life; international students; student professional organizations • check OU's experts directory: http://www.ohiou.edu/news/experts/index.html • This does NOT include simple "happenings" on campus like speeches or conferences.

CITY GOVERNMENT

- Athens City Council (get updated list of members and their phone numbers)
- Clerk of Council, City Bldg
- Agendas for city council meetings and council committee meetings
- Mayor's office
- Mayor's Wednesday news conference (usually at 1:30 pm)
- Municipal agencies (i.e., zoning, civil service, safety; Board of Commissioners)

COUNTY GOVERNMENT

- Athens County Commission (get updated list of members and their phone numbers)
- Agendas for county commission meetings—usually meet Wed at 9:30 am—and committee/boards meetings
- County agencies

COURTS

- Federal, state courts
- Local courts (i.e., municipal; county; appellate; juvenile)
- Prosecutor's office; public defender
- Court dockets for upcoming trials available 4th floor, Athens Co. Courthouse

CONSUMER

- Recalls, product problems—check Consumer Product Safety Commission Web site—www.cpsc.org
- Shopping trends, innovations, hot new products, internet shopping
- Product pricing and service (i.e., gas prices, airline fares, rebates, food prices)
- Check with OU Home Economics department for experts in retailing and consumer issues—also OU Marketing department for consumer research

ECONOMY

- Labor unions; layoffs
- Monthly jobless rate reports
- New industries; business closings; development in city or county
- Find contact people for area unions
- Localize national economic issues
- Check OU's experts directory:
  http://www.ohiou.edu/news/experts/index.html

EDUCATION

- Athens city and county schools (get list of local superintendents and phone numbers)
- List of school principals with their office phone numbers
- Hocking Technical College
- Agendas for school board meetings (get list of current board members and phone numbers)
- School fundraisers; current legal battle over equity in schools

EMERGENCY/CRIME

- OU Police
- Athens Police
- Athens County Sheriff
- Ohio Highway Patrol (Athens and Hocking Counties)
- Southeast Ohio Emergency Medical Services (SEOEMS)
- Athens Fire Department, Station 1, Columbus Road
- Athens Fire Department, Station 2, Richland Ave.
- Jails; rescue; ambulance service; hospitals; medical examiner
- Check for breaking news; get updates on crime/accident reports
- Develop feature ideas—programs law enforcement authorities are doing with the community or schools for crime prevention/education.

ENTERTAINMENT

- Educational and cultural events @ OU (i.e., International Street Fair, Parents Weekend, Homecoming, Dads Weekend, Moms Weekend, Sibs Weekend)
- Check OU "Calendar of Events" Web site: http://redbud.cats.ohiou.edu/calendar/
- Check Baker Center
- Ohio University Office of Continuing Education and Workshops, 115 Haning Hall
- Kennedy Lecture Series; Office of Public Occasions
- School of Theater; School of Dance; School of Music; Kennedy Museum of Art
- University Program Council
- Cultural/education events in the Athens community
- Collect fliers on upcoming events in the Athens community
- Athens County Convention and Visitors Bureau, 667 E. State St.
- Community theater; holiday events (i.e., Memorial Day, parades, etc.)
- Dairy Barn, 8000 Dairy Lane, Athens
- Athens County Historical Society and Museum, 65 N. Court St.
- Stuart's Opera House, 34 Public Square, Nelsonville
- Story ideas must be more than just a calendar listing of events—need to express how the story could be developed into a pkg!!

ENVIRONMENT/SCIENCE

- Dysart Woods; Chad Kister—mining and reclamation
- Recycling; landfills; water and air pollution
- Flooding issues
- State and National parks
- Research on OU's campus possible source for idea development: Science Writer, OU News Services
- Check OU's experts directory: http://www.ohiou.edu/news/experts/index.html

HEALTH/MEDICAL
• Local medical news—Obleniss Hospital • Develop feature ideas; localize national stories—from www.WebMD, www.CNNmedical • Athens AIDS Task Force • Hudson Health Center, Health and Wellness (contact Char Kopchick, director) • Wellworks, Education Outreach/Special Events • Check OU's experts directory: http://www.ohiou.edu/news/experts/index.html

POLITICS/STATE GOVERNMENT
• Governor's office • Local elections; state political campaigns • Election board; political parties • Candidates and elected office holders • State legislature (i.e., bills introduced, laws passed) • Legislative Information Office: (800) 282–0253

SOCIAL ISSUES/COMMUNITY AFFAIRS/RELIGION
• Altruistic organizations; community improvements; social betterment • Youth agencies; 4-H; Girl Scouts; Boy Scouts • Elderly; United Seniors of Athens County/Athens County Senior Center • Welfare; poverty; WIC • Race relations; women's affairs • Goodworks; Salvation Army • American Red Cross (local blood drives); • United Appeal/United Way; My Sister's Place; Careline • Area churches

SPORTS—HIGH SCHOOL
• Local high school sports (i.e., wrestling, basketball, baseball, football) • Get names and numbers of all high school coaches • Get schedules for all upcoming high school games • Little League; other organized sports in the community

SPORTS—OU
• Bobcat sports
• Intramural/club sports
• Get schedules for all OU games
• Get names and numbers of all coaches
• Get season media passes for games (contact: weather, sports, information, director of media services)

Appendix C:
How Do They Figure
Out the Ratings?

As mentioned earlier in the book, ratings are very important in the radio and television business because they indicate how many, and what kind of people are listening to or watching a particular station. Two top companies dominate the ratings industry: Nielsen Media Research[1] in television and Arbitron[2] in radio.

These two companies are commonly referred to, on a day-to-day basis, as "the Arbs," "the Nielsens," "the ratings," or just simply "the numbers." And whatever you do, do not make the mistake of thinking ratings aren't important. According to Nielson, not just millions, but billions of dollars a year hinge on their findings alone. Nielsen reports, "That information is the currency in all the transactions between buyers and sellers, which adds up to more than $60 billion in national and local advertising spending in the U.S. each year."

Ratings are important because they affect the bottom line. If the numbers are low, it is harder for a station's account representatives to sell advertising. When advertising sales go down, the station loses money.

On the other side of the coin, when ratings are up, everybody is happy. The sales manager and general manager are happy because it is easier to sell advertising, and the station can raise its rates because more people are listening or watching. The program director or news director is happy because people like what he chose to put on the air, the air talent is happy because more people are tuning in to watch or listen to them, meaning their job security is solid. Off-air people are happy because everyone else is happy.

RADIO RATINGS

You may wonder how exactly these companies are able to find out how many people tune into what stations at what times. Let's start off with the radio ratings first. Arbitron conducts four different surveys a year, each lasting twelve weeks. Each of these ratings periods, known as "books" in the industry, are named after the season in which they are released. The four ratings periods in Dallas in 2007 were as follows:

Winter	2007	January 11–April 4
Spring	2007	April 5–June 27
Summer	2007	June 28–September 19
Fall	2007	September 20–December 12

All but twenty-eight days of the year were a part of a ratings period, but usually stations put more emphasis on the spring and fall books. Some program directors forbid key air talent from taking vacations or unnecessary time off during the spring and fall ratings periods.

Now that we know *when* Arbitron is rating stations, you may wonder just exactly *how* they rate stations. Abritron is in the process of implementing a new ratings system called "people meters" using new technology. It is currently being tested in a couple of test markets, but, believe it or not, despite all the advances in technology, for the time being, Arbitron still relies on good old-fashioned diary keeping. They contact over five million people over the course of a year to see if they would be interested in keeping a detailed listing or diary of when they listen to the radio. According to Arbitron, about 75 percent of those contacted agree to keep a diary; 2.6 million diaries are mailed to participants each year.

Even though each rating period is twelve weeks, the diary keepers are asked to fill out surveys in one-week increments. These seven-day diaries are designed to be maintained by each member of a household, up to nine people over the age of twelve. All participants are asked to record details of each time they listen to the radio, including the actual times they tuned in and tuned out, where they listened (car, work, home, etc.), or if they did not listen to the radio at all.

Diary-keepers are also asked to provide personal details that help Arbitron know exactly what kind of person is listening. These questions include the diary-keeper's age, sex, employment, and place of residence, as well as twenty-one other questions that help describe the listener in detail.

Arbitron uses this information to show radio stations how many people are listening and what kind of people they are. This includes details such as age demographics, social and economic standing, buying preferences and lifestyle. This information helps those of us who work at radio stations in a number of different ways. Air personalities find out whom they are talking to and how many people are listening at any given time. Program directors find out whom they are reaching and who is not tuning in. The information also helps sales managers steer their account reps to businesses that are interested in reaching that station's particular audience. National advertising agencies buy commercials at specific stations based on these numbers and the information gleaned from the diary-keepers.

TELEVISION RATINGS

As I have mentioned, Nielsen Media Research dominates how television ratings are measured. Nielson calls itself the "Official national measurement service of the television industry," and it is hard to argue since its ratings are truly the industry standard. Nielsen tries to answer two questions: who is watching and what are they watching.

According to Nielsen Media Research, there are over ninety-nine million households in the U.S. with televisions. In order to find out *who* is watching, Nielsen uses a sample of 5,000 households, containing over 13,000 people who have agreed to tell Nielsen what they watch and when they watch it.

Nielsen goes high tech for information on *what* people are watching. In specially selected sample homes, Nielsen installs metering equipment on television sets, VCRs, cable boxes, and satellite dishes. These meters keep track of when television sets are turned on and what they are tuned to. The meters are connected to a black box, which calls its information into central computers at night and gives them instant ratings. This process gathers ratings on a national level, and in some larger cities, has been refined enough to offer local stations detailed information, as well. In cities that are not set up with the most cutting edge black box technology, Nielsen relies on viewers' handwritten diaries, just as Arbitron does. These diary-keepers record their TV viewing during a given week. "Sweeps" is a term that refers to the four months during the year (February, May, July, and November) during which Nielsen Media Research conducts a complete diary measurement across the country. In several larger markets, there are as many as three more ratings months (October, January, and March) during which diaries are used for more ratings.

MARKET SIZE

The following lists illustrate the way radio (Arbitron) and television (Nielsen) lists the markets according to size, starting with radio. I have listed the top fifty markets for radio and the entire list of television markets, according to size. The bigger cities are considered major markets. Cities with medium-sized populations are called medium markets, and the least populated towns are called small markets.

ARBITRON RADIO MARKET RANKINGS: SPRING 2006

Note: Metro 12+ means from the age of twelve and older are counted. There are other numerical breakdowns of the ratings that count various age groups and demographics but the 12+ is a counting of every listener twelve years and older.

Rank	Market Name	Metro 12+ Population
1	New York, NY	15,332,000
2	Los Angeles, CA	10,790,100
3	Chicago, IL	7,698,300
4	San Francisco, CA	5,829,700
5	Dallas–Ft. Worth, TX	4,730,200
6	Philadelphia, PA	4,354,900
7	Houston–Galveston, TX	4,353,000
8	Washington, DC	4,132,800
9	Detroit, MI	3,892,600
10	Atlanta, GA	3,860,100
11	Boston, MA	3,841,100
12	Miami–Ft. Lauderdale–Hollywood, FL	3,505,100
13	Puerto Rico	3,250,400
14	Seattle–Tacoma, WA	3,204,800
15	Phoenix, AZ	2,938,500
16	Minneapolis–St. Paul, MN	2,632,400
17	San Diego, CA	2,484,900
18	Nassau–Suffolk (Long Island), NY	2,393,800

19	Tampa–St. Petersburg–Clearwater, FL	2,262,900
20	St. Louis, MO	2,262,000
21	Baltimore, MD	2,249,900
22	Denver–Boulder, CO	2,157,700
23	Pittsburgh, PA	2,015,100
24	Portland, OR	1,963,400
25	Cleveland, OH	1,799,900
26	Sacramento, CA	1,758,100
27	Riverside–San Bernardino, CA	1,756,600
28	Cincinnati, OH	1,705,200
29	Kansas City, MO–KS	1,553,300
30	San Antonio, TX	1,552,100
31	Salt Lake City–Ogden–Provo, UT	1,485,600
32	Las Vegas, NV	1,438,600
33	Milwaukee–Racine, WI	1,429,200
34	San Jose, CA	1,413,100
35	Charlotte–Gastonia–Rock Hill, NC-SC	1,409,800
36	Providence–Warwick–Pawtucket, RI	1,404,000
37	Orlando, FL	1,402,300
38	Columbus, OH	1,401,300
39	Middlesex–Somerset–Union, NJ	1,383,100
40	Norfolk–Virginia Beach–Newport News, VA	1,314,600
41	Indianapolis, IN	1,312,200
42	Austin, TX	1,204,800
43	Raleigh–Durham, NC	1,143,700
44	Nashville, TN	1,125,000
45	Greensboro–Winston–Salem–High Point, NC	1,113,300
46	West Palm Beach–Boca Raton, FL	1,098,000
47	New Orleans, LA	1,079,200
48	Oklahoma City, OK	1,059,600
49	Jacksonville, FL	1,057,600
50	Memphis, TN	1,047,900

TELEVISION MARKET RANKINGS ACCORDING TO NIELSEN:

RANK	Designated Market Area (DMA)	TV Homes	% of US
1	New York	7,375,530	6.692
2	Los Angeles	5,536,430	5.023
3	Chicago	3,430,790	3.113
4	Philadelphia	2,925,560	2.654
5	Boston (Manchester)	2,375,310	2.155
6	San Francisco–Oak–San Jose	2,355,740	2.137
7	Dallas–Ft. Worth	2,336,140	2.120
8	Washington, DC (Hagrstwn)	2,252,550	2.044
9	Atlanta	2,097,220	1.903
10	Houston	1,938,670	1.759
11	Detroit	1,936,350	1.757
12	Tampa–St. Pete (Sarasota)	1,710,400	1.552
13	Seattle–Tacoma	1,701,950	1.544
14	Phoenix (Prescott)	1,660,430	1.507
15	Minneapolis–St. Paul	1,652,940	1.500
16	Cleveland–Akron (Canton)	1,541,780	1.399
17	Miami–Ft. Lauderdale	1,522,960	1.382
18	Denver	1,415,180	1.284
19	Sacramnto–Stkton–Modesto	1,345,820	1.221
20	Orlando–Daytona Bch–Melbrn	1,345,700	1.221
21	St. Louis	1,222,380	1.109
22	Pittsburgh	1,169,800	1.061
23	Portland, OR	1,099,890	0.998
24	Baltimore	1,089,220	0.988
25	Indianapolis	1,053,750	0.956
26	San Diego	1,026,160	0.931

27	Charlotte	1,020,130	0.926
28	Hartford & New Haven	1,013,350	0.919
29	Raleigh–Durham (Fayetvlle)	985,200	0.894
30	Nashville	927,500	0.842
31	Kansas City	903,540	0.820
32	Columbus, OH	890,770	0.808
33	Milwaukee	880,390	0.799
34	Cincinnati	880,190	0.799
35	Greenvll–Spart–Ashevll–And	815,460	0.740
36	Salt Lake City	810,830	0.736
37	San Antonio	760,410	0.690
38	West Palm Beach–Ft. Pierce	751,930	0.682
39	Grand Rapids–Kalmzoo–B.Crk	731,630	0.664
40	Birmingham (Ann, Tusc)	716,520	0.650
41	Harrisburg–Lncstr–Leb–York	707,010	0.641
42	Norfolk–Portsmth–Newpt Nws	704,810	0.640
43	New Orleans	672,150	0.610
44	Memphis	657,670	0.597
45	Oklahoma City	655,400	0.595
46	Albuquerque–Santa Fe	653,680	0.593
47	Greensboro–H.Point–W.Salem	652,020	0.592
48	Las Vegas	651,110	0.591
49	Buffalo	644,430	0.585
50	Louisville	643,290	0.584
51	Providence–New Bedford	639,590	0.580
52	Jacksonville	624,220	0.566
53	Austin	589,360	0.535
54	Wilkes Barre–Scranton	588,540	0.534
55	Albany–Schenectady–Troy	552,250	0.501

56	Fresno–Visalia	546,210	0.496
57	Little Rock–Pine Bluff	531,470	0.482
58	Knoxville	516,180	0.468
59	Dayton	513,610	0.466
60	Richmond–Petersburg	510,770	0.463
61	Tulsa	510,480	0.463
62	Mobile–Pensacola (Ft Walt)	501,130	0.455
63	Lexington	478,560	0.434
64	Charleston–Huntington	477,890	0.434
65	Flint–Saginaw–Bay City	475,500	0.431
66	Ft. Myers–Naples	461,920	0.419
67	Wichita–Hutchinson Plus	446,820	0.405
68	Roanoke–Lynchburg	440,390	0.400
69	Green Bay–Appleton	432,810	0.393
70	Toledo	426,520	0.387
71	Tucson (Sierra Vista)	422,480	0.383
72	Honolulu	414,960	0.377
73	Des Moines–Ames	413,590	0.375
74	Portland–Auburn	407,050	0.369
75	Omaha	399,830	0.363
76	Syracuse	398,240	0.361
77	Springfield, MO	395,820	0.359
78	Spokane	389,630	0.354
79	Rochester, NY	385,460	0.350
80	Paducah–Cape Girard–Harsbg	383,330	0.348
81	Shreveport	382,080	0.347
82	Champaign& Sprngfld–Decatur	378,100	0.343
83	Columbia, SC	373,260	0.339
84	Huntsville–Decatur (Flor)	370,820	0.336
85	Madison	365,550	0.332
86	Chattanooga	354,230	0.321

87	South Bend–Elkhart	333,190	0.302
88	Cedar Rapids–Wtrlo–IWC&Dub	331,480	0.301
89	Jackson, MS	328,350	0.298
90	Burlington–Plattsburgh	325,720	0.296
91	Tri-Cities, TN–VA	323,690	0.294
92	Harlingen–Wslco–Brnsvl–McA	318,800	0.289
93	Colorado Springs–Pueblo	315,010	0.286
94	Waco–Temple–Bryan	310,960	0.282
95	Davenport–R.Island–Moline	308,380	0.280
96	Baton Rouge	305,810	0.277
97	Savannah	296,100	0.269
98	Johnstown–Altoona	294,810	0.267
99	El Paso (Las Cruces)	290,540	0.264
100	Evansville	288,800	0.262
101	Charleston, SC	283,730	0.257
102	Youngstown	276,720	0.251
103	Lincoln & Hastings–Krny	274,150	0.249
104	Ft. Smith–Fay–Sprngdl–Rgrs	273,000	0.248
105	Greenville–N.Bern–Washngtn	271,130	0.246
106	Ft. Wayne	270,500	0.245
107	Myrtle Beach–Florence	265,770	0.241
108	Springfield–Holyoke	264,840	0.240
109	Tallahassee–Thomasville	261,250	0.237
110	Lansing	256,790	0.233
111	Tyler–Longview (Lfkn&Ncgd)	255,770	0.232
112	Reno	255,090	0.231
113	Traverse City–Cadillac	247,600	0.225
114	Sioux Falls(Mitchell)	246,020	0.223
115	Augusta	245,590	0.223
116	Montgomery–Selma	245,090	0.222

117	Peoria–Bloomington	241,800	0.219
118	Fargo–Valley City	234,190	0.212
119	Boise	230,100	0.209
120	Macon	229,870	0.209
121	Eugene	229,280	0.208
122	SantaBarbra–SanMar–SanLuOb	224,290	0.204
123	La Crosse–Eau Claire	224,090	0.203
124	Lafayette, LA	220,030	0.200
125	Monterey–Salinas	218,080	0.198
126	Yakima–Pasco–Rchlnd–Knnwck	211,610	0.192
127	Columbus, GA	205,300	0.186
128	Bakersfield	201,850	0.183
129	Corpus Christi	192,380	0.175
130	Chico–Redding	191,190	0.173
131	Amarillo	190,250	0.173
132	Columbus–Tupelo–West Point	186,510	0.169
133	Rockford	183,090	0.166
134	Wausau–Rhinelander	182,620	0.166
135	Monroe–El Dorado	174,370	0.158
136	Topeka	170,650	0.155
137	Duluth–Superior	168,650	0.153
138	Columbia–Jefferson City	167,860	0.152
139	Wilmington	167,810	0.152
140	Beaumont–Port Arthur	167,430	0.152
141	Medford–Klamath Falls	163,090	0.148
142	Erie	158,660	0.144
143	Sioux City	156,950	0.142
144	Wichita Falls & Lawton	154,960	0.141
145	Joplin–Pittsburg	153,720	0.139
146	Lubbock	152,150	0.138
147	Albany, GA	152,140	0.138
148	Salisbury	147,890	0.134
149	Bluefield–Beckley–Oak Hill	145,850	0.132

150	Terre Haute	145,630	0.132
151	Bangor	142,790	0.130
152	Rochestr–Mason City–Austin	142,770	0.130
153	Palm Springs	142,730	0.130
154	Wheeling–Steubenville	142,020	0.129
155	Anchorage	141,290	0.128
156	Binghamton	138,560	0.126
157	Panama City	136,450	0.124
158	Biloxi–Gulfport	135,540	0.123
159	Odessa–Midland	135,100	0.123
160	Minot–Bismarck–Dickinson	133,910	0.122
161	Sherman–Ada	124,060	0.113
162	Gainesville	117,190	0.106
163	Idaho Falls–Pocatello	114,560	0.104
164	Abilene–Sweetwater	112,510	0.102
165	Clarksburg–Weston	108,730	0.099
166	Utica	106,130	0.096
167	Hattiesburg–Laurel	105,000	0.095
168	Missoula	104,700	0.095
169	Quincy–Hannibal–Keokuk	103,890	0.094
170	Yuma–El Centro	103,170	0.094
171	Billings	102,620	0.093
172	Dothan	98,370	0.089
173	Elmira (Corning)	97,210	0.088
174	Jackson, TN	95,010	0.086
175	Lake Charles	94,090	0.085
176	Alexandria, LA	93,120	0.085
177	Rapid City	91,070	0.083
178	Watertown	90,930	0.083
179	Jonesboro	89,530	0.081
180	Marquette	89,160	0.081
181	Harrisonburg	85,870	0.078
182	Greenwood–Greenville	76,800	0.070

183	Bowling Green	75,420	0.068
184	Meridian	71,210	0.065
185	Lima	70,940	0.064
186	Charlottesville	69,750	0.063
187	Grand Junction–Montrose	65,190	0.059
188	Laredo	64,410	0.058
189	Great Falls	64,130	0.058
190	Parkersburg	63,990	0.058
191	Lafayette, IN	63,330	0.057
192	Twin Falls	60,400	0.055
193	Butte–Bozeman	59,300	0.054
194	Eureka	58,340	0.053
195	Cheyenne–Scottsbluff	54,320	0.049
196	Bend, OR	54,250	0.049
197	San Angelo	53,330	0.048
198	Casper–Riverton	52,070	0.047
199	Ottumwa–Kirksville	51,290	0.047
200	Mankato	50,930	0.046
201	St. Joseph	45,840	0.042
202	Zanesville	33,080	0.030
203	Fairbanks	32,310	0.029
204	Presque Isle	31,140	0.028
205	Victoria	30,250	0.027
206	Helena	25,810	0.023
207	Juneau	24,130	0.022
208	Alpena	17,790	0.016
209	North Platte	15,320	0.014
210	Glendive	5,020	0.005
Total		110,213,910	100.000

Now that we have a basic idea of how radio and television are rated, let's take a look at how stations try to get the best ratings possible. We will start off with radio.

HOW TO IMPROVE RADIO RATINGS

Keep in mind that radio ratings are actually quite complex. The most basic number is the *overall ratings*. These are generally the ones the newspapers report, and it consists of ratings gauged Monday through Sunday, 6 AM to 12 midnight, age twelve and up.

The overall ratings provide the broadest common denominator when it comes to radio ratings, but, according to Dallas program director Tyler Cox, those are not the numbers stations themselves are most interested in. Cox says, "Nobody from a radio station perspective sells their advertising based on their 12+ [twelve years of age and over] share. 'Twelve plus' is pretty much a bragging rights demographic. Each station has its own core that it is shooting for, and then targets advertisers based on what is appropriate for that core."

DEMOS

There is much more to ratings than just who has the best overall numbers. When it comes to ratings you will hear people talking a lot about demographics, or "demos." Demos are the different groups of people whom stations are trying to turn on and make into regular listeners. Identifying the different demos is a pretty intuitive process. According to Cox, "A news-talk radio station is going to look at primarily adults ages thirty-five to sixty-four as a general rule. An oldies station is going to look [for people] forty-five plus. An adult contemporary current music station is going to really focus on twenty-five to fifty-four, youth oriented stations eighteen to thirty-four, an all sports station is really going to focus on men eighteen plus. Every station has a different demographic target that it shoots for."

Since radio stations shoot for different age groups, there can be a lot of winners each ratings book. For example, the station that has the top thirty-five to sixty-five audience can claim to be number one in that age group, so can all the other stations that crunch the demographic numbers in their favor for different demos. A station does not have to have the most listeners anymore, just the most in the area that it is targeting.

DAY PARTS

There are a few more areas into which the ratings can be broken down. Radio programmers divide the day into different time segments, or day parts, generally broken down like this:

- Morning drive, 5 AM to 10 AM

- Mid-day, 10 AM to 3 PM

- Afternoon drive 3 PM to 7 PM

- Evenings or nights, 7 PM to midnight

- Overnights midnight to 5 AM

Mornings and afternoons are called "drive time" because that is when most people are driving. When people commute they tend to listen to the radio, thus drive time is primetime when it comes to total number of radio listeners. During drive time, radio stations have a captive audience.

Just as they do with the demographic groups, stations can sell different day parts based on the ratings. If the morning show did well, but the rest of the station came up lacking in the ratings, the sales department could focus on selling higher priced ads during the morning show. Generally, the morning drive is the most listened-to day part, which is why most stations put a great deal of their resources into the morning show.

SHARE, CUME, AND TIME SPENT LISTENING

There is yet another area where radio ratings experts break down the numbers. There are three important categories of ratings: share, cume, and time spent listening (TSL).

The share is the percentage of listeners or viewers a station has. If a station has a five share, that means they have five percent of the audience tuning in.

Cume refers to the total number of different people who tune into a radio station during the course of a daypart for at least five minutes. Time spent listening is how long people spend listening to the station. TSL is based on a complicated ratio that Mr. Cox explained as, "an estimate of the number of quarter hours that the average person spends listening to [the station] during a specific time period." That basically boils down to the total amount of time a listener spends tuned into the station.

Stations with high cumes can sell the fact that they have more overall listeners than the competition. Stations with higher TSL can sell the fact that their listeners are more loyal and stay tuned in longer.

Breaking down and reading all the information that comes back in a ratings book is a big job. Most major market stations have people who are experts at breaking down the ratings numbers. These people make the numbers work to the station's advantage so that the sales department has some ammunition to make the station money. Usually these experts are the program director, general manager and/or sales manager.

As complicated as radio ratings may seem, they are still based on concepts initiated a long time ago. "It's kind of funny," Cox says. "Radio ratings are built around a formula that involves something called an average quarter hour and it's a throwback to the early days of radio when *The Green Hornet* and *The Lone Ranger* were fifteen-minute radio shows. So average quarter hour is a carry-over from those days. We've just never gotten away from it."

Since these quarter hours are so important in the ratings, there are things a program director and an air personality can do to try and make the system work in their favor. The most notable strategy is something called "sweeping the quarter hours." A station gets credit for a quarter hour in the ratings if a listener tunes in for five of the fifteen minutes, so if you can get them to listen from ten minutes past the hour to twenty minutes past, you get credit for two quarter hours in the ratings. The same dynamic takes place if a listener tunes in from twenty-five to thirty-five past, as well as forty to fifty, and fifty-five after to five past. Tyler Cox described some of the tricks stations use to do this, "At the top of the hour you will frequently hear a news station giving teases for what is coming up in the next newscast, trying to keep that listener tuned in beyond the top of the hour and into the next quarter hour. As you prepare to do a sportscast at fifteen past the hour, at thirteen past the hour you might tease ahead that sportscast and some other story coming up, again trying to keep them listening longer."

RADIO PROGRAMMING TRICKS

There are also tricks programmers and personalities use to help ratings diary-keepers remember their station. You have probably heard your favorite station give its call letters over and over again, time after time. That is no accident. Stations do this so that the listener will remember the call letters and write them down in the diary book.

There is also something called "day part recycling," which is nothing more than having one show during the day promote another show. You have probably heard it a million times. For example, the morning disc jockey will say, "Be sure to tune into Big Jack this afternoon—he'll be giving away a trip to Bermuda." This is day part recycling; he is promoting another show in the hopes of getting the listener to come back later or stay longer.

The same idea applies to produced promo spots. For instance, during a promo, the station announcer comes on the air in the afternoon and reminds you of what happened during the morning show, and plays a funny piece of audio from that show. The announcer then comes back and says, "When you miss a morning, you miss a lot," or something to that effect. The station is hoping it can entice the listener to come back and listen the next morning. Stations use all these different tricks to try and build up cumes and time spent listening.

TELEVISION PROGRAMMING

The way television stations pursue ratings is a bit different. Most television programming is dictated to individual stations by their mother network. For instance, NBC, ABC, Fox, and CBS demand that their affiliate stations carry a large percentage of their network programming every day. The local TV station program director is pretty much at the mercy of the network to supply the station with good shows that will earn good ratings.

Local television stations make their mark in local programming during their local newscasts and a few hours, usually three to five hours a day, of open time. During this time, they can program syndicated shows outside of their network, shows like *Oprah* or *Wheel of Fortune*. Brian Hocker, the vice president of programming and operations at KXAS, NBC 5 in Dallas, said, "We program thirty-five and a half hours of news per week for a seven day week." That breaks down to about five hours of local news a day. Some will do two or three hours in the morning, another hour at five or six o'clock at night, and then again for an hour at ten or eleven.

Just like radio, television ratings are based on winning quarter hours. National programs build suspense as their show continues so that the viewer has to stay tuned in order to see what happens next. This strategy applies to all different kinds of programs. In reality shows, viewers have to stay tuned until the end to see who gets eliminated, and in a mystery you have to stick around to see "who done it." Even in a comedy you have to stay for the punch line.

LOCAL TV NEWS

While the national programming is out of their hands, local television station programmers focus on their local news shows. This is vitally important for several reasons. Firstly, each station has an obligation to the community; it is part of the station's job to serve the community, and offering live local programming achieves that goal. Doing hometown news also allows the station to become a part of the community. Secondly, news programs greatly contributes to the station's bottom line. For many stations, doing live community programming is their best opportunity to sell commercials to area companies at higher rates. Brian Hocker says, "Because it is all our time to program, it's also all our time to sell, with respect to commercials. So in any given half hour, we have more opportunities to sell advertising than we do in a prime [time] half hour."

Since doing the local news is the most important element of local programming for most television stations, how do program directors go about getting higher ratings? Hocker says, "I don't want to say never, but you don't want to put a commercial break at a quarter hour (:15, :30, :45, :00), because that's the perfect opportunity for somebody to tune out. In news one of the things that you do is, you are constantly teasing deeper in the show, so in that first quarter hour you are teasing or highlighting stories that are not going to be seen until the second quarter hour. You often try and hold the main weather story, because weather is a primary reason for viewing news, you try and hold that to the second quarter hour, to carry people through the first into the second."

Even though the networks are responsible for a large part of a local station's programming, the ratings are still important. Hocker explains, "The numbers are critically important because, remember, the network gives us avails [commercial availabilities], opportunities to sell commercials inside network programming, so we've got to know the makeup of that audience as well." It is important for local television stations to know the demographics of the people watching their shows, because that tells the sales staff the type of companies they need to target for commercial sales.

EVERYONE MATTERS

While programming is vitally important for a station to get good ratings, so is the work of each individual on the air. Program directors can use every trick in the book to get good ratings, spend large amounts of money on advertising, and dream up contests that give away tons of money, but in the end it comes down to how good the air personalities are. This is why it is important for an aspiring air personality to hone their on-air skills and work their voice into an instrument. The programming of a station is important; it is the structure for the station, but the air personality has to attract an audience by offering his or her intrinsically special and unique personal qualities. It is the air personality's job to use the format and the programming around them to shine and to reach the person on the other side of the speaker.

End Notes

[1] *www.nielsenmedia.com*

[2] *www.arbitron.com*

Author's Page

Chris Schneider has worked on the air in radio and television in Los Angeles, Chicago, London, Dallas and Cincinnati for great organizations like CBS, ESPN International, Prime Sports, Sporting News Radio, and the BBC.

Schneider was born and raised in Wyoming, so he has a unique perspective on how to build a career in broadcasting from the bottom up. This book is not just for those starting out, but also for those already in the business looking for ways to move up.

When he is not writing or on the air, Schneider is an inspirational speaker giving keynote addresses, speeches at industry luncheons, and broadcasting lectures to schools and professional organizations. Schneider is a proud and devoted Christian and would be happy to answer any questions readers might have about the book, radio, television, or anything else he can help with at www.RadioActive Speaking.com.

Photography by Steven Elliot-Hendrix
Photo courtesy of
Newsradio1080 KRLD

Index

Books from Allworth Press

Allworth Press is an imprint of Allworth Communications, Inc. Selected titles are listed below.

The Radio Producer's Handbook
by Rick Kaempfer and John Swanson (paperback, 6 × 9, 256 pages, $19.95)

Voiceovers: Techniques and Tactics for Success
by Janet Wilcox (paperback, 6 × 9, 208 pages, $24.95)

VO: Tales and Techniques of a Voice-Over Actor
by Harlan Hogan (paperback, 6 × 9, 256 pages, $19.95)

How to Audition for TV Commercials: From the Ad Agency Point of View
by W.L. Jenkins (paperback, 6 × 9, 208 pages, $16.95)

So You Wanna Be on Reality TV
by Jack Benza (paperback, 6 × 9, 224 pages, $19.95)

The Art of Auditioning: Techniques for Television
by Rob Decina (paperback, 6 × 9, 224 pages, $19.95)

They'll Never Put That on the Air: The New Age of TV Comedy
by Allan Neuwirth (paperback, 6 × 9, 256 pages, $19.95)

Writing Television Comedy
by Jerry Rannow (paperback, 6 × 9, 224 pages, $14.95)

Career Solutions for Creative People
by Dr. Ronda Ormont (paperback, 6 × 9, 320 pages, $19.95)

To request a free catalog or order books by credit card, call 1-800-491-2808. To see our complete catalog on the World Wide Web, or to order online for a 20 percent discount, you can find us at ***www.allworth.com.***